Thinking the Art of Management

Thinking the Art of Management

Stepping into 'Heidegger's Shoes'

David M. Atkinson

First published 2007 by
PALGRAVE MACMILLAN
Houndmills, Basingstoke, Hampshire RG21 6XS and
175 Fifth Avenue, New York, N.Y. 10010
Companies and representatives throughout the world

PALGRAVE MACMILLAN is the global academic imprint of the Palgrave Macmillan division of St. Martin's Press, LLC and of Palgrave Macmillan Ltd. Macmillan® is a registered trademark in the United States, United Kingdom and other countries. Palgrave is a registered trademark in the European Union and other countries.

ISBN-13: 978–0–230–55374–3   hardback
ISBN-10: 0–230–55374–5   hardback

This book is printed on paper suitable for recycling and made from fully managed and sustained forest sources. Logging, pulping and manufacturing processes are expected to conform to the environmental regulations of the country of origin.

A catalogue record for this book is available from the British Library.

A catalogue record for this book is available from the Library of Congress.

10   9   8   7   6   5   4   3   2   1
16   15   14   13   12   11   10   09   08   07

Printed and bound in Great Britain by
Antony Rowe Ltd, Chippenham and Eastbourne

For my sons, Mark, Gareth, Ryan and Finlay

Contents

List of Figures, Plates and Tables

Figures

Plates

Tables

Preface

This work is the culmination of a PhD, in Critical Management, gained at Lancaster University Management School. However, it does not, as some might imagine, and despite my background as an experienced practicing manager, offer a typical empiric examination of a socio-cultural managerial phenomenon. This immediately sets the reader up for what I hope is an interesting yet challenging read. Can management be seen as an artform? And if so, to what extent is such a concept of use in furthering both management knowledge and the education of future managers? Such questions are not the standard research questions to be addressed as a PhD topic; neither is the outcome – in essence, what has been described as a quasi-complete philosophical framework for positioning an art of management – a focused application of a specified research technique in identifying and closing a gap in some existing body of management and organizational literature.

This book then, is published in my 50th year; it carries with it a background of some experience, history and (more recently) academic preparation. The goal of exploring what is a big question has benefited from a certain luxury – in that the research was entirely self-funded – and consequently the only driving factor was one of my own mental curiosity. No specific agenda, political or otherwise, intervened in this work and I hope, therefore, that the reader will benefit from what is an *a political* perspective. However, I do note the political nature of my conclusions with wry humour. Although not siding with any specific agenda, as a contribution to knowledge I have set the discussion rather loosely in the frame of critical management studies (CMS). Here I must recognize that some readers may question this relevance. Lest this issue cloud the nature of my argument, I have kept any CMS discussion to the opening and closing of the text. Knowledge of certain extant CMS positions should not, therefore, be seen as central to my conception of artistic management. I merely see CMS as a useful forum within which the concept might, in future, be usefully explored.

As the outcome of a PhD project I believe it will be useful to the reader to highlight some of the critique resulting from the process. Here I separately and warmly acknowledge the part that Professor John Hassard and Dr Bogdan Costea played in the "coming out" of this work. The text itself provides a highly philosophical and abstract conceptualization of a management as it might be practiced as an artform. However, the reader will note that I have not engaged in a protracted analysis based in the work of the "founding fathers" of philosophy and social science. Contrary to the indication that the title of this book might suggest, Heidegger's philosophy and thinking are not central to this book's thesis. Rather I have practiced a degree of intellectual eclecticism in borrowing from such founding fathers as Kant, Heidegger, Marx, Weber, Ruskin, and so on, rather than centering on them. Thus I only borrow from Heidegger, in a form of pastiche, in relation to his specific interpretation of Van Gogh's painting *Old Shoes With Laces*. There are, perhaps, other valuable books waiting to be written about how such founding fathers would contemplate the form of social art theory I advance in this work. However, I would leave such work to those who clearly possess a more extensive knowledge of these individuals than I myself possess at this time.

Although I had not set out on this project with a conscious awareness of C Wright Mills' (1959) *The Sociological Imagination*, I am subsequently indebted to John Hassard's critique that my work might be seen in terms of crafting research along such lines. Indeed, as Mir and Mir (2002) observed, research that attempts to avoid '*...a blind obeisance to "grand theory" and an over reliance on "abstracted empiricism"*', through the exercise of a "sociological imagination", might help transcend the artificial gap between theory and practice. This is exactly where this work is situated. The theory/practice divide. What I present the reader within this text is, therefore, a logical, structured argument in which a broad range of concepts are introduced to help a certain "thinking about management as an artform". Here I must accept a persistent weakness within this structure. There are few illustrations of a concrete nature that help to explain some of the concepts. My approach has been the attempt at "quasi-completeness" in describing a cohesive paradigm. But this has, however, been at the expense of individual concept development. Again there is scope for further work here.

As a final point, it might be seen by some that this work sets itself up to turn "management" ontological. As Bogdan Costea offered in critique, the question remains whether management as an object of a philosophical investigation is truly a philosophical object at all. My own response to this is the basic premise that I advance in the Introduction. Management, in practice, is management – it is no more than that, it is certainly not (in my view) ontological; management is neither a science, nor an art, nor a craft. Management is whatever managers do; it is not what an individual *has* to do to be a manager.

Pickhill   D M A

Acknowledgments

This work is the result of a journey of exploration upon which I have had the immense good fortune to have been richly influenced by a great number of individuals. Here I would like to acknowledge a few who are particularly representative of the many. Most fundamentally, as a past student of Lancaster University's M.Phil/Ph.D in Critical Management (Cohort 5), I am indebted to its co-founders Professor Julia Davies and Dr Jonathan Gosling. Particularly, it was Julia's passion for the course that encouraged me to challenge conventional wisdom, and to embrace the alternative thinking implicit in CMS.

As a practicing manager, and therefore only a part-time academic, I have been privileged by a group of excellent academic mentors. In an eclectic work such as this, these mentors have hailed from vastly different backgrounds. Dr Emily Brady was instrumentally responsible for guiding my understanding of art and aesthetic theory. But it was, perhaps, Professor Peter Anthony's healthy skepticism of my aesthetic point of view – delivered with his immense good nature – that helped me frame this understanding within my arguments. Peter's invaluable contribution to my understanding of organizational sociology, despite my discursive ventures into the realm of aesthetics and philosophy, ensured that I never lost sight of my intended objective. Without Peter's immense breadth of knowledge and challenging comments on my work, I am sure that my reaching a closure in this application of art and aesthetics to management would have proved greatly more problematic. I am also indebted to Professor Fred Botting and Dr Isis Brook for their contributions to this work. In particular, Fred provided a keen cultural critique in closing out some of the "aesthetic" and "philosophic" issues in its later stages.

I would also like to acknowledge the following: Dr Jonathan Vickery for his helpful comments on my definition of Art (an early and much shortened amalgam of Chapters 4 and 5), presented to the 2nd Art of Management conference in Paris, 2004; and Vincent Degot, not only for the illuminating nature of his original work, but also for his kind encouragement of its critique. Finally, from the non-academic world, I owe a debt of thanks also to: the staff of my firm, for providing me with the space and forbearance to practice what I preach; to David Norris-Jones who, in a non-executive role, has provided a crucially valuable sounding board for the growth of my own commercial management experience; and finally to my wife Yvonne, for her long suffering forbearance of my generally nocturnal and weekend research habits.

List of Abbreviations

C1	Consequence 1 (or Preferred Consequence)
CA	Constructive Alternativism
CJ:nn	Used in Reference to Kant (1790:nn), Critique of Judgement
CEO	Chief Executive Officer
CMS	Critical Management Studies
CTA	Conjunctive Theory of Art
D:nn	Used in Reference to Degot (1987:nn)
DBA	Doctor of Business Administration
DE	Dependent Entity
DE_{sf}	Self-Dependent Entity
ECT	Epistemological Culture Theory
FE	Fictional Entity
H1.. H4	Hypotheses 1 to 4
IE	Independent Entity
KBAT	Knowledge Based Affect Theory
M1K	Mode 1 Knowledge
M2K	Mode 2 Knowledge
MBA	Master of Business Administration
NK	Narrative Knowledge
NK_n	Naïve Narrative Knowledge
NK_s	Sophisticated Narrative Knowledge
P1.. P4	Premisses 1 to 4
RAEs	Research Assessment Exercises
SK	Scientific Knowledge
SNA	Socially Negotiated Alternativism
YBAs	Young British Artists

Introduction

Principles for the Development of a Complete Mind: Study the science of art. Study the art of science. Develop your senses – especially learn how to see. Realize that everything connects to everything else.

Leonardo DaVinci

Enlightened management: the root of all evil?

This book presents a critical, philosophically informed exploration into what, if anything, the world of management and organization – its practice and its study – can learn from the world of art. From the outset I do not argue, as Dobson (1999) has, that management is "best perceived" as an artform; nor do I argue, as Mintzberg (2004) has, that it "appears" like an artform. Rather, in this book, I merely advance a central Art-aesthetic, paradigmatic thesis in which – given the general and growing uncertainties and constraints inherent in running a business in a "real" world – management might, under certain circumstances, be beneficially practiced as an artform. In noting Adler's (2006:488) comment that, *'[l]eading business schools worldwide are [now] adding arts-based courses to their curriculum,'* this thesis steps beyond a mere empiric observation of the potential of artists to contribute directly to managerial practice and its teaching. Instead, I seek to use the lens of art to accelerate an understanding of managerial practice. That is to say, the concern of this book's central thesis is the gaining of an art-like understanding of practice that might provide a beneficial input to the process of management and organizational education. However, as I shall argue, this objective is philosophically problematic from the outset.

First a contradiction: given an objective of improving academic support for practice, why is this book positioned within what has become academically "signed" – through, for example, the work of Alvesson and Willmott (1992) – as Critical Management Studies (CMS)? Here, the dominant CMS critique is now, almost traditionally, seen as anti-managerial and thus a CMS critique is least likely to be seen as a managerial partner.

It is axiomatic that, in the so-called "real" world of operating a modern business, what the management practitioner is concerned with is the application of acquired managerial knowledge, experience and practical skills as a "means" towards some organizational "end". From this I advance three further axioms of managerial practice. Firstly, successful managers exist today who have received no "formal" management knowledge. Secondly, "trained" managers exist today, frustrated by the inability of much formally acquired knowledge to meet the exigencies of their practice; and thirdly, managers exist today frustrated by the fact that what appeared to work for them yesterday, or in their last job, or what they had heard had worked for someone else, has failed to work for them today. Together, these axioms can be construed as an argument. If "formal" management knowledge is no essential antecedent of successful management practice, yet a manager's knowledge may be found wanting – preventing the fulfilment of managerial responsibility – then there must therefore be a further type of knowledge that is not formal, but which, nevertheless, can be "instrumental" in contributing to managerial success. Therefore, if the academic business school is to more fully support managerial practice, it becomes a valid concern to attempt an understanding of the nature and production of this "other", non-formal (or tacit) knowledge. This concern is the book's rationale.

Most managers are faced, from time to time, with determining actions to take under uncertain circumstances; a concern with ordering apparent chaos. It is here, in the "reality" of management, that any "lack" of knowledge is most evident. However, in addressing this knowledge deficit, an evidential route for many managers is the purchase of such "popular" management texts as may be found in airport and railway station bookshops. Such books appear to offer reading around many of the notable management concerns of their day. Indeed, Peters and Waterman (1982), The Arthur Young *Manager's Handbook* (Liddane and Chandler, 1986), Peters (1987), and Harvey-Jones (1991) have, over the years, informed my own management practice. However, rather than being critical of a managerial practice that appears to eschew much of what is both established and contemporary (socialized) management theorizing, my concern tends to a critique of theorizing itself. This text arises then, not through a conscious accession to the form of CMS advanced by, say, Grey (2005) – such form being a Marxist-like concern over a bourgeois managerialism – but through my own involvement on the Lancaster University Management School's (now closed) masters of philosophy in CMS. Here, Lancaster's critical agenda, observed by Mintzberg (2004), was no more than an imperative to question conventional wisdom.

Given the CMS context, I return to the philosophical problematic that is inherent, I believe, in the definition of what management might be. Here, drawing on MacIntyre's *After Virtue* (1981), I consider a proposition of the "self": that is, I am a manager with a job of managerial work to do. This job is, itself, set in a context of an organization and its practices. I am neither a scientist, nor a craftsman, nor am I an artist. I am a manager. However, I would accept that, since many managers are rarely managers first, my managerial capability – as a smorgasbord of knowledge and experience – is influenced by whatever I might have been before taking on a managerial role. From this I advance the basic premiss that management, in practice, is management – it is no more than that; management is neither a science, nor an art, nor a craft. Management is whatever managers do; it is not what an individual *has* to do to be a manager. Management in this sense cannot, therefore, be described as an autonomous activity; one that might be objectively studied to produce a set of prescriptive "management practices" fully defining the social role of manager. What can be said, however, is that whatever it is that managers do, they are *responsible* – to the socio-cultural grouping that recognizes them as a manager – for the performance of their role. But, the conceptual definitions of any socio-cultural grouping are context sensitive. While an individual organization may have a relatively clear conception of what it requires of its managers, this conception cannot be held to be "universally" applicable. In the context of a larger grouping, a more generic concept of manager becomes subject to the greater, and inherently conflicting, requirements imposed by, for example, individual rights, representative bodies and other political, social and economic policies and critiques. Such a grouping might, for example, relate to an academic business school that, on the basis of some abstract concept of management, has developed a certain programme of study in attempt to satisfy the varied expectations of multiple, diverse socio-cultural subgroupings.

The problematic of the "social definition" of the manager is, I argue, similar for the engineer, the teacher, the professor, and so on. Here, the notion of *responsibility* is crucial. It is *responsibility* that invites us to extrapolate the concept of (social) performance into some future reality and to answer for performativity's past promises. Consequently, because of the social imperative for the practicing manager to meet their responsibility to "manage", even under complex, ambiguous or otherwise unknown conditions, I argue that we cannot adequately define the individual practitioner solely by reference to an accepted historio-social, rational conception of what a manager might be. We cannot, therefore, begin to fully define the requirements for the selection, education and training of managers based merely on an empirical, *a posteriori* description of their envisaged role.

We can, it is true, identify certain skills. An individual seeking assignment to the role of *teacher of geography* can be taught a knowledge of geography and techniques for the presentation of this knowledge; but does this make them a teacher? The individual seeking the social status of *engineer* can be taught elements of electrical or mechanical knowledge and how certain materials might perform in conjunction, but does such teaching make that individual an engineer? The painter may be taught how to mix colour, how to represent, by the manipulation of paint and brush-stroke, certain aspects of light and shade; but is the painter then an artist? By what authority does an individual seeking a social role actually occupy that role? This, I argue, is the essence of my philosophical problematic; it is a problematic of "social definition" that arises through an authority that can only be expressed in terms of its origin in a specific socio-cultural grouping. The moment we step outside that group we no longer possess a role authority.

An alternative to the idea of a social role lies in MacIntyre's (1981) social "*character*": a stock figure which provides an interpretation of the actions of those individuals who act *in character*. It is, as MacIntyre suggests, a knowledge of the *character* which informs the behaviours of such individuals; the notion of a *character* imposes a certain "moral" constraint on those who are "in" *character*. *Characters* are thus "moral" representatives of their socio-cultural origin; they are responsible to their socio-cultural grouping for their performance *in character*. In this sense, the manager, scientist, artist, and so on, are amongst the "essential" stock *characters* and, in this sense, the manager, scientist, artist, and so on, are, as *characters*, "mutually exclusive". *Characters* represent separate moral imperatives; though they might share some similar characteristics. Individuals might also – from time to time – change or even combine *characters.*

The question of what management might be: "is it an art, a science, or a craft?" arises from the conventional wisdom that suggests that "management", as a "proper" concern of the *character* of a manager, is an appropriate field of academic study. To address this question is to form the basis of an ontological perspective. However, my point of departure in a CMS perspective – in which I am encouraged to challenge such conventional wisdom – is to suggest that, if management is merely what managers do, then management itself cannot be the proper object of this book's study. I can, I suggest, only relate to the general "reality" of management indirectly – and it is *with* the general reality that I must identify, in order to explicate what can only be "generally" unknown – by understanding the "manager" as "object". However, as I have argued above, I can only come to terms with what a manager is, by reference to some social construct of "the manager", derived from an historical perspective of what it is that those we have come to regard as managers "do". In order to overcome the circularity that is inherent in this argument, conventional research practice would compel me to set my "object" construct of either "manager" or "management" (organization or organizational practice) in stone, in order that I could then describe its corollary. In short, conventional research would compel me to establish both an ontological and epistemological starting point at the outset of study. As Easterby-Smith *et al* (1991) would concur, following convention I would simply hide the problems of philosophy in my method. This, I suggest, is a tradition of unresolved circularity that is a legacy of the Enlightenment project.

Despite the ardent criticism of the Enlightenment (for example see Schmidt, 1998) an understanding of its origin is germane to this text. In short, the Enlightenment project held that human nature (and thus the social) was to be related to certain timeless, immutable laws; a historical progression of humanity towards an enlightened condition of human association based on principles of reason. As Friedman (1986) described, this implied the existence of some grand narrative; the duty of rationalistic thought being the unfolding of the truth of that narrative: a form of eschatological progress. However, despite the dismantling of any form of "grand narrative" (see, for example, Lyotard, 1979), thinking about reality has retained the fundamental character of the Enlightenment project's process: a dominant paradigm of rationalism and its mode of autonomous thought. Here, as Whitton (1988) recalled, the "truth" of a social knowledge and its propositions is established through an objective process of verification and falsification; a process that has remained to characterize much of what is the scientific form of "modern Western culture".

The Enlightenment's philosophy of thought lay in the division of reality into separate spheres of existence: an instrumental, a moral and an aesthetic reality. It is a separation visible in Kant's three critiques of *Pure Reason* (published in 1781), *Practical Reason* (published in 1785) and *Judgement* (1790); it informs, as Postone (1990) comments, Weber's thinking on the separation of logics into the "value spheres" of science, art, and legal and moral representations. It is a gross simplification of the Enlightenment, but we might say that (in the West at least) the birth of all that is modern science, all that is modern (social) moral and legal practice, and all that is autonomous (modern) art can be seen as stemming from the autonomous logics arising from this great division of thought. Here Guillet de Monthoux (2000) argues that:

> If pure reason takes over we forget about ethics and our freedom. If the logic of practical reason conquers the realm of pure reason we end up with the kind of madness called rationalism.

In commenting on one key critique of Enlightened thought, Mueller (1958) noted that, to Hegel, the dialectic nature of rational, autonomous thought meant that any "ism" (for example instrumental*ism*) that is a special viewpoint that leaves the "other" to itself must be criticized by the logic of philosophical thought, whose problem is reality itself. Therefore we see that Hegel's critique turned to the uncovering of processes by which rules, concepts and laws could be found to make general, public and common, the "reality" of law, art, philosophy, religion, literature, science and other spheres of thought (see, for example, Knapp, 1986).

In Weber's critique, the paradox of autonomous thought was, *inter alia*, the loss of any theoretical and ethical unification of the world; a consequential loss of meaning crystallized in the form of the postmodern condition and a certain *crisis of representation*. In the "Weberian social", while thinking about reality is achievable, in an abstract sense, through any lens, paradigm, model, metaphor or sphere that a researcher may wish to define, parameterize and describe, generalizing the practice of *a social reality* is problematic. Yet, paradoxically, free of moral, legal and aesthetic consideration, instrumental rationalistic thought has provided for great advances in the understanding and control of the physical world; it has lead to greater efficiencies and effectiveness. But, as Postone (1990) observed, Weber argued that this freedom of consideration led to a corresponding loss of "social freedom" through the institutionalization of a "cognitive-instrumental rationality" within the economy and the state. The legacy of the Enlightenment leads us to study management through, in essence, holding *ceteris paribus* any thought of a management reality's aesthetic, and moral and legal implications. Here, from the CMS view at least, many academic studies "describe" a reality devoid of emotion and feeling and with no concern over any moral or legal prescriptivity. Conventional (scientific) wisdom merely causes us to rationalize the instrumentality of management practices. If this is the case, why – as academics – might we be surprised that the theorizing of management appears to be of little direct application in practice?

Without autonomous thought we cannot push the boundaries of our knowledge – this "pushing" is the traditional role of academe. But it is problematic if a *Realpolitik* increasingly subordinates the academic role merely to the support of social practice. This is nowhere more relevant, nor more visible, than within the contemporary "academic business school". It is a particular concern when (as in the UK) academe is faced with reduced "state" financing and an imperative to seek financial support from the very institutions that are likely to seek (as a return on their investment) an increased relevance of theory to practice. Thus, while managers may well hold valid concerns over their lack of a knowledge that might better prepare them for the unknown, the existence of the Management Gap (as, for example, described by Starkey and Madan, 2001) is more appropriately considered a concern for the agenda of business schools, set as they are in a context of increasing commercialism.

The groundwork is done for the foundation of a critique on the social theorizing of management and organization that is, I argue, still rooted in the division of the Enlightenment's spheres of existence and its paradigm of rationalism. Here as Friedman (1986) describes, contemporary social science has developed under the twin influences of Marx and Weber; the primary difference between them being seen to lie in the potential relationship between the "order" of an institutionalized rationality and the observed "order" of the social. To Marx the relationship was one of historical progress towards some political eschaton; to Weber, whatever order there was was aesthetic. This difference leads me to highlight the two clear critiques of a rational instrumentalism that, in turn, characterize the two contemporary "critical" turns in social theorizing that inform this text.

In the first critique of instrumental rationalism, I single out the "critical" social researcher drawing from the ethical nature of a social morality – thus we witness *a turn to culture*. Yet, as I have argued above, academe – trapped in a paradigm of rationalism – merely objectively reifies an abstraction of a moral and legal management and organizational reality. The *"cultural turn"*, seemingly set against the politics of an institutionalized rationalism (and its neglect of the moral and legal sphere of prescriptivity) has undoubtedly led to many advances in management and organizational thinking. Gradually however, over the 1980's onwards, while some of this social theorizing was co-opted into mainstream teaching, the separate voice of welfare and paternalism (for example see Walsh and Weber, 2002) and the potential of a Marxist critique of management and organization, has faded in line with what Friedman (1986) has termed the general retrenchment of Western Marxism's "theoretical moment". Here, outwith the CMS agenda, the *realpolitik* of capitalism simply outweighs Marxism's eschatological hope.

The second critique of instrumental rationalism lies in a cognizance of the Weberian observation of an "aesthetic" social order. Thus, in the manner of the cultural turn, as Taylor and Hansen (2005) observe, the last decade has seen an *"aesthetic turn"*: the growth of interest in the aesthetic sphere of our existence in organizations. From Weber's viewpoint then, the history and science of the social (and thus management and organizations) merely represents a ground for contemplation, where the aesthetic of a social order might reveal "an order" but it is, ultimately, one without an "end"; fascinating in its intricacy, but altogether meaningless in its ability to transcend its own context. This again leaves capitalism's development triumphant.

Although there is an argument that much of western (capitalist) business is being increasingly "aestheticized"; that is to say the GDP of advanced economies is being increasingly influenced by the "aesthetics" of business (see, for example, both Baudrillard and Lyotard's observations on "image" and "signs"), this is not, I argue, the same as an "aestheticization" of business management. Here, an aesthetic critique of rational management order suffers the potential to see its own demise in management and organizational practice. Without the realization of an "end" to an (*apolitical*) aesthetic order, what has aesthetics to offer the reality of practice? What has aesthetics to offer a practice that is set within a firmly entrenched (bourgeois or otherwise) *realpolitik* of capitalism? "It is all very well *feeling good* about this *beautiful* solution you present, but will it add value to my business?"

There is, certainly in the aesthetic "means" to advertising's "end", a rational argument "for" the instrumental reification of an "aesthetic" voice; that is to say its co-option as an *aesthetic* "for" business. However, where is the cogent argument for an aesthetic voice "about" business; that is, an aesthetic "of" management and organization? Here, in the increasing cross-fertilization of the arts and management observed by Adler (2006), there is now a clear distinction to be made between concepts and possibilities such as the *Art of Management* and of *Art and Management*.

Autonomous writing on the aesthetics of management and organization, as was the case with the morality and law of a Marxist critique, is undoubtedly providing new and valuable insights. Edited works, such as Linstead and Höpfl's *The Aesthetics of Organizations* (2000), and Carr and Hancock's *Art and Aesthetics at Work* (2003), are providing new insights that, Taylor and Hansen (2005) surmise, "fill in" the less understood spaces in organizations. Yet, as the product of an academic world, such abstractions from reality provide little immediate promise for management practice. As Taylor (2002) advances, aesthetically informed management and organizational research is merely characteristic of the researcher's rational perspective of an "aesthetic" reality. Here, an epitome of the hypostatization of an autonomous theorizing on managerial and organizational aesthetics can be found in Dobson's *The Art of Management and the Aesthetic Manager: The Coming Way of Business* (1999). Dobson construes an argument for the "management aesthete", from which he derives a prediction of the eclipse of rational and moral management ideologies by the aesthetic. Here, from the neo-Enlightenment metaphors of the Technical, Moral and the Aesthetic universes; Dobson's "aesthetic voice" asserts that crises in business management develop when '...*the universe in which management believes it resides conflicts with that of the surrounding society.*' It is, Dobson argues, the time for businesses to move to the aesthetic universe, and for managers to shift their "management paradigm".

The aestheticization of business does not infer a *de facto* call for the supremacy of an aestheticization of business management. Dobson's claim for the "autonomously aesthetic" manager, in some way exposing the "vacuous essence" of all that is rational, moral and legal certainly appears to throw the baby out with the bathwater. This is not the project of aesthetic thought initiated by Kant, in which – as Guillet de Monthoux (2000) argues – Kant's *Critique of Judgement* was seen to hold the promise of managing the dualism of pure reason and practical reason. In the "reality" of management and organizational practice, if we refuse to bury the philosophical problematic of a Hegelian "reality" in a web of ontological, epistemological and methodological intrigue, we might rationalize that there can be no such thing as the "technical manager", the "moral manager" or the "aesthetic manager", for managers are, in fact, all of these. It is, I argue, a mistaken belief in the primacy of an "academic" knowledge over a "practical" or "narrative" knowledge that has shifted the perception of the "Management Gap" to a problem to be solved for the benefit of management, from one to be solved for the benefit of academe's support of management.

Aesthetics is concerned with how knowledge might be construed from sensory experience. I argue, here, that it is an aesthetic sensibility that allows us to reach out to the unknown, to the complex and to the ambiguous. Yet an autonomously aesthetic view of management and organizational practice can be argued to merely add to the post-modernistic *crisis of representation* that Taylor and Hansen (2005) argue lies at the root of the aesthetic turn. Here the Art of Management Conference series, started under the auspices of the University of Essex, might in a sense – certainly to a management practitioner – appear to be the epitome of a crisis of representation; seemingly lacking any purposive "end" to which it might be progressing, yet fascinating in its intricacy. Post-Enlightenment, in the postmodern condition and its growing crisis of representation – a surfeit of context sensitive, rationalistic knowledge – we ask the question (coined by Adler, 2006) *Now That We Can Do Anything, What Will We Do?*

Post-Enlightenment, for a theorizing of practice to be of benefit to practice, I argue that there must be some support for the reconciliation of autonomous rationality. The requirement for this support does not undermine the value any individual paradigm for an ontological reality used for the purposes of advancing understanding. Such purpose is, after all, the *raison d'être* of the academic world. However, for business schools in particular, the *raison d'état* arising from the *realpolitik* of managerial practice, calls for a constructive paradigm that goes beyond any mere appreciation of morality, law and aesthetics. It calls for a paradigm that highlights the potentiality of all spheres to enhance the instrumentality of objective knowledge in "creating" new narratives of practice. The identification of such a paradigm is, I argue, a worthy aim of a non-idealized, non-Marxist critical voice; one that challenges conventional wisdom specifically for the benefit practice.

The above argument justifies this book's Art-aesthetic paradigm, specifically one of management pointillism. Here, I make the distinction between an *aesthetic* and an *Art aesthetic* to clarify what I advance as a non-autonomous conception. Art infers, at any level, the creativity required of constructive paradigm, whereas an autonomous aesthetic merely relates to a sensual perception of a reality. An Art aesthetic introduces the possibilities of creating new or changing existing realities; whereas an autonomous aesthetic merely infers new perceptions of existing realities. An Art aesthetic offers a paradigm of perception shifting; whereas an autonomous aesthetic merely offers a paradigm of new perceptive disclosures. The paradigmatic conception of the management pointillist suggests a manager with the faculty to infer new meanings from fragmented, objective instrumental, moral and aesthetic knowledge; one who can visualize connectedness in complex structures. The pointillist practices a technique using dots of colour which, through the spectator's eye, merge – they take form – through some abstract, towards some simulacrum; a copy of a reality perceived without a basis in the "truth" of an *a priori* visible reality.

What follows then, is a narrative disclosure of a paradigm of management pointillism, revealed through the process of an exploratory philosophical argument. In advancing this book's Art-aesthetic thesis, I follow its own constructive paradigm in three parts. Part I presents a discourse arising from autonomous thoughts from the field of management; Part II presents a discourse arising from autonomous thoughts from the field of Art. In the final Part III, I offer the constructive possibilities of a paradigm of *management art*. This emerges as a mediated rationalization of the critiques of Marxist and Weberian social order, not to introduce some new grand narrative of management and organizational purpose, but to introduce art's potential to construct new "localized" teleological purpose, purely as the basis for managerial action.

Part I

From the Management World

1
Framing an Art of Management

> We might say that the Greeks understand the quality of the unknown, but so great was their faith in order that the unknown, although always symbolized, functioned for them as a part of reality, and entered as a real attribute in all their relationships.
>
> Mark Rothko (1940/41)

Overture: on cultures and the matter of art

In the academic world of universities and their business schools, a concern of some scholars is that the output of research appears little adopted by the world of practice.[1] Conversely, railway station and airport bookshops reveal volumes of management secrets marketed to this *alter*-world; they offer its population of managers the seven, ten, 20 or so key steps to take to solve this or that management issue. These books present a *populist* management science; a symptom of a culture of practice. Here, in a May 2006 search of the online bookshop Amazon.com, a significant number of business-related titles (over 2,900) connected with the search words "Art of", including: *The Art of Managing People; The Art of Being an Executive; The Art of Using Science in Marketing; and The Art of Strategy*. Such books tell stories of successful individuals and of their excellent companies; they are packaged for managerial consumption, with the promise of a share in their narratives of success. But from within the world of academia, Henry Mintzberg (2004:10) has followed others in suggesting that, rather than being a science, management appears more like an "artform", with characteristics of "insight", "vision" and "intuition". The word *Art,* in a management context, has become legitimized with a certain relevance to management studies. However, viewed critically, the concept of a *management art* is not supported by a coherent body of theory. Mintzberg himself neglects to offer any insight into what *management art* might be. There is, therefore, an overriding presumption that when the word *Art* is invoked, both the practicing and academic readership is assumed to interpret its use as a valid premiss to what might follow.

In the complex, ambiguous world of practice, full of management and organizational ills, the market for popular management books grows and, as Ford *et al* (2005) observe, the academic world laments an apparent rejection of their own remedies. Is there a valid concern? Two cultures, two illnesses; or one syndrome, two treatments? The management-world "patients" continue with their "success" treatments; some organizations survive and flourish, others wither and die; yet economies continue and growth continues (although not perhaps consistently); capitalism reigns. Is the syndrome or illness acute – in need of innovative treatments from the world of science – or is it chronic and merely controlled within its own culture through naturalistic treatments and placebos? Is the naming of an *Art* of management an exercise in "control" in the name of culture; an attempt to sign *that* which cannot be fully understood?[2]

If the concept of *Art* is to hold significance in a management and organizational context, then what is "that" which we cannot so fully understand? Here, a simple vignette will serve as an overture. Michael Eisner (1999:4), as Chairman of *The Walt Disney Company* in July 1994, wrote in the opening chapter of *Work in Progress* of his struggle to "fill the void" of Frank Wells' (Disney's President) unexpected and untimely death in a helicopter accident. Not withstanding his obvious and overwhelming sense of sadness and loss, Eisner relates his "anger" at Frank for his death, for '...*not [being] around to help [him] deal with a very difficult situation...*' Indeed, less than 36 hours following the death of Frank Wells, Jeffrey Katzenberg, the *de facto* Number 3 in the ranks of Disney executives, had laid the ultimatum on Eisner that '...*Either [he got] Frank's job as president... or [he was] going to leave the company.*' As Eisner (1999:299) recalls:

> Plainly, passions were running high. For Jeffrey to quit immediately after Frank's death would only prompt more media attention, compound the company's trauma, and exacerbate the sense of anxiety that our employees were already feeling. On a practical level, we were just two weeks from opening *Beauty and the Beast* on Broadway

and eight weeks from releasing *The Lion King* in movie theaters. I was especially loath to lose Jeffrey before those projects were launched. As I had done so often before, I found myself operating on two separate tracks. On one level, I was fed up, angry, and absolutely convinced that the only solution was to let Jeffrey quit. On another level, I still valued his strengths running our movie division and continued to believe that somehow things would all work out in the end.

Under "normal" business conditions the challenge of management and organizational practice is often about the introduction of change to achieve some vision, purpose or function. When we now consider the inevitability of unexpected scenarios, such as that painted by Eisner, even the best efforts to manage effectively become prone to ambiguity, emotion and seeming irrationality. While large global corporations of the size of Disney Corp. are easily related to organizational complexity, the challenge faced by many smaller firms, competing in the greater economy and faced with increasing legislative and cultural pressures, is no less an issue of complexity and ambiguity.

All organizations are prone to a dialectic of chance and necessity. The *de facto* market for popular remedies indicates that the patient might indeed have a legitimate concern over their health; one for which academe appears ill-equipped to provide its own remedies. Here I introduce a key premiss for the argument to follow: *it is the complexity of the totality of relationships involving the sub-universe[3] of the contemporary organization that adds burden to the management challenge; that is management's malaise.* It is the often overwhelming nature of the mathematically and dynamically complex environment that contributes ambiguity, uncertainty and a certain unease of the "unknown", or the "absent other". I shall go on to argue the organization as a potentially "sublime" environment, within which the contemporary manager will be advantaged by possessing an *aesthetic* faculty to approach the unknown, the complex and the ambiguous, in order to facilitate the management of issues within it. It is one thing to use the word *Art* in a popular management title, as a "marketing edge", separating a book's concepts and ideas from those that have gone before, lifting it into a privileged position in the manner of a highly regarded Artwork. It is another thing to reach a critical understanding of the consequence of drawing a parallel between the artistic process and the processes of contemporary management.

Given the foregoing, the central issue I address with this text is *"**how appropriate is the concept of an art of management for reconceptualizing management and organizational practice?**"* The challenge of this book is to offer an explanation for a hitherto unexplained requirement to understand that management might legitimately be practiced as an artform. How managers visualize their organizational sub-universe; how they react to and cope with the ambiguity and complexity within it; how they manage the unexpected is, I argue, a question of the acquisition of a requisite knowledge. And it is here in the domain of knowledge that practice and science frequently divide.

The cultural paradox

Scientific knowledge (SK) does not represent the totality of knowledge; as Lyotard (1979:7) argues, SK exists in addition to, and in competition with, another kind that he refers to as narrative. Narrative knowledge (NK) is not meant to supplant SK; rather NK acts to form *an equilibrium* within the mind of the knower. Narrative – and one of its key corollaries, storytelling – represents a creative description of the world in which hidden patterns and previously unexplored meanings unfold. In this respect narrative need only be provisional; NK need only satisfy the knower's immediate information requirements, that is to say NK need only be plausible as the basis of a judgement for action. Narratives provide for the unfolding of provisional truths about an empirical existence; they provide an existential sought-for-equilibrium between the known and the unknown within the mind of the knower. In this sense, NK is therefore a question of competence about how the individual relates to their *existence-in-the-world*: Lyotard's (1979:18) *savoir-faire*, *savoir-vivre*, and *savoir-écouter* for example.

Narrative knowledge frames an individual's thinking, feeling and *acting-in-the-world*. It transcends the need for an eternal truth; it relates, for example, to Lyotard's (1979:18) criterion of efficiency, justice, happiness, and the audio and visual sensibilities; in short, I argue, it also relates to aesthetic sensibilities. In this respect NK subsumes the notion of a knowledge that emanates solely from the senses; what Strati (2007:62) refers to as "sensible knowledge". Narratives therefore embrace what is perceived, judged, produced, and reproduced through the senses and which, in the *sensible individual,* constitute a basis for aesthetic judgement. As Strati continues, sensible knowledge '*...generates dialectical relations with action and close relations with the emotions of organizational actors'*. This individualized "sensible knowledge", realized as a shared NK, represents a consensus that is a social phenomenon; it is a construction of social relationships that also constitute the culture of a people. As Hofstede (1994:5) has described, this is the anthropological view of culture; it represents patterns of thinking, feeling, and acting that influence a given universe's population.

Culture, in the above sense, is epistemological; it provides a population with the ability to understand its experiences. As Demerath (2002:208) argues:

> [culture] makes us feel as if we know our world and our place in it. …By sharing our [narrative] interpretations with others, we verify, strengthen, and expand our understandings of our environment. In doing so we create consensual meanings and, thus, [our] culture.

We therefore understand our place in our world by reference to our culture; a relationship to the narrative of our existence. But, the modern act of privileging scientific knowledge has led to a *postmodern* phenomenon of "controversion". Our perceptions of our experiences are organized around the central meanings of our culture, and a controversion of that meaning implies that our relationship with our world is not what we have believed it to be. Frequently, the controversions created by the objectivity of science undermine the provisionality and predictivity of our narratives. Modernity's repositioning of narrative as a truth to be sought for (if not identified and verified) through (social) science has acted to supplant the very foundations of its own rationale. The equilibrium of mind between the known and the unknown is lost. Bush's (1908) concern that the *scientific community* was critical of a "provisional" (narrative) knowledge was prophetic of Lyotard's (1979:41) postmodern condition, in which our culture has lost its nostalgia for our own narrative.

The writings of Lyotard and other social theorists are symptomatic of the late 20th century interest in culture. Contemporary social theory has been said to have undergone a "cultural turn", with a body of academic research[4] giving increasing exposure to the study of culture and, therefore, to the narratives of the sub-universes that these "cultures" represent. As Eyerman (2004:25) argues, culture itself – as the narrative of the people – has become the object of empirical measurement and theorizing. Paradoxically, this objectification of culture fuels the concern of postmodernism, because it fails to encourage the interpretative value of narrative and its corollary of a "good story"; where, as Demerath (2002:208) comments, good stories may be both about something good as well as something bad. Rather, as Nash (2001:79) observes, the paradox of the *cultural turn* is that postmodern theory sees social life as radically unstable; where a measure of stability is only maintained through the manipulation of symbol and meaning to secure collective identities. But the objectification of culture is not just a function of social theory. Insofar as management and organizational practice are functions operating within a social body of *people-in-the-world*, there has been a "management turn" to culture where, equally, the objectification of management and organizational practice as a basis for knowledge can be critically questioned. Here, Costea and Introna (2004:4) observe, lies management's late 20th-century "neo-liberalistic" turn toward the human subject.

The existence of narratives, myths and stories is a fundamental feature of a social existence and is thus, implicitly, also a feature within organizational and managerial practice. However, although there are exceptions (for example Watson, 2001a), Rhodes and Brown (2005:168) argue that both organizational and managerial theory appear limited by a meta-theoretical perspective that sees NK and SK as separate domains – that is, I argue, the province of the domains of art and science respectively – rather than as different forms of knowledge. Although modern science holds the promise of controlling the world around us, the paradox of the turn to culture is that knowledge is increasingly divorced from any narrative. The pursuit of rationality in the modern, within the arts and the social, has been undermined by an irrepressible suspicion that its foundation – the everyday world – is unstable and unknowable; that is, deeply non-rational or even irrational. As Chaney (2002:29) argued, for the dominant rationality of the academic world, this paradox is unwelcome and profoundly absurd.

An understanding of the sociological nature of knowledge, of both the scientific (SK) and the narrative (NK), is a key requirement in coming to understand the process of management and organizational practice. But, in order to transcend the dominant meta-theoretical perspective that limits this understanding, I argue that a new meta-theory is required to allow for a creative integration of both SK and NK. Such a meta-theory should allow a "scientization" of the domain of art in order to collapse the socially constructed boundary that exists between it and the domain of science. This then allows for a critical discussion of both NK and SK within a common paradigm – that is, towards a scientization of narrative and a narratization of science.

On rational theories of practice

The development of a knowledge base (both SK & NK) of the management and organizational sub-universe is, I argue, of fundamental importance to management and organizational practice. This is the *raison d'être* of research-led university business schools. Here, in what might be conceived of as the instrumental sphere of our existence, a rational[5] management knowledge is seen to be the desirable consequence of theorizing practice. People are considered mechanistically, as another functioning part of an often technologically-based system. It is rationalized that, if the actions of people can be controlled with the same predictivity as technical elements, then the application of scientific management will enable successful outcomes and the risk of failure to be averted. Individuals and organizations both assume the status of objective entities. Here the scholar has traditionally sought to support management and organizational practice through a "dominant" process of inductive theorizing. From observations of the sub-universe of the organization and its environment, the role of the academic researcher has been to establish a certain knowledge with which managers may seek to make sense of future performance. Here, to paraphrase Magee's (1973:19) Popperian induction:

> [t]o comprehend the complex organization the aim is to make carefully controlled and meticulously measured observations at some point on the frontier between our knowledge and our ignorance of the organization and, in the course of time, to accumulate a lot of shared and reliable data. As the data grows, general features emerge from which general hypotheses are formulated to fit all known facts and explain how they are causally related to each other.

The presumption of a "scientific" approach to management is therefore that of a certain uniformity within the organization. However, Popper rejected inductivism on the basis that the assumption of uniformity cannot be secured, either through logical argument or further observation, since future events cannot be observed. Thus, despite the general intent of inductive research, Malan & Kriger (1998) have observed that, rather than searching for sense-making data from within a "researched" pool of comparative organizational studies, managers "normally" practice management on the basis of experience and observations within their own "localized" environment. They concluded that '...*practicing managers do not find a great deal of relevance in...*

scientific studies... Instead, manager's bookshelves are lined with books by executives that share their experiences in single organizations.' Table 1.1 depicts Malan & Kriger's key assumptions from the "dominant researcher" and "practicing manager" perspectives.

The difference in world-views, between researcher and manager, appears to evidence a gap in understanding between the two. If, therefore, one of the purposes of management and organizational research remains the informing and guiding of practice, then one of research's functions must be to develop an adequate knowledge of the domain, cognizant of the nature of the difference between theory and practice. Here I introduce the concept of *poiesis* as being relevant. A simple

Table 1.1   Dominant Research v Management World-views

Current Dominant Approach (Researcher)	Alternate World-view (Managerial)
Individuals, groups, and organizations are objects to be studied that are relatively stable over time.	Individuals, groups, and organizations are characterized by complex, continually changing patterns of relationships suggesting organizations as "socially constructed networks of relations and patterns of cognitive processes".
The behaviour of individuals, groups, and organizations is best studied through an examination and comparison of means across populations.	Managers tend to prefer concrete observations over abstract generalizations.
The interaction effect between the object of study (for example, a set of organizations) and the researcher(s) should be minimized controlled, or eliminated.	Organizations may be treated as learning laboratories; the interaction between the manager as participant-observer and the organization is of more interest than the organizational phenomena separate from the observer.
'Occam's razor' should be applied so that the largest amount of variation can be explained with the fewest explanatory constructs, variables, or factors.	Managers are perceived to regard organizations as complex, dynamic, fast paced patterns of relationships in which the application of simplified assumptions distorts the nature of what they wish to know and understand.

understanding of this concept (from ancient Greek translation) is to "make, create or produce"; however this is neither a technical nor a *Romantic* notion of creation – it is more a bringing forth of something. A *poietics of management knowledge* is thus the bringing forth (or *poietic* realization) of a knowledge (within the "self") that is both relevant and useful to the "self" as a manager. This is a desired outcome of management studies where, I argue in the positivistic tradition, a *poiesis* represents a rationally based assimilation, within the manager, of an extant knowledge base of managerial facts.

The bringing forth of knowledge infers an antecedent of thought in which the primary mode of *poietic* origin can be seen as a significantly refined form of trial and error. Here, "trial and error" is characteristic of the "pragmatic maxim". But, as Popper (1963:313) had argued, in the significantly refined, consciously developed form of *trial and error* we have "scientific method" and its dialectic triad of *thesis, anti-thesis* and *synthesis*. Although Popper is ultimately critical of dialecticism, in this preamble to my argument, management knowledge may traditionally be seen to be brought forth along some continuum, between the trial and error of an uninformed management practice and the formal dialectic of management science.

A useful distinction can now also be made between the Hegelian dialectic of *existence* and the Marxist dialectic of *materialism*. As Mohun (2003) describes, Hegel's dialectic initially abstracted a material reality – for example the "reality" of the management world – into thought, and then interpreted this idealized, abstract reality as the hypostatization of thought. For Marx however, the issue was the reverse: the relationship between a reality and theorizing about a reality was not how thought is used to construct reality, but how the theorist comes to a knowledge of an *independent* material reality. Therefore, in contrast to the idealistic Hegelian dialectic, the Marxist dialectic is synonymous with the contemporary project of Realism. It can now be seen that a *poietics of management knowledge* might be rationalized in terms of a tri-polar relationship (Figure 1.1) of competing, underlying (largely positivistic[6]) philosophies.

Within this rationalistic paradigm, the idealist philosophy is that the real world is not independent of the cognizing mind; that is to say, reality is reflected in (and by) the workings of our mind. This is a largely *subjectivist* ontology,[7] in which entities do not exist independently of the conscious being. Realism, on the other hand, admits an objectivist thesis, in which entities of the world do exist, their character being independent of the conscious being. The study of

Figure 1.1   Rationalizing Positivism: The Rationalist Paradigm

management practice under these philosophies provides the foundation for what Gibbons *et al* (1994) has described as Mode 1 Research; that is, the generation of a Mode 1 knowledge (M1K).

Looking at "Heidegger's Shoes"

Malan & Kriger (1998:243) develop the hypothesis that it is the "nuances of variability" in the socially constructed networks of "patterns of cognitive processes" – that are representative of organizations – that interest managers the most. To address this interest, they suggest that researchers require an ontological (or world-view) shift from an objective reality to social-construction and beyond, to other more holistic models. Their own move is towards a *Theory of Organizational Variability*, in which they assume that managers act as dynamic interpreters of fine shades of variability, within complex cognitive networks of socially and personally constructed meaning. However, I argue here that their reconceptualization of organizations in this manner can be said to fall victim to their very argument against objective induction.

Malan & Kriger's work presents a welcome departure from a strictly objectivist-rationalist paradigm. It offers a sensitization to the existence of alternative, culturally informed views of management. However, their assignment of *Variation* within a framework that aligns levels of managerial ability against each of six classifications – approaching a Theory of Management Wisdom – suffers from the potential to turn further research into objectively misplaced concreteness. The focus is on effect rather than cause. A *Theory of Variability* compressed into six classifications denies the manager the freedom to utilize the full range of their senses (hearing, sight, feeling, taste, smell). To take the example of one popular translation within a business text, in Sun Tzu's *The Art of War*,[8] the primary colours are noted as being only five in number, but their combinations are infinite.

Mintzberg's (2004:93) view is contemporaneous. He invokes, as one of three management poles,[9] an artistic process of "imagination", "creativity", "novelty", and "inductive reasoning", in a comprehensive synthesis of "insights and visions". In this *matter-of-Art*, "vision" becomes a factor in the unfolding of managerial narratives. Here, I juxtapose the concept of *management art* against such managerial narratives. "What is the *Artist* trying to achieve?" As Schopenhauer would have argued, the Artist sees a world that is different to the world of the non-Artist.[10] Is, then, the potential of *Art* that the organizational *vision-holder* (the CEO, the Entrepreneur, for example) holds an *artistic responsibility* to interpret and communicate his or her vision in a manner that can be related to by the non-Artist? Here, the concept of the Artist's self-expression in *Art* may be acknowledged as a disclosure of <u>a</u> *truth* content of their world. This is a *mimetic* process, in which *mimesis* – from its Greek origin – simply means "imitation" or "representation".[11] However, I argue a wider interpretation that provides for *mimesis* being a learning experience. *Mimesis* presents an alternative to *poiesis*,[12] as a bringing forth of a narrative (and provisional) knowledge of the artist's world.

In supporting my argumentation for a *mimetic* bringing forth of aesthetically informed narrative, I introduce Heidegger as my protagonist, and his note on Van Gogh's 1885 painting *A Pair of Shoes* (see Plate 1.1).[13] I argue metaphorically that *in "Heidegger's Shoes"*, Heidegger's interpretation supports the view that one function of Art (and the role of the Artist) lies in the disclosure of *"a truth of being"*; a position that places ontology as a function of the aesthetic experience. As Heidegger (1935:423) interprets Van Gogh's painting:

> From the dark opening of the worn insides of the shoes the toilsome tread of the worker stares forth. In the stiffly rugged heaviness of the shoes there is the accumulated tenacity of her slow trudge through the far-spreading and ever-uniform furrows of the field swept by a raw wind. On the leather lie the dampness and richness of the soil. Under the soles slides the loneliness of the field-path as evening falls. In the shoes vibrates the silent call of the earth, its quiet gift of

Plate. 1.1   **Vincent van Gogh (1853–1890)** A Pair of Shoes (F 0255), Paris, 1886

Oil-paint on canvas – 72 x 55 cm
Inventory number: s 0011 V/1962
Courtesy: Amsterdam, Van Gogh Museum (Vincent van Gogh Foundation)

the ripening grain and its unexplained self-refusal in the fallow des-
olation of the wintry field. This equipment is pervaded by uncom-
plaining anxiety as to the certainty of bread, the wordless joy of
having once more withstood want, the trembling before the
impending childbed and shivering at the surrounding menace of
death. This equipment belongs to the *earth*, and it is protected in
the *world* of the peasant women. From out of this protected belong-
ing the equipment itself rises to its resting-within-itself.

Heidegger's interpretation provides a frame of reference for the interpretation of the aesthetic experience of a work of "fine" Art. Here
Heidegger's interpretation has much in common with the observations
of Ruskin in contemplation of the '*...blunt head of a common, bluff,
undecked sea-boat, lying aside in its furrow of beach sand.*' In *The Harbours
of England* Ruskin (1856:13) provides an interpretation of the complexity

within the ship building-process – drawn, in part, from his contemplation of the bow of that small sea-boat: '...*[t]hat rude simplicity of bent plank... has in it the soul of shipping.*' As Ruskin (1856:28) continues:

> Take it all in all, a Ship of the Line is the most honourable thing that man... has ever produced. By himself, unhelped, he can do better...; he can make poems and pictures, and other such concentrations of what is best in him. But as a being living in flocks, and hammering out, with alternate strokes and mutual agreement, what is necessary for him..., to get or produce, the ship of the line is his first work. Into that he has put as much of his human patience, common sense, forethought, experimental philosophy, self-control, habits of order and obedience, thoroughly wrought handwork, defiance of brute elements, careless courage, careful patriotism, and calm expectation of the judgement of God, as can be put into a space of 800 feet long by 80 broad.

In both Heidegger's and Ruskin's syntheses, the exercise of an aesthetic judgement suggests an overriding idea that art must do more than faithfully recreate the images of man's creation. There is, I suggest, a powerful notion in seeking to learn through a faculty for exercising an interpretive aesthetic judgement of *Art*, to apply the same *mimetic* faculty within the complex organization by identifying that within it that embodies the whole. Aesthetics provides, as Collingwood (1938:vi) observed, an approach '...*to reach, by thinking, the solution of certain problems arising out of the situation in which artists find themselves here and now.*' That the artist's work might conceivably be interpreted in different contexts by different individuals, and yet still provide *plausible* explanations of a *world view*, leads to the notion of the *mimetic* copy-without-the-original; what Baudrillard (1981) describes as "*simulacra*". I argue that a "*Heideggerian simulacrum*" invokes a *mimetic* bringing forth of an aesthetically informed *knowledge-of-the-world*, one that previously did not exist. This presents a contextually relevant, provisional *truth* value that does not, necessarily, require hypostatization as "concrete" scientific knowledge.

Management pointillism?

Commercial organizations – as socio-technological systems – are introduced to meet some vision or purpose of consumer exchange value. However, academe's dominant viewpoint of contemporary *management practice* within the realm of an empirical, rationalist *management science* belies the fact that the vision being sought must be communicated within a "social" structure. The dominant science discourse suggests a requirement for the introduction of instrumental control systems, in which positivistic measurement, quantitative risk analysis, and other characteristics of "science", cocoon the socio-technological system firmly within the rationalist paradigm. But the paradox of this paradigm is that measurement implies a treatment for that which is already known and/or knowable; science cannot reliably address the ambiguous and the unknown.

A known or knowable event is observed, quantified and the resultant data is communicated and compared – within some established protocol; an accepted convention of management practice – against a known and/or desired outcome. But here we have also seen that people cannot be relied upon to obey a given set of processes in the achievement of some defined and measurable goal. Conventions of management practice therefore imply that action and its preceding judgement occurs against data that has undergone some manipulation within social processes that cannot, themselves, be fully controllable. Processed data does not, therefore, necessarily provide a true representation of an event itself. Such data is, I argue, secondary-level data. However, within a purely social context, perceptions of events are often based upon our sensory faculties; these provide a source of rich primary data. But, given the management conventions of an instrumental sphere of existence, such perceptions are neglected in the exercise of judgement. Common sense, gut feeling, intuition and emotion are not measurable; they have no defined place within a rational management practice. The limitation of a rationalistic management theory can therefore be seen as an inability to assimilate the richness of primary data that might act to influence judgement. Within this limitation, the value of the dominant paradigm is, however, not undermined; there is a value to a science and measurement that aids a better (instrumental) understanding of the current environment. Rather the concern lies outwith this limit. Here it requires a new paradigmatic approach to understand what might be perceived in practice, but remains unknowable.

As I have argued in the Introduction to this text, the turn from a purely instrumental mode of study, to include a rationalization of the cultural sphere of our existence, is a symptomatic response to both the successes and failure of the Enlightenment's great division of thought. Following this *cultural turn*, the later decades of the 20th century saw the rise of significant body of work on rationalizing the aesthetic sphere – *the aesthetic turn*. Here, aesthetics calls into play emotion. For example, "marketing" plays on emotion and, as rational practice gives way to the power of rhetoric, policy, plans, and other change devices can all be viewed as being produced to appeal to (or play upon) human emotions. Particularly now, in the consumer society aptly portrayed by Baudrillard (1970), judgement is often exercised within the realm of the aesthetic. I therefore extend the interest of those already highlighted, and others, in applying aesthetics to the study of management and organizations. However, rather than submit to a rational (or, I argue, an autonomous) aesthetic, I advance the notion of an Art aesthetic.

In suggesting a new paradigm of *management art* I will draw on a heuristic analogy from the field of Fine Art. In *Impressionistic* terms, I envisage the *management pointillist*[14] who possesses the ability to infer new meanings from fragmented, objective and aesthetic knowledge; one who can visualize connectedness in complex structures. The pointillist practices a technique using dots of colour which, through the spectator's eye, merge – they take form – through some abstract, towards some simulacrum. The spectators' exercise of aesthetic judgement in viewing a pointillistic *mimetic* representation yields just one example of where Polanyi (1958, 1966) has observed the focus of analysis shifts from a dynamics for which explanations can be given to a dynamics more closely associated with tacit knowledge. As Guillet de Monthoux (2000:41) argues, it is the dimension of aesthetic judgement that allows the widening of art's creative discourse into one of interpretation.

Negotiated alternatives

A paradigm of management pointillism – a distinctly sensory, emergent and pluralistic notion – provides the promise of new insights in developing a cognitive basis for understanding management challenges in complex and ambiguous organizations. Returning to the narrative of practice, at the highest levels of management, the Senior Executive must come to know his organization. Like the Disney Corp., the larger and the more complex the organization is, the more prone it is to ambiguity and the more difficult it is to know. The fundamental question posed is therefore:

> What can we learn about cognition from the role of the Artist and Spectator, and the artistic process, in the context of developing a Manager's faculty for management and organizational practice?

To paraphrase Collingwood, I seek to apply aesthetic theory in an attempt to reach, by thinking, the solution of certain problems arising out of the situation in which managers find themselves here and now. However, despite the growth in the interest of aesthetic theory in management and organizational study, few authors have attempted to describe the concept of the (aesthetic) manager as an artist. Preceding Dobson (1999), whose work suggests a fairly evangelical vie of the *management aesthete,* one notable (though overlooked) exception is Vincent Degot's (1987) article: *A Portrait of the Manager as an Artist.*[15] Degot's article, while presenting a valuable discourse on the concept is, I argue, flawed by a weak correlation of parallelism between the world of art and the world of management. That is, there is only a loose fit between this book's problematic, its underlying question, and Degot's potential answer. This, I believe, is a consequence of an inadequate philosophical basis for the conceptual linking of the two worlds. I argue that what is required here, is a dissolution of the boundary between art and science, rather than the building of a conceptual bridge linking them.

While there are currently a number of diverse themes forming the mantle of aesthetic interest within organizational and management studies, as Linstead and Höpfl (2000:2) observe, such themes merely *draw attention* to the *possibility* of developing an *aesthetics-of-the-organization* as a legitimate field of inquiry. Aesthetic interpretation, and its antecedent of aesthetic affect, is generally unmediated by knowledge; it is enhanced by an imagination that offers a capacity to both experience mental images (for example thinking, dreaming, perceiving, and remembering) and to engage in creative thought. However, this is not at the expense of rationalist thought. Indeed, metaphorically, *pointillism* offers a capacity to play imaginatively with elements of scientific knowledge and rationalistic thought, together with sensory perception, in order to explicate new meanings and insight. Here, aesthetics suggests that the study of art might provide understanding and insight into the social, and into our beliefs and knowledge about the world we live in. However, although the American philosopher Goodman (1976) held that aesthetics is a branch of epistemology, Novitz (1998:120) noted that this position challenges the mainstream. Art is, after all, creative and fictional. Thus, while Goodman describes an aesthetic epistemology based on an understanding of art that comprises the act of "correct" interpretation, I argue that the value of a paradigm of art lies in the full variability of the interpretation of aesthetic affect. Here, Novitz continues, '...*it is through our capacity to play imaginatively by combining or suspending... ideas, concepts, or images that we discover new possibilities, many of which are insightful, instructive, helpful, and informative.*'

There is an increasing body of significant work in the application of aesthetics to organizational and management issues. However, as I have previously introduced, there appears little, clear philosophical argument upon which this autonomous theorizing of the "aesthetic" voice is founded. As Carroll (1999:11) intimates, such a philosophical basis will not be found within the social science of management; it will, rather, stem from analytical philosophy. Therefore, in order to gain the greatest value from the field of aesthetics and its application to management and organizational practice, I argue that, given the state of relative immaturity of the field, an exploratory critique is required to build a sustainable philosophical position. From such a position, further (more empiric) work can then be proposed in the study of management and organizational practice through an alternate, Art-aesthetic paradigm. In rehearsing the argument to follow, in order to be able to proceed to explore the concept of an Art of Management, it also becomes necessary to address the basic question: **what is art**? Here a new conception of *Art* – bound to the social and cultural nature of its production – requires the description of a similarly new philosophy of Socially Negotiated Alternativism (SNA). This provides a meta-theoretical framework that will permit a new ontological view of a negotiated reality to form the basis for a socio-cultural narrative of existence. This will overcome what I will subsequently describe as the Weberian *aesthetic problematic*. It is such a meta-theory that will permit the drawing together of the seemingly parallel, but previously unrelated, socially contrived sub-worlds of organizational management and Art.

A paradigm of management pointillism

Why should the concept *Art* be extended to consider anything other that what it is generally taken to mean? Degot (1987:41) noted that '...[c]ost-benefit accounting is no longer sacred, and [managers] must increasingly take on board certain sociological and cultural considerations'. In a weak argument of parallelism he sought to draw inspiration from the fields of Aesthetics, The History of Art, and Art Criticism. Here, it is not sufficient to be able to interpret (and respond to) Malan and Kriger's *fine shades of variability* within organizations. From my own position it is also necessary to be able to play imaginatively with the organizational environment in its totality. As Degot went on to suggest, '...a "good" managerial work... takes the best advantage of the degree of freedom, and adapts best to the constraints, inherent in the social, *cultural and political environments.'* But, while Degot went no further than offering a sensitizing to the implications of an alternative paradigm, he did so avoiding any drift into positivistic frameworks, or premature classification systems. However Degot's central idea that Management had evolved more in character with artistic activity, than it had with the "rationalistic" model failed to engage a reasoned debate. Thus, in order to overcome the short comings of Degot's work, and to fully engage with a contemporary critical debate, "rescuing" what I believe are the valuable insights obtainable from his *Portrait of a Manager*, I inform this book's general thesis of an Art-aesthetic paradigm of management and organizational practice with a specific thesis. It is preferable, in the selection and training of (future) senior managers for critical[16] management positions, that account is taken of the candidate managers' aesthetic sensibility and that they are both sanctioned and facilitated to apply such sensibility within the management cycle of sense-making, judgement and action.

Rather than suggesting an undermining of extant thought, an Art-aesthetic thesis (both in the general and the specific) can be thought of as an integration of empiricist theorizing with more creative (fictional) theorizing. This enables the representation of a narrative of an organizational reality to an enlightened organizational audience; serving to lift a *poiesis* of a "concreted" abstract knowledge to the level of a *mimetic* instantiation of a plausible, relevant reality. In turn this will, I suggest, set new parameters for the study of a history of management and organizational practice, and its critique in the manner of a Heideggerian realization of potentially multiple plausible simulacra. However, as I have observed, while an *"Art of management"* may be an accepted colloquialism, there is a noticeable paucity of explicit definition, theorizing or narrative concerning what this might mean. Therefore, as I have already highlighted, the objective of this book is an exploration of the concept of Management Art. In order to achieve this objective – Framing an Art of Management – I will adopt the strategy of presenting what amounts to a philosophical argument through the following structure:

1. I will describe the broad, socio-cultural nature of management and organization, highlighting three themes of an instrumental rationalism's autonomous thought: the objective, the subjective and the pragmatic;
2. I will describe a focus on the landscape of management "aesthetic" studies by critically illuminating the potential within an aesthetic

understanding of a management art, as first described by Vincent Degot;

3. I will describe a conjunctive theory of art (CTA) and offer a definition of art's principal aesthetic categories; illustrating the theoretical framework of CTA with an empiric review of established Artists;
4. I will argue a philosophy of socially negotiated alternativism (SNA) in order to overcome CTA's problematic of ontological perspective;
5. I will describe the "preferred" hypothesis of an art of management based on the framework of CTA/SNA, and develop a critical reframing of Degot's original work; and finally,
6. I will describe a paradigm of management art as a meta-extension of a knowledge-based affect theory (KBAT).

This book is therefore set firmly within the context of a "challenge to conventional wisdom". Given this context, the broad and eclectic nature of the field of management and organizational study suggests a post-disciplinary view that sees management and organizational practice through the lens of art (itself another broad and eclectic field). The notion that management might be practiced as an Artform requires that I explain, in some detail, concepts that are firmly rooted in an Artworld. Although there are many forms of Art: dramatic, performance, music, and poetry for example, I have elected to discuss art in the context of what are commonly referred to as the plastic arts; specifically the *Fine Arts* of painting and of contemporary installation work. Therefore, in Part I of this book I enframe the tradition of autonomous thinking from the world of management (I include here extant organizational aesthetics and Degot's writing). In Part II, it becomes necessary for me to balance Part I with a review of autonomous thought from the world of art. There is a danger, I suggest, in any preemptive correlation between the two. Therefore, it is not until Part III that I turn to the constructive possibilities of a paradigm of management art. In the first instance, I revisit Degot's writing and then develop this – through an exploration of interpretation – towards the book's conclusions.

Argument structure

Continuing both Part I and this Chapter's origin in past and current management and organizational study, Chapter 2 delineates this broad field from a socio-cultural perspective. I draw on an Argyrian Model I/Model II theory-in-use construct, structuring the discussion around the major topics of the organization as a bounded universe, organizational culture, the Fayolian character of the manager and conceptualizing managerial space. Model II management is presented as a premiss for the "effective" manager's requirement for new information in managing complex and/or ambiguous situations, in which the desired outcome of theorizing is explicated as facilitating this requirement. Here, Academe's capacity to support managerial practice, through the dominant paradigm of rationalism, leads to the identification of three hypotheses of narrative knowledge production. My point of departure from this broad field is a call to an explorative social aesthetic.

In Chapter 3 I provide a focus that links Chapter 2 to the problem of conceiving an art of management through a critical review of Vincent Degot's *A Portrait of the Manager as an Artist*. Although relatively obscure, this work stands apart as one of the few attempts to conceptualize a management artform. I argue that, despite a flawed premiss, the narrative contains real insight, the intent of which is worth rescuing. This insight is revealed under the emergent themes of: 1) historicity, 2) creative management, 3) management artwork, 4) philosophy and 5) "audience" clarification. I argue that, to realize the potential of Degot's insight, a concept of a management artform requires a (new) definition of art that transcends any notion of a specific skills base; whether it be painting, drama, literature, or music or, indeed, management. This is the rationale behind Part II – a need to explore the world of autonomous art.

In Part II then, the focus shifts from *thinking-within-the-management-world* to *thinking-within-the-artworld*. In Chapter 4, I derive CTA from an explorative theorizing about art, drawing on *Art-as-Expression, Art-as-Craft* (Resemblance, Representation and Imitation), *Art-as-Mimesis* (through Functionalism), and *Art-as-Seeing & Telling* (Language, Intention & Communication). I define CTA as a tripartite relationship of innovation, mimetic learning and a non-specific notion of a craft skill set. This advances a richer view of *mimesis* than that of Platonic "imitation", in which an Aristotelian *mimesis* invokes character and emotion, and an experiential aesthetic attitude of disinterested contemplation.

In Chapter 5 I further develop CTA's Art aesthetic of disinterested contemplation; explicating the fundamental aesthetic categories of sublimity and beauty. I argue that an understanding of this aesthetic is necessary to develop an empirically informed validation of CTA. Chapter 5 therefore presents an aesthetic discourse on the sublime and the beautiful, culminating in revisiting the notion of *Art-as-*

Communication. This discourse is based on an explication of sublimity as the "object" of Art, and an argument that the concept of beauty possesses two distinct modes: the Attractive and the Judgemental. In preparation for a reframing of Degot's portrait, I also seek to lay some foundational connections between the Art aesthetic of sublimity and beauty, and management and organizations.

In Chapter 6 I present a provisional validation of the theoretically based CTA as an epistemic model of art; one that mediates the individualism of the sublime experience through a communication of the sublime discourse. This validation culminates in an empirically informed discussion of acknowledged Artists – drawn from BBC interview archives – including Dali, Hodgkin and Warhol. I draw a conclusion from this discussion that all Art (from a CTA perspective) exists in a temporally fluid state bounded by the dimensions of its mimetic, innovative and craft content. Through a discussion of the psychology of the artist and the creative process, the artist's education and training, and their responsibilities, CTA is shown to be able to describe relative, spatial, positions for multiple classes of art and artists.

In Chapter 7 I recognize that, although CTA advances the conjunction of craft, innovation and *mimesis*, a temporal disconnect exists between the mimetic facilitation engaged in by the artist and the mimetic learning of art's audience. While this disconnect is theoretically dealt with by CTA's process of socialization, this is problematic. The aesthetic nature of CTA presents a complex notion that is antecedent to any ontological position. It complicates any suggestion that an art of management might be a useful concept for future empirical study. Therefore I argue for a philosophy of SNA that is at least cognizant of the aesthetic problematic. This follows from a discussion of the transmission of meaning, in which the dichotomy of language is explored, positing SNA as a non-foundationalist epistemic philosophy. Part II therefore presents CTA/SNA as the philosophical and theoretical foundation for the paradigm of art into which the craft of management is then set.

Part III presents CTA/SNA as a value contribution to the field of management and organizational study and practice. In Chapter 8 I represent Part I's key themes of historicity, creativity, management (art) works, and management's audience. On a "value" basis, CTA/SNA allows (for example) an explication of organizational power-politic relationships that is in no sense hyper-critical. It also allows for a clarified positioning of Degot's roles of management art Historian and Critic. I also advance a framework for the graphical mapping of managerial space. The philosophy of CTA/SNA offers a paradigmatic shift from an instrumental, rationalistic thinking about a given management reality (an ontological position) to a negotiation of multiple plausible interpretations of (artistic) images of management and organization.

In Chapter 9 I develop the paradigmatic view of CTA/SNA, in which its value to management and organizational theorizing lies in understanding the concept of *management art* as a paradigm of artistic interpretation, in which a plausible (narrative) knowledge emerges through a negotiation of shared meaning. I go on to conclude by suggesting CTA/SNA as a paradigm for perception shifting; one in which the study of fiction production – argued as necessary within management and organization practice – is facilitated. I discuss the role of this paradigm in theorizing about management and organizational practice by revisiting the notion of the Management Gap; positing the Art-aesthetic agenda within a knowledge-based affect theory that address such theorizing in terms of the affect of "play". Here a *Sociology of Management Art* is an empiric possibility. My protagonist, Heidegger, allows the essence of an emergent fiction as the origin of a "truth" to be revealed.

Finally, in Chapter 10 I reargue this books central thesis in the context the contemporary CMS project, against which I offer CTA/SNA as a candidate for what is perceived to be a requirement for a new research agenda. I provide a brief overview of an extant "anti-bourgeois" challenge to the dominant authorities and the distribution of power, status and material claims within management and organizations. I argue that CTA/SNA's contribution to CMS is a critique of theorizing about practice, in which I present conclusions about the question of the value of a concept of management art, and its implication for future theory, policy and practice.

2
A Portrait of the Organizational Manager

> Good managers are not born, they are made. They are fashioned by experience of business and the realities of the workplace. They grow in stature and skill largely from their encounters with people and problems, not from studying the notes and theories catalogued in text books.
>
> John Darby, Chairman, Arthur Young, 1986[17]

The organization, a bounded universe

Management is a feature of everyday social life within which culture lays claims to an organization of the social. As Magretta and Stone (2002:5) observe, contemporary management has an overarching role as organizations increasingly become the vehicle of choice for implementing the work of society. Management is a theme that pervades government, commerce, art galleries, theatres, and even the home. But, as Hales (1993:1) observed, the terms "management" and "manager" are beset by ambiguity, confusion and obfuscation. The concern of this text is, however, the specific use of these terms in the context of a commercial organization. Here, the term "organization" presents a socially constructed boundary around a region of the universe – our social world; a "bounded" universe.[18] Within this bounded universe, I follow Chaney (2002:8) in noting that the term "culture" is profoundly effective, in that it makes sense of the variety of the social, offering a mode of explanation with infinite scope. Contextually therefore, culture is something an organization is; it is a representation that Anthony (1994:28) describes as a pattern of '...*economic and social cooperation reinforced by custom, language, tradition, history, and networks of moral interdependence and reciprocity.*' But the organization is also commonly to be understood, in concretized terms, as this or that organization. It might, for example, be a legal entity in its own right, with a specific location, and employing a given population. It may, in case-study fashion, be measured. We can thus describe: the organizational entity; its legal responsibilities; its geographic location; its function; its employees, and its successes and failures.

Within the concretization of an organization's boundary, the practice and the study of management leads to the formation of organizational narratives, in which patterns of economic and social cooperation are described. These patterns are, as Anthony (1994:3) relates, the implied systems of values and beliefs; they are the values-in-action revealed in the behaviour, policies and practices of the organization's population and its history. Such patterns describe a level of naïve narrative knowledge (NK_n) of the constructed sub-universe of the organization "as is". It is a description which is naïve in respect of its innocent relationship to other organizations within the universe of organizations. Therefore NK_n is existential; it is inferred from statements about the organization, as "object", that depend upon the information at hand about it. But, because of the naivety of other organizations, there can be no suggestion of a claim to universality of any NK_n. We deny that NK_n can be representative of alternatively constructed sub-universes. Outside of the organization, NK_n remains descriptive – it cannot claim to be prescriptive in any other organization. My company is *my* company; it is *not* like yours, although we might be in the same business. Intuitively, the single organization as representative of the universe of organizations creates a very limited sample from which "information at hand" about organizations can, in general, be drawn.

Within the organization, its own narrative may be prescriptive. From within that narrative, "stories" of effective action prescribe the organizational culture. Here, drawing on Argyris' (2004) Model I/Model II conception of "theories-in-use",[19] such "prescriptive" stories can be argued to form typical Model I theories.[20] These theories-in-use influence organizational practice by way of an effective action loop. Under Model I theories, managers learn and/or adopt strategies[21] that require skills in the reading of narrative and, as the basis of effective action, in the selection and dissemination of appropriate organizational stories. The effective action loop perpetuates the existing sub-universe. But, following Argyris' observations, the most important consequences of an organization managed on a Model I basis, rooted in what I have described is NK_n, are: 1) the potential for misunderstanding – that is, I argue, the incorrect reading and dissemination of narrative; 2) the escalation of errors – that is to say the reading of incomplete or incorrect narratives; and 3) the use of self-sealing, self-fulfilling, counterproductive and self-fuelling processes – that is the reading of inappropriate narratives.[22]

"Stories of excellence" abound; but such narrative abstractions of managerial and organizational "excellence" are rooted in the NK_n of individual managers and of individual organizations. Media, the movement of managers between organizations, the growth of management consulting and the strategies of managers practicing Model I theories-in-use, all feed a perception of "achievable excellence". In an appeal to Model I strategies, particularly the maximization of gain, NK_n stories are offered through the non-academic management literature.[23] As an exemplar, *In Search of Excellence*, by Peters and Waterman (1982), presented a sub-universe of excellent organizations and their excellent managers. However, the "fictitious" boundary employed in such a presentation limits the information at hand about the objects in question, by virtue of all those excellent companies and managers that might not be included in its analysis.

The "faux" universalization of a culture of excellence denies the arrival of additional "information-at-hand" from organizations and managers outside the fictitiously constructed boundary. It acts to deny the progressive revision of the description of excellence where, to paraphrase Bush (1908:184):

> ...the progressive revision of what constitutes a culture of excellence approaches a limit where all the information concerning the universe of excellent organizations and managers is to hand; despite the fact that this limit may never be reached.

The phenomenon of a market-driven "turn-to-culture" fuels a premature regression of the revision process. Here, as Anthony (1994:15) observed, the conclusion to be drawn from the cultural narrative is that the possession of, or creation of, a strong culture is the key to economic success. But the paradox of the *cultural turn* in management theorizing is that the foundation on which managerial expertise and "excellence" rests – the everyday world – is unstable and unknowable because it appears deeply non-rational or even irrational.

Fayol's organizational manager

Although assuming a general context of commerce, I wish to advance the proposition that it is necessary to consider a generic perspective of organizational management. Here a level of abstraction from the detail of management work becomes essential, in order to overcome certain contemporary issues that fuel the management debate. This potential for a generic perspective is illuminated, for example, by an intuitive sense of the convergence of many functions in the gamut of public and private, profit and non-profit organizations; all constrained by their common existence within a contemporary milieu that is increasingly characterized by legislative and environmental constraints. However, while in theory we might conceive of a generic role called *the manager*, as Bartlett and Ghoshal (1997:92–93) have observed, in practice this view has always been very different.

In conceptualizing the generic manager I shall borrow from the grounded theory of Glaser and Strauss (1967). This allows me to transcend description and its associated problems: for example what is accurate and factual, what is interpretation and so on. Importantly, conceptualizing the manager allows me to develop an idea that is abstract from time, place and people. This is an abstraction in a formal, Lockean empiricist sense, as the process by which particular ideas – in this case the "idea" of *the manager* – are made general. I do not argue that an abstract conceptualization of the manager is, in any sense, the only way to explain managers, but simply that it provides a valid approach in the context of this text. As Glaser (2002:3) confirms, traditional "description" arising from empiric study, is neither "bad", nor "wrong", nor "unfavourable"; it is just different with different properties to conceptualization.

As an abstraction of managerial narratives, the *idea* of the *manager* provides a simple and attractive device. To paraphrase Taylor (1978:99) and therefore, indirectly, Locke:

> We notice recurring features in the immense variety of our [narratives of] experience of what it might... be to be a manager; for example we notice something similar in the work of the manager we met today and the work of the manager we met yesterday. We pick out this feature of the complex patterns of information we receive, isolate it from the features which accompany it on the particular occasions of our meetings (whether the manager was male or female, tall or short, busy or relaxed, and so on) and assign to it a label, *viz.* a descriptor (or characteristic) of what it is to be a manager. Somebody is "a manager", and is to be classified "a manager" if and only if they conform to the [appropriate, culturally] identified pattern of information.

The conceptual *idea* of *the manager* therefore arises as a distillation of a body of experiential instances of *a manager*; a synthesis of managerial narrative. To further paraphrase Taylor: *an abstract idea of a manager may serve, in this Lockean sense, as both: a paradigm postulated in order to explain our ability to classify a person as being a manager; and as a sign postulated to explain how particular terms related to being a manager have general application to particular managers.* However, to some (for example Bartlett and Ghoshal, 1997) the idea of a "universal" manager remains intrinsically impossible.[24]

Putting abstraction into context, Magretta and Stone (2002:19) described the role of "management" as about "value creation". However, this view may be too abstract. The theoretical concept of a generic manager invokes the image of Russian Dolls: each manager being a similar, but bigger, version of their subordinate manager; each involved, therefore, in "value creation". But, as Bartlett and Ghoshal (1997:93) report, in practice top-level managers are seen to set direction, while front-line managers find themselves in the role of operational implementers and are more concerned with directing aspects of production and service delivery, than in a conscious and explicit desire to "add value". A breakdown between theory and practice becomes evidential in too high a level of abstraction. However, Magretta and Stone (2002:215–217) go on to suggest that management is also about building organizations that work; that is, moving from a purpose through design to execution. This further perspective may elaborate certain facets of managerial work but, I argue, its principles do no more than restate what Henri Fayol (1916b) advanced as the five cornerstones of managerial work, specifically: planning, organizing, commanding, coordinating, and controlling the organization and its purpose.

All managerial models, be they organizational or individual, represent some level of abstraction; generally based on assumptions. For example, in a contemporary vein, Bartlett and Ghoshal's (1997:94) own framework of "New Management Roles" was drawn up on the basis of assumptions concerning '...*the major elements of the emerging organizational framework that is shaping them.*' In their "New Organizational Model", such assumptions – concerning changes to the "old" structures and processes of management – represented a distinct challenge to the more classical, hierarchical structures like, for example, Taylorism. However, as a general scientific principle, any model developed on the basis of assumptions, particularly of a temporal nature, must be considered in the same context as those assumptions.

Therefore, in developing an *ahistoric* concept of "the manager", it is necessary to avoid assumptions concerning time, both relative and absolute. An *ahistoric* model of a manager invokes management features that are not, or have not been, at variance – to the greatest extent discernible – over history. Seen in this light, Fayol's management model presents a generic, *historically insensitive* approach and, in the context of this text, presents a viable abstract concept of managerial work.

Fayol at the limit of style

Fayol is not without his critics. Notably, Henry Mintzberg (1971:108) stated that '*Fayol's fifty-year-old description of managerial work is no longer of use to us.*' But, as Lamond (2004:353) has argued, in such cases it is possible to reconcile differing managerial models through the discussion of management "styles". The identification of managers by reference to a greater degree of *recurring features* eventually presents the dilemma of widening the managerial discourse into the realm management style; each style (or "class") being appropriate to some defined managerial context. Increasingly, as Ferrario (1994:112–113) has noted, style has become recognized as one of the "qualities" – together with personality, motivation, attributes & skills, and competencies – commonly assumed to be characteristic of managers in general.

Although the concept of "style" presents a powerful argument for the reconciliation of differing management models, I believe that it detracts from management's *esse objectivumm*. Therefore, while the question of "style" is important in understanding management and organizational practice under defined contexts, I argue that it is necessary to transcend issues that the term "style" implies; for example issues of gender and stereo-typing. Although too high a level of abstraction is problematic, as the veils of abstraction are lifted – revealing the details of a context-specific management role – the less useful a theoretical model of management is as a reference signifier, postulated to explain how the particular features related to being *a manager* have a "general" application to *individual managers*. Also, the suggestion of a management style is very subjective; it is crucially dependent on the individual person as manager, their behaviour and their relationships within the organization – that is their individual *narratives-of-existence*. As Lopez (1970:61) observed:

> The managerial role has probably been misinterpreted more than any other in history. …[I]ts dimensions depend, not only on what is

to be done, but on the personality of the doer and the cultural milieu in which [s/he] does it…. In fact, it appears that as a role increases in complexity, significance, and status its dimensions become more ambiguous and vague.

Giddens (1984:284) related that the study of management, as a phenomenon of the social sciences, is constituted by both the actions of the actors (in this case the management theorists) and the meta-languages invented for its purpose. Therefore, from a social science perspective, management is not only affected by how those *in* society perceive it, but at the same time it becomes an effective agent in shaping itself. The narrative (NK_n) of managerial activity acts, through Model I theories-in-use, to shape and reinforce itself. To paraphrase Ghoshal (2005:77):

> …a management theory – if it gains sufficient currency – changes the behaviours of managers…. Whether right or wrong to begin with, [a Model I] theory can become right as managers – who are both its subjects and the consumers – adapt their behaviours to conform with the [theory]… this is precisely what has happened to management practice over the last several decades, converting our collective pessimism about managers into realized pathologies in management behaviours.

The more managers are classified by reference to a set of managerial features, the more Model I theories-in-use are developed and the easier it is to identify managers fulfilling our criteria for a certain "managerial style". But, to return to the cultural paradox, a well-defined conception of what it is to be a manager – reliant on a low level of abstraction in the "Model I" manager – can only be achieved in relatively stable and specific contexts with clearly stated assumptions. However, the management environment is characterized by an *everyday world* that is unstable and unknowable, because it appears deeply non-rational, or even irrational. The cultural paradox undermines both context and assumptions. Here, change, ambiguity and irrationality, as recurrent features of the organizational landscape, preclude management from being reduced, in a Tayloristic sense, to a series of elements of *management work*. I argue, therefore, that the essence of a manager lies within an *ahistorical*, abstract concept of a manager in an embedded relationship with their organization. It lies in the psyche of the individual acting out their managerial role within the socio-cultural context of *the* organization. Management, as an individualistic activity, is mediated by personalities and conventions of existence in some society characterized by a market economy and constrained by legislative and environmental requirements and societal norms. It is enacted under conditions of constant change; within a fluid environment about which the manager can only ever hold an imperfect level of knowledge.

The Model I manager (after Fayol)

Hales (1993:2) has suggested that the socio-cultural concept of management arises as a function of human agency – through (*inter alia*) the quintessential human capacity to stand back and regard experience: "prospectively" in terms of what will happen; "reflexively", in terms of what is happening; and "retrospectively", in terms of what has happened. This explanation is coherent with the development of narratives, stories and metaphors (that is NK_n), as the manager's sensemaking of the "what will", "what is" and "what was" of management and organizational practice. The manager, as an "agent", is therefore seen to possess the capacity to shape the organization, rather than to simply react to it. From this agential relationship, Hales derived five conceptually distinct managerial activities: deciding/planning work objectives; time/resource allocation; motivating/generating work effort; coordinating/combining work effort; and monitoring/controlling effort in line with objectives.

Although Hales' managerial activities resemble Fayol's categories of planning, organizing, commanding, coordinating and controlling, Hales argues a divergence in three respects. Firstly, he suggests that Fayol's conceptualizing of management offers a distinct separation from planning whereas his own concept integrates the planning/forecasting activity but separates out decision-making. I argue that this is conceptually semantic. Citing Fayol (1916a:48) Cuthbert (1970) discusses Fayol's foresight and planning as coming under the principle of *Gouverner c'est prévior* – to govern is to foresee. Conceptually, it is only necessary to relate to the activity of planning since, by its very nature, planning is concerned with future events and involves both the forecasting of objectives and/or likely outcomes, and the selection of (or decisions regarding) those outcomes.

Hales' second divergence is his use of motivation as a concept that subsumes Fayol's "more restricted" term: *commanding*. Here I argue that "command" offers the more general expression. Again referring to Cuthbert's (1970:117) commentary, in Fayol's notion of command

'*...the manager himself [sic] [is] to set a good example and to aim at making unity, energy, initiative and loyalty prevail.*' Fayol's manager develops initiative by allowing his or her subordinates the maximum share of work consistent with their position and capabilities. In this sense motivation is a factor that rests within command. Thirdly, Hales relabels Fayol's "organizing" as the allocation of time and effort (that is resources), in order that he can reuse the label "organizing" to describe the process by which all management elements are brought together and conducted on a large scale. Fayol's concept of organization is, however, broader than that suggested by Hales. Cuthbert (1970:114) observes that Fayol's "organization" referred not only to resource allocation, but also to the structure and processes involved in the achievement of work's objectives.

In critiquing these divergences, I simply indicate that Hales' concept of management is even closer to Fayol's than Hales suggests; as even Hales (1993:3) admits, Fayol's basic formulation endures. However, as Cuthbert's own reading of Fayol suggests, there are analytic weaknesses within Fayol's theory. Certainly, if Fayol's work is used in a descriptive sense, then contemporary interpretations might well disagree with Fayol's classical position. However I argue that, in the abstract, Fayol's five concepts of planning, organizing, commanding, coordinating and controlling, begin to look like an *ahistoric* framework for the basic social process that is *managerial work*. They appear to hold as valid today as they did at their inception nearly 100 years ago.

Notwithstanding such contributions as Fayol's and others, management – as evidenced in other cultures – is arguably an occupation of ancient standing. As Wren (1990:141) noted, this view is often neglected in favour of an academic interest that is generally restricted to recent (20th-century) history. Therefore, as Lui (1996:391) suggests, we also find that:

> ...management is no stranger to the Chinese culture... Over 3000 years ago, during the Chow Dynasty, there was an official by the name of Lui Shang, [also] known as Kiang Tai Kung, whose writings Tai Kung Luk Tao could be regarded as the oldest publication on the art of management in China.

Certainly it has not been lost on some contemporary management writers that, amongst other notable Chinese, Sun Tzu had much to say that has relevance to management (see, for example, McNeilly, 1996). As Lui continues, the idea of drawing comparisons between the early Chinese approaches to management, and those of contemporary western practitioners, identifies and upholds a certain universality to the managerial concept. Therefore, in conceptualizing the work of a manager, I concur with Wren (1990:142) in noting a remarkable continuity – between Fayol and others – in the abstracted descriptions of managerial activities. This does no more than reaffirm what Carroll and Gillen (1984:135) observed as the fact that:

> ...classical management functions have endured for many decades simply because they have been found to be... useful [for] classifying the... thousands of different activities carried out by managers as individuals or groups for purposes of teaching and communication.

I argue, therefore, that Fayol's *classical* concept provides a sufficient basis upon which to outline a portrait of the Model I manager; I shall refer to this subsequently as the *five classical functions* of managerial work *(after Fayol)*. Although these functions have been added to significantly over the years, as Watson (2001b:37) has argued, contemporary research does not require us to dismiss this "classical" approach.

Management's responsibility

Juxtaposing the *five classical functions* of managerial work with Watson's (2001b:30) sociological concept of an occupation, the gamut of planning, organizing, commanding, coordinating and controlling activities ensure that a manager is, at any time, "engaged" with the organization on any number of tasks. As Watson continues, this engagement is with a set of '... *ongoing human relationships utilizing various technologies in which people cooperate to achieve [other] tasks which would otherwise not be possible[.]*' As an *a priori* engagement with other people, managerial ability therefore depends on facets of the manager's wider social abilities; this ensures that the individual *psyche of the manager* is as important as the nature of their work. The individual manager is someone who both "interests others" and has "interests". Consequently there is, in a manager's exercise of reasoning and judgement, a powerful notion of communication and negotiation with, and between, "others" and their "interests". As Watson (2001a) discusses:

> [The] very process of thinking and decision-making involves us in a dialogue in our minds with the arguments of human others, whether these be remembered arguments of particular people... or cultural norms... Thinking and deciding has a dialogic form.

But communication is, I suggest, broader than just the concept of dialogue, and negotiation is inherently influenced by power and politics. The notion that managerial communication is not just a *face-to-face* dialogic exchange is crucially important.

A manager's reliance on communication is evident in other descriptions of managerial work. Penley *et al* (1991) argue that organizational management is fundamentally tied to communicating; both appear inextricably linked because of the nature of management and its responsibilities. In reviewing the literature in this area, Penley *et al* point to two general perspectives that characterize a manager's communicative faculty. Firstly they identify a "skills" perspective. They argue the hypothesis that a manager's abilities are influenced by both oral and written skills, as well as a faculty to articulate and a certain sensitivity to various communications media. Secondly, they point to a "social cognitive" perspective: a manager's faculty for construing social processes and their perceptions of social realities.[25] We may also add Sypher *et al's* (1989) highlighting of listening as a further aspect of communication. Therefore, from these perspectives, we can reason that our perceptions of our social reality – and of its social processes – rely, not only on the information received from a variety of sources (of which the aural is only one), but also the ability to interpret and act on that information. Social cognition broadens the concept of communication – beyond the aural – to include the realm of aesthetic senses and judgement. Communication, in this broader concept, is about a manager's ability to gather, process, and disseminate information about the environment in which they practice the *five classical functions* of managerial work.

The aesthetic of a social cognitive discourse, as central to the concept of a manager's communication abilities, can be related to MacIntyre's (1981:12) notion of "Emotivism" – the philosophical doctrine that evaluative judgements are nothing but expressions of preference; they are evaluative in character. Whereas aesthetics is an individualistic notion of "the self", MacIntyre's (1981:23) *emotivism* presupposes a sociology and, while it is more often used in moral argument, I shall generalize its use here and advance the idea that the essence of the manager – involved in the planning, organizing, commanding, coordinating and controlling of his/her web of organizational relationships – is embedded within an emotive philosophy.[26] Here, MacIntyre continues:

> [there is] at least a partial conceptual analysis of the relationship of
> [a manager] to his or her reasons, motives, intentions and actions,

and… generally…some claim that these concepts are embodied or at
least can be in the real social [and therefore management] world.

MacIntyre's organization is characteristically engaged in a competitive
struggle for scarce resources to put to the service of its given *ends*. Here,
managerial responsibility is to "manage" as effectively as possible
toward those *ends* and, in doing so, make choices. But questions of *ends*
are questions of values on which reason is silent, and managers are
simply seen to make choices in their dealings within the network of
relationships that constitute their businesses. Yet, as Lopez (1970:
10–11) had observed, such choices are neither necessarily free, nor
inherently self-interested, and while it is true to say that individuals
behave in a way best guaranteed to satisfy their own needs, this is
simply not the whole truth. Individuals, acting under strong cultural
influences, do mostly what they are expected to do. Therefore, while
we might empirically rationalize the elements of managerial work, it is
apparent that the *actual* execution of that work tends to a question
of *constrained* individual choice. Managerial choice, particularly in a
complex and uncertain environment, now hinges on the manager's
"emotive" sensibility to a broad concept of communication. That is to
say, managerial choice hinges on a manager's social-cognitive abilities
and their (cultural) perceptions of the *managerial world.*

Drawing further from MacIntyre (1981:27), his concept of *the character* is particularly useful in attempting an abstract conceptualization
of *the manager*:

> There is a type of dramatic tradition – [for example] Japanese Noh…
> and English medieval morality plays… – which [possess] a set of
> stock characters immediately recognizable to the audience. Such
> characters partially define the possibilities of plot and action. To
> understand them is to be provided with a means of interpreting the
> behaviour of the actors who play them, just because a similar under-
> standing informs the intentions of the actors themselves[.]

I therefore advance the notion that MacIntyre's *character* of *the manager*
bears a close resemblance to the manager of whom I am attempting *a
portrait*. Such a *character* appears possessed of the attributes required
of my Lockean *abstract manager*; a sign postulated to explain how particular terms related to being a manager have general application to
individual managers. A knowledge of the *character* of the manager provides an interpretation of the actions of those individuals who have

assumed the character *manager*. The individual, with his or her "self" embedded within an emotivist philosophy – assuming the character of the manager – has the capacity to evade any necessary identification with any particular contingency of what it might be to be a manager. Hales' principle of "human agency" is preempted by MacIntyre (albeit in the form of moral agency). *Managers* now require the ability, to some degree or another, to be able to stand back from any situation they might find themselves in and to pass judgement on it from a universal and abstract point of view that is, as MacIntyre (1981:33) might argue, detached from "all social particularity". But, as Watson (2001b:12) observes:

> [g]iven the complexity of the world around us... its unpredictability, and ...the limited mental ability of the human animal to gather and process information about [it], we can never really know what is going on around us. Neither can we ever be sure what the outcome of any action... will be.[27]

A Model I characterization of management becomes limited by the socio-cultural perspective of the world in which it operates.

The Model II manager

In an Argyrian Model I sense, it is within MacIntyre's *character* of the manager that I find the limits to the application of Fayol's *classical functions of managerial work*. I have already introduced the premiss that part of a manager's real challenge is in taking effective action in the face of excessive complexity and/or ambiguity. I have argued that, in taking action, managerial choice hinges on the manager's "emotive" sensitivity to a broad conception of communication – to his or her social cognitive abilities and perceptions of their "management world". But how do managers *effect* managerial choice when there is incomplete or insufficient knowledge of a given complex and/or ambiguous situation, in which they are expected to initiate and direct organizational practice – frequently under increasingly stringent time constraints? This is a problem exacerbated by the cultural paradox.

To paraphrase Lamoreaux (2001:633), I am no longer concerned with the day-to-day choices of managers, such as product placing, recruitment, or the plethora of ongoing routines of an extant managerial or organizational narrative. I am, rather, concerned with ambiguity, complexity and matters such as change in the political, economic, societal and technological environment in which commercial organizations operate. Here such matters act to undermine the predictivity of naïve narratives; where Model I theories-in-use cease to be reliable as an effective guide for action. I am concerned with how a break from the past can lead to the development of new (or revised) narratives, in order to provide effective responses to such change, under conditions of risk and uncertainty.

Faced with a failing reliability of their narrative(s) of existence, Model I practitioners would direct organizational practice on an uncritical Model I assumption that the (external) narratives of others (for example Peters and Waterman) were sufficiently prescriptive to effect action. That is, until the consequences of such action might be determined as effective or not; making any correction after the fact – a single loop process. There is, in effect, a (sub)conscious denial of the requirement for an *equilibrium* within the mind, between what is known and what remains unknown. This, I suggest, provides a reinforcement of the limiting cultural boundary, through a "belief" in the validity of "un-validated" knowledge. A Model I management and organizational practice, founded on the narratives of others – a practice of narrative substitution – can therefore be seen to lead to a greater risk of Model I's negative consequences. Here, as Anthony (1994:15) observed, the case for the deliberate change of organizational culture in order to *manufacture* success, goes beyond the cultural associations claimed by such as Peters and Waterman. Following Peters and Waterman's identification of the population of their *excellent* sub-universe, Anthony (1994:16) observed that further information came to hand, from outside their fictitious boundary, to suggest that the subsequent performance of the excellent companies was no better than that of other companies existing within the universe of companies. Stories of excellence give way, through progressive revision, to the reframing of such excellence as no more than a revised narrative of organizational culture in general. The fictitious boundary of *excellent* companies dissolves into an historical artefact of naïve narrative.[28]

The danger inherent in the limits of Model I theories-in-use lies in an assumption that any NK_n might be universally prescriptive; that is, the validity of a narrative external to *the* organization is not questioned before that narrative forms a *faux a priori* justification for action. The importation of NK_n from some other sub-universe is, under Model I management, rarely subject to a process of validation. Here, Argyris' (2004:10) Model II theory-in-use offers a potential solution. Model II management still provides for strategies that: advocate one's position; call for the evaluation of the action of the self and others; and make attributions concerning their intentions; it is not, therefore, an opposite of Model I. However, under Model II, these strategies are now applied to the new governing values of 1) the production of new information; 2) the exercise of *informed* choice; and 3) the monitoring of the effectiveness of actions. In this sense, Model II management practice extends effective Model I action by creating an imperative for enquiry and testing. Model II management requires managers, rather than merely engaging in some form of narrative substitution, to go beyond their "own" sub-universe boundary for new information that can be admitted to the process of progressively revising their own NK_n. Seen in this way, Model II is not a replacement for effective Model I management; it is an adjunct. I argue, therefore, that the values of control, maximization of gain and minimization of loss, suppression of negativity, and rational action, that are central to Model I, remain part of Model II. It is this adjunctive nature of a Model II theory-in-use that is reflected in Argyris' notion of double-loop learning.

A Model II practitioner would not rest on the assumption that any narrative represented the limit of what was knowable at the time. As a basis for action, the Model II manager does not, therefore, rest on assumption, but seeks to form *an equilibrium-of-mind* between what is known and what is not. In this respect, the revision of NK_n need only be plausible and provisional, and the achievement of a new equilibrium can be seen as a dissolution of the cultural boundary obstructing narrative revision.[29] The Model II practitioner questions beliefs. However, while highlighting a manager's imperative to engage in narrative revision through the acquisition of new information, an Argyrian Model II solution leaves open the question of what "theories-in-use" might constitute acceptable methods of information generation? Here, I argue, the process of narrative revision at the limits of the organizational boundary or, more accurately, at the point of dissolution of the present boundary, calls for an understanding of an unbounded management space.

Unbinding the management space

> I am brother, cousin and grandson, member of this household, that village, this tribe... These... characteristics... [define] partially at least and sometimes wholly my obligations and my duties.
>
> (MacIntyre, 1981:33).

The manager, as an *embodied self*, while possessed of an ability to judge from whatever perspective it chooses, is nevertheless a derivative of, and inherits from, a particular social space within an interlocking set of social relationships. Here, paraphrasing MacIntyre (1981:34), to know the "self" as a manager is not to occupy a static and fixed position. It is to find oneself placed at a certain point on an organizational journey with set goals. Moving through management life is to make (or fail to make) progress towards a given "end". The manager is thus inextricably linked to his, or her, own environment; one that includes not only the organization within which managerial responsibilities are enacted, but also the social world and its cultural milieu within which the organization is, itself, embodied. But, as Watson (2001b:20) argues, we cannot "know" our environment; its ambiguity is so great, and the human mind is so limited in cognitive capability, that we cannot "know" all the facts; the cultural paradox is that we can only make and act upon our interpretation of it. As Argyris (1973:254) has previously written, '*In fact [the environment] is so complex that [we] cannot make decisions without having constraints imposed upon [it] to help make it manageable.*'

The manager, in the exercise of managerial choice, employs reason and judgement and decides. In doing so, the manager processes information about his or her environment. This information is, however, much less than an approximation to the real environment; it is information in which perception and cognition intervene. As Simon (1959:272) has argued:

> ...the perceived world is fantastically different from the "real" world. The differences involve both omissions and distortions, and arise in both perception and inference. ...The decision-maker's model of the world encompasses only a minute fraction of... the relevant characteristics of the real environment, and his [sic] inferences extract only a minute fraction of all the information that is present even in his model.

Our knowledge about our environment and its situation is therefore limited. As Watson (2001b:20) has confirmed, '*...we fall back to a considerable extent on recipes, formulae, legends, folk tales and intuition to make sense of these situations.*' We come to rely on our narratives-of-existence. However, given such a reliance, the classic (Model I) rationality of, for example, Simon's (1959:272) economic man(ager) – exercising managerial choice by choosing between fixed and known alternatives to managerial actions, each with their own (known) consequences – is invalidated. Neither, as Argyris (1973:254) observed, would the concept of a *bounded rational man* find favour – in which, *inter alia, man* is provided with givens or premises, created as boundaries within which managerial activity may be directed to a presumed rationality. A descriptive social science based on rationality, bounded or otherwise, tends to the normative, in which generalizations become coercive of human behaviour. Here, as Ghoshal (2005:75) recalled, a Keynesian *practical man* – slave to the theories of others – leads to what Argyris (1973:266) argued was the probability that social science will increasingly produce self-fulfilling prophecies.

From a Model I concept, the more we attempt to define the commercial organization within which the manager operates (that is, the more we map the managerial space), the more we might be inclined to shape it towards an ideal that would tend to the empirically normative. Here, Stubbart (1989:326) has noted that such a "normative" idea of management – *the Russian Doll:* each manager possessed of the same knowledge, the same reasoning, and responding to the same threats and opportunities in pursuit of the same goals – is not a viable foundation for management and organizational study. As I have argued, the cultural paradox of the gap between managerial theory and practice is that a normative conception of what management and the organization might be – reliant on a low-level of abstraction in the "model" commercial organization – can only be achieved in relatively specific contexts with clearly stated assumptions. Here the Model II manager must, however, eschew the normative in favour of a faculty for, potentially constant, revision; a more abstract idea of the organizational space occupied by the Model II manager is therefore required.

As Reed and Anthony (1992:609) argued, organizations which conduct commercial enterprise are themselves communities, and the networks that compose them engage in *'activities and dependencies which are not susceptible to mechanistic description and measurement.'* The manager enacts his or her role within, and constrained by, the activities and dependencies of a community of individuals that is, itself, influenced by a wider community of other individuals; and indeed other communities. This broad conception of a management space is indeterminate; it has no imposed, tangible or fictional boundaries. However, to move from a context sensitive view of an organization – where assumptions about the network of influences from external relationships form the boundaries of rational comprehension – to the abstract conceptualization of an indeterminate management space, requires a significant shift in belief structures. Here, as Fuchs (2002:7) argues:

> ...[t]here is a shift from predictability to nonpredictability; from order and stability to instability, chaos and dynamics; from certainty and determination to risk, ambiguity, and uncertainty; from control and steering to self-organization of systems; from linearity

to complexity and multi-dimensional causality; from reductionism to emergentism; from being to becoming; and from fragmentation to interdisciplinarity.

However, this shift does not represent a total break from rationality and its attendant predictability. It respects what I have argued is the necessary adjunctive differentiation between Model I and Model II theories-in-use. In this sense, the abstraction from the real sets up a dialectic of chance and necessity; that is, there are certain aspects of the managerial space that can be determined and described by general laws, at the same time other aspects become governed by the principle of chance.[30] To adopt chance as an equally legitimate aspect of the management and organizational space implies the possibility of a form of "Brownian motion" in MacIntyre's journey of self-realization. The manager, as a social person, is devoid of a static and fixed position. At any point in time, the manager simply occupies a space at a certain point on a journey through management life, progressing – or failing to progress – toward a given "end".

Effective managers: the constitution of new universes

An unbounded, indeterminate management space amounts to what Fuchs (2002) has argued is a self-organizing space; it is a space characterized by multi-dimensional social systems, where managers are not only *managers* but they may also be '...*patriarchs, patriots and professionals, capable of drawing resources and inspiration from all of their social identities.*' Therefore, within an abstracted Model II theory-of-action, managerial agency can be distilled into fundamental questions of social identity. That is to say that the *character* of an *a historical, a temporal* "manager" can also, *in character*, be an "explorer". It is with this Model II conception of the *manager-as-explorer*, coupled with the *aesthetic of a socio-cognitive responsibility*, that I fully mark the point of departure from the rational, socio-cultural, nature of management hitherto described. Here, the manager who is effective under conditions of complexity and uncertainty appears to possess a certain innate competence concerning their *existence-in-the-world* that appears to transcend scientific knowledge. This competence acknowledges their *thinking-, feeling-,* and *acting-in-the-world* through Lyotard's (1979) criterion of efficiency, justice, happiness, and the audio and visual sensibilities. At the limits of the usability of their extant narratives, the effective organizational manager is seen to be able to create (a new) or change a (rare) universe through the origin of new narratives. Effective managers appear as subjects who have the skills to define and describe a new universe. Effective managers can be perceived of as possessing an ability to map an unbounded, indeterminate space.

Clearly there are a great many effective organizational leaders and managers; people, either with or (notably) without appropriate levels of "formal" management education. These are frequently the objects of study within the popular management narratives such as *In Search of Excellence*. I do not suggest that these managers are necessarily conscious of their competence in mapping the unbounded managerial space; these managers appear to just "manage effectively". But, in order to define and describe a new organizational universe, "subjects" (that is managers) are needed who have the skills to do so. Moreover, as Argyris (2004:6) suggests, it would also be necessary to have norms that sanction and encourage such behaviour (or competence). If we assume, therefore, that the skills to create the new universe, or to modify the "as is" universe, exist in the "as is" universe, then what appears as a limiting factor in the creation of new narratives is the universe's capacity to sanction, and even encourage, an individualistic, knowledge-acquisition behaviour. Such behaviour transcends socio-culturally accepted norms of scientific knowledge; it also draws on the critical concepts of power and politics.

In the development of effective managers, the task of academe becomes one of improving and/or facilitating a manager's capacity to employ narrative and storytelling in their organizational practice. Here, in considering the mainstream objective of organizational and management research, Argyris (2004) has noted that the task of the scholar is to describe their chosen organizational/management universe "as is", as completely and as validly as possible. I will describe such research as naïve;[31] it may also be referred to, as others have,[32] as Mode 1 research leading to Mode 1 Knowledge (M1K). Such naïve research yields a scientific knowledge concerning the sub-universe "as is" (SK=M1K). However, as I have alluded to, the significant concern of some scholars and practitioners[33] is that, while SK features as a commodity of the academic world, it finds little application in the sub-universe it describes. Here, I argue, new knowledge need only be provisional and plausible as a basis of action, in order to contribute to the continued unfolding of an organizational narrative.

The academic rigour attached to the production of SK introduces an abstraction of the organizational universe "as is". This places SK outside the culturally constructed boundary of the manager. For Mode 1 research to bring managerial value, either SK needs to be reinserted into the manager's universe, as a (sophisticated) narrative (that is $SK=NK_s$),[34] or managers require that their own cultural boundary is repositioned to include the academic world as a relevant source of new knowledge. However, to suggest that SK need only be considered as provisional narrative in a new practice, is to appear to devalue the rigour of its production. Herein lies an origin of the conflict between stories and science noted by Rhodes and Brown (2005). Therefore the cultural environment – that is to say the business schools – in which SK is presented in the education of managers (the generation of management expertise[35]) serves to "preserve" a state where $SK \neq NK_s$, by virtue of an almost political attachment to the "privileged" process of scientific knowledge production.

The preservation of attachment to academic rigour is manifest in the appearance of the Management Gap, where MacIntyre (1981:106) has argued that organizational success and organizational predictability exclude each other. One academic response to this gap has been developed by Gibbons *et al* (1994) in their work *The New Production of Knowledge*, which presents a conception of Mode 2 knowledge (M2K). This is what Watson (2001a:387) has described as a concept of managerially "biased" knowledge for the advantage of managers; a concept that is flawed, in that it remains attached to a requirement for academic rigour. However, in a Model II conception of management, knowledge is emergent through practice; the effective manager does not merely engage in narrative revision, but "creates" new narratives-of-existence. As I have argued, this practice is suggestive of a managerial ability (conscious or otherwise) to effect the repositioning of what is a socio-culturally defined boundary of NK_n – in effect remapping the managerial space. If, therefore, an objective of academic research is to retain a contribution to this practice, then such research must contribute to the following desired consequence of management practice:

- **Consequence C1:** through generating and applying new, plausible narrative knowledge, a manager is better able to resolve ambiguity and complexity within management situations, and to manage to successful outcomes.

My point of departure from a strict Model II theory-in-use, is the call to the aesthetic that lies in conjunction with the concept of the manager as an explorer. This is argued in my discussion of managerial responsibility, and it is implicit within Lyotard's concept of narrative. It is of a philosophically individualistic origin, but with a strictly socio-cultural consequence.

A portrait of the manager (after rationalism)

I now recall Malan & Kriger's (1998) observation that managers practice their craft of management on the basis of their experiences and observations – that is, on the basis of their narratives-of-existence within their own "localized" environment. These narratives are generally a synthesis of both NK and SK and include (*inter alia*) the "craft skills" of management set within a framework of the *five classical functions of management* (*after Fayol*). These skills represent the accepted conventions of management practice. In a critical context, the dominant rationalist paradigm infers that there are at least three plausible hypotheses for the study of management and the development of its conventions of practice. Therefore, from the viewpoint of academic rationalism, management knowledge is frequently understood through the form of *skills* which, having been identified, empirically rationalized and generalized into some "theory" or other, can be taught to prospective managers to enable them to cope with the challenges of management; generally as Model I theories-in-use. Here, as Vermeulen (2005) has described, the positivistic theorizing of management that is embedded within both the Hegelian and Marxist dialectic processes of thesis, anti-thesis and synthesis, lies at the root of much discussion of the relevance of theory to practice. Firstly, the Hegelian dialectic invokes a subjectivist ontology in which idealist abstractions of a socially dependent reality are made available as instantiations of new knowledge relevant to practice. We therefore have the following premiss:

- **Premiss P1:** management is practiced on the basis of the application of an *a priori* knowledge base of socially "innovated" *postmodernistic* instantiations of knowledge.

Secondly, a realist theory of management would observe managers rationalizing within themselves that very little of what is produced under the academic theorizing of P1 (that is SK) appears to have immediate practical relevance to their role as a practicing manager. Such managers appear to prefer the anecdotal relevancy of a *real* knowledge that exits independently of them – as evidenced in the popular practice of others. Therefore we also have:

- **Premiss P2:** management is practiced on the basis of the application an *a priori* knowledge base of tried and tested "real world" management solutions.

Thirdly, many managers may be observed to go about the business of management applying, adapting, and improving on, their own internalized knowledge base. Indeed, there are a decreasing[36] number of those who practice management without ever having been introduced to formal training. The "fly-by-the-seat-of-the-pants" (or trial-and-error) approach to management provides the final contending premiss:

- **Premiss P3:** management is practiced as a craft in which a working knowledge is developed *a posteriori* through (academically uninformed) experience.

Given an academic imperative to contribute to the desired consequence of managerial practice, **C1**, the above premises combine to provide a set of three competing hypotheses. The dominant paradigm of rationalism can now be expressed by the following hypotheses:

- Hypothesis **H1**, Idealism: H1 {P1 $\rightarrow$ C1}
- Hypothesis **H2**, Realism: H2 {P2 $\rightarrow$ C1}
- Hypothesis **H3**, Pragmatism: H3 {P3 $\rightarrow$ C1}

From the above discussion, hypotheses **H1** and **H2** are characteristic of Model I theories-in-use. They are both based on *a priori* concepts, where practice is influenced by knowledge. Hypothesis **H3** offers the potential of the desired Model II theory-in-use since, with an *a posteriori* basis, it is implicit that knowledge is emergent as a consequence of practice. However **H3**, as the hypothesis of pragmatism, does not admit as necessary the prior knowledge that I have argued is required of the adjunctive nature of a Model II theory-in-use. Neither does **H3** address an *imperative* for the generation of new information – it is evolutionary rather than revolutionary. The study of management, informed by the hypothesis **H3**, merely tends to a catalogue of management history with, arguably, little to satisfy any requirement of academic rigour or pretence to prescriptivity.

It is perhaps axiomatic that, in the practice of management, although managers might prefer concrete observations over abstract concepts, in the paradoxical situations they frequently inhabit, they must exercise choice on the basis of their cognition of the moment. Here, although an *accuracy* of perception might be a worthy aim, a perceptive ability is a managerial prerequisite. This is supported by Mezias and Starbuck's (2003:15) observation that most management problem solving does not require accurate knowledge of current situations. However their conclusion that an accuracy of perception is therefore an "important research topic" is, I argue, misconceived. As Das (2003:25) comments, a more convincing premiss would be that the *inaccuracy of perception* should be "taken as a given". Therefore, innocently preempting the tenor of this book, Das (2003:27) remarks that:

> ...there is a case to be made for developing the *conceptual* architecture of managerial work much more strenuously than hitherto... certainly before [taking] a headlong plunge into empirical endeavours.

The inaccuracy of managerial perceptions in the context of research (from whatever perspective) implies that the "researcher" possesses a primacy of knowledge. From the context of managerial action however, then can be no such primacy since, I argue, the manager's cognition at the time of action is *of the moment* – it simply represents knowledge (neither accurate nor inaccurate). As Das (2003:23) observes, '*...the closer one gets to an actual managerial position, the less significant some of the explanations and recommendations in the academic research literature appear.*' This observation on the competing hypotheses {H1, H2, H3} and their relationship to the gap between management research and management practice is as well rehearsed as it now appears traditional.[37]

Within the context of this Argyrian Model I/II portrait of the manager, I appeal to Richardson's (1991:173) postmodern sensibility of a doubt that any theory holds a universal and general claim to authoritative knowledge. A portrait of the manager (after Fayol) simply presents one perspective on management. This book's problematic is, however, to discover how useful the concept of *management art* is in reconceptualizing this field, in order to provide additional, critical insight into the academic world's capacity to support the desired consequence of management practice.

3
Degot's Portrait of the Manager as an Artist

> And at once it struck me, what quality went to form a man of Achievement... I mean Negative Capability, that is when a man is capable of being in uncertainties, mysteries, doubts, without any irritable reaching after fact and reason.
>
> Keats, letter of 21 December 1817[38]

A critical reading

Although Degot's *Portrait of the Manager as an Artist* is very much an antithesis of a profit-performance motivation, his contribution appears to have been largely overlooked for its potential to contribute to the post-rationalistic, postmodernistic management debate. As Degot (1987) observed:

> We live in a society where the yardsticks of performance, [both individual and corporate], are expressed in quantitative terms: earnings or profits. The "best" executive or manager is generally regarded as being the one who has the most successful career and earns the most money. (D:47)[39]

Reading this quote in 2007, one can intuitively relate to the fact that such quantitative sympathies – despite an acknowledgement of the appeal of other, socially based, phenomena – remain current for a great many managers and their observers. As a practicing manager myself, I can intuitively rationalize the quote as a valid, if not wholly exclusive, observation in today's commercial environment. Therefore, in critically exposing a weakness in Degot's work, it is my intention to rescue what I believe is the essential insight that Degot's *portrait* of the *manager-artist* contains. This insight emerges within five key themes (Atkinson, 2006); these are: 1) historicity, 2) creative management, 3) the work of the manager-artist, 4) the need for a philosophical basis and 5) the need for "audience" clarification. However, the rationale for a critical reading of Degot is not merely to seek the reason why his portrait failed to engage with the critical post-rationalistic, post-modernistic debate that is witnessed within management and organizational theory's own cultural and aesthetic "turns" – but also to identify how that debate can be rejoined.

Why is it then, that Degot's discourse on the realm of a possibility: *what if management was an art*; and its potential contribution to management knowledge, appears overlooked? Perhaps one answer lies in his claim simply to "explore" the central idea that management, as it evolved (certainly during the 1970s and 80s), looked '...*more like an artistic activity than the rationalistic model which business economists [of the day had] been trying for so long to impose.*' (D:45). Even at the time of its writing, it would have been possible to mount a strong counter-argument to this position. For example, management writing of the era was not, in fact, as suggestive of a continued, or even strong, tradition in rational-economic thought, such as an initial contextual reading of Degot's portrait might suggest. As recent readings of "classical" management theorists suggest,[40] and as I have described in Chapter 2, there has always been more to management than the empirically derived, stereo-typical economic profit focused "caricatures" to be found in some management writing.

The gradual dismantling of the classical (and simplistically) positivistic notion of management can be argued to have existed for some considerable time. Furthermore, Chapter 2 introduced an air of complexity within the three hypotheses of rationalistic managerial practice that, following the cultural turn, has now embraced for itself the promise of a *sociological understanding*. Indeed, Degot's portrait hints that both rational and social phenomena have co-existed in the practice of management for as long as management *per se* has been an identifiable function. Degot refers to this as *the latency of management*. (D:24). Therefore a new paradigm, as suggested by a management artform might appear, at first sight, unnecessary in contemporary management theorizing.

A further factor – arguably the most visible in its potential to discourage readers of Degot's portrait from a meaningful engagement with its content – is his choice of language in putting forward his core premiss: '*If it is not too far-fetched, a parallel [between the field of Art and] the management field might be discerned...'* (D:14). This parallel is based on an evolutionary analogy: that because management can be identified as evolving from one outdated tenet (rationalism) to another and that because art has evolved from one outdated tenet (naturalism) to another (impressionism) that therefore management is like art. This simplified argument does not act to encourage an appropriate level of engagement. It is an improbable correlation and an indefensible argument.

One final reason to highlight as an explanatory factor in the lack of appeal of Degot's portrait is the notion of its audience. It is not clear for whom the portrait was written. At times Degot appears to offer an appeal to academic policy makers in seeking to justify alternative avenues for research, with academia becoming the custodian of "management heritage" (D:18). As custodians, universities and academic business schools would have a decisive role to play in enhancing the role of management (D:19). Yet in concluding his narrative portrait, Degot appeals directly to the practicing manager, by offering a stance of *anti-neoclassic* economics in the hope of arousing their interest (D:45). I believe that it is not that Degot implied neoclassic economics had, in some way, accounted for the longevity (or even resurgence) of the rationalistic debate, but that the management writing he referred to, appeared to have failed to influence the culture of management practice. In this way Degot's insights might be seen as a precursor to the more recent debate on the gap between management theory and management practice.

My objective in this opening critique is simply to park these obvious concerns, and to suggest that a critical reading of Degot's portrait is worthy of renewed interest – providing a rich source of ideas relevant to this book's problematic. In a more immediate defence of Degot's work I stress that at no point did he suggest, within his rhetorical narrative, a definitive position *argued* from a basis of empirically derived premisses. Degot does not advance an argument with the intent of influencing his audience to accept, as fact, that management is an art. Nor does Degot claim any other academically privileged status for his view. Indeed, his phrase "this article" (D:45) sets an appropriate context for the reader of its day. My objective here is to represent Degot's portrait in a new and coherently critical context.

History and all that

Firstly then, I turn to examine the argument that there exists a parallel between the fields of art and of management. Though not explicitly stated as an argument this parallelism nevertheless provides the rationale for Degot's portrait. The general form of this argument is a counterfactual one – it is based on the conditional form: *if premiss A then conclusion B*. That is, <u>if</u> there is a parallel between art and management, <u>then</u> aesthetics, history and criticism[41] are to be seen as valid disciplines for the study of management. Here, a counter position might readily be adopted, in which there is no need to consider management as an artform, given the immediacy of existing studies, for example: 1) aesthetics in management and organizations (for example Linstead and Höpfl, eds, 2000); 2) management history (for example Goodman and Kruger, 1988; Cuff, 1996; Carson and Carson, 1998; Gibson *et al*, 1999; and Booth, 2003); and 3) critical management studies (for example Linstead *et al*, eds, 2004). Given even these limited examples, in which there is no explicit suggestion that management is indeed an art, it would be easy to question the value of maintaining Degot's line of management art thinking. Could we not entertain as similar a position (*B*) as Degot, without the need to establish the acceptability, relevance and adequateness of Degot's underlying premiss (*A*)?

Counterfactual arguments, of the form *if A then B*, are usually made in knowing, or at least assuming, that one or more premisses are false. In this way Degot might be seen as exploring the consequences of the occurrence of a (potentially) hypothetical situation, *viz*: what "might" we learn of management if we "were" to assume it is an artform. In this respect, Degot's attempt at establishing his argument for a parallel between Art and Management is, I argue, not critically relevant to his position. Indeed, as I have introduced it undermines his position by establishing a dubious premiss when all that might reasonably be required is an appeal to *counterfactual conditionals* as a legitimate analytic device. Therefore, following the counterfactual form a statement that *some* management might be an *artform* might be proven to be true by assuming it to be false and then deriving a contradiction from that assumption.

Looking a little further at Degot's central "parallel" argument however, this argument makes the assertion that, because of a degree of similarity between the evolution of art and the evolution of management, then management can be likened to art. The term evolution in this context lies strictly in an historical treatment of the subject. Here Degot draws on just two of the definitions associated with Art over the long period of Art history – those of naturalism and expressionism. Degot describes an evolutionary process occurring between the two periods. As I shall go on to examine in Chapter 4, in

Transcending Art's Craft, this description cannot be so clearly made. For example, on a simple counter-example basis, expressionism has been a feature of the art landscape since the 19th century, while a certain return to naturalism can be detected in the works of Andy Warhol and, more recently, the Young British Artist's (YBAs) Tracey Emin and Damian Hirst. The evolutionary context in which Degot portrays the movement of art from an outdated tenet of naturalism to one of expressionism is an unacceptable premiss. Indeed, Degot offers his own rebuttal in that, despite expressionist art being viewed on its own terms, it cannot be described as being independent of social and historical influence. This rebuttal is indicative of the sense in which art is still very much open to interpretation.

Using the same counter-example basis as above, it is also possible to refute the premiss that management has evolved from one outdated tenet to another. Here, I have already indicated (both above and in Chapter 2) that: as there are examples of rationalistic, economic management thinking today, so there are examples of other softer, people-orientated non-profit-centred management thinking as far back as circa 1000 BC. However, if we dispense with the notion that there might be a parallel between art and management and adopt, explicitly, a counter-factual argument, we might begin to explore the emergent historic theme that Degot's notion of management activity, seen as through art, allows us to forge a link between contemporary management and its pre-capitalist traditions. Here, citing Gergen (1973), Booth (2003:96) notes that:

> ...any social enquiry is inevitably historical rather than scientific in nature... because the world is so bounded by cultural, spatial and temporal specificities that our knowledge cannot transcend these boundaries; in other words, the particularistic and inherently complex nature of the objects and subjects of our enquiries require historical perspective.

From an historical, counterfactual perspective, we might then reasonably assume that management *is* an art and explore where such an assumption might then lead us. To take one example, we might conceive of an "institutionalist" conception of management art, based on (say) Dickie's *The New Institutional Theory of Art* (1983). Here functional theories of art – of which expressionism is merely one such theory – may be justified in terms of their own individual context. However, as Dickie describes, it is the narrow nature of specific contexts that make individual, functional theories necessarily open to repudiation by counter-examples. A consequence of such an "institutionalist" conception of management is therefore that management "works" seen through (art) aesthetic, (art) historic and (art) critical perspectives are simply likely to lead – from an academic point of view – to individual functional theories of management.

An analogy can be drawn with the earlier discussion of management "styles" in Chapter 2. If "institutionalist" theories of management are only justifiable in terms of their own individual context, they are open to repudiation by counter-examples. Therefore "functional" or "institutionalist" theorizing about management tends to suggest that, as Goodman and Kruger (1988:316) describe, any management research developed from a historiographical method would A) lack objectivity, B) lack direction, and C) lead to conclusions that are merely tentative and not easily generalizable. The suggestion, therefore, of many individual functional theories of management tends merely to a discussion of management "styles". Certainly, from an institutionalist conception, this leads to a limit in the usefulness of an abstract concept of a *manager as an artist* – a lack of any transcendent notion of a general theory of management that might be applied to management. It is not surprising that despite a period of two decades since Degot's portrait, and a growing force of historical interest in management and organizations – as Booth (2003:96) notes – the importance (or relevance) of an historical perspective appears to remain elusive.

If the progress of management evolution can be characterized by a surfeit of theories, justifiable in terms of individual (institutionalized) domain contexts, what benefit might an historical perspective bring that is not already served by contemporary management thinking under the dominant paradigm of rationalism? Here Degot's own art-historiographical theme presents an interesting and alternative take on what, at first, appears inconclusive. Given the existence of an established artworld relationship between aesthetic theory, art history and art criticism, might not an *understanding* of art be one route to an understanding of the relationship that might exist between the current thinking on the aesthetic, the historic and the critical within management and organizations? However, seeking to recontextualize the decontextualized, such an understanding presumes a clarification of the assumed role of an art in (or of) management. Such a presumption is, I argue, not well served by a lack of an effective conception of art *per se*. But, at this point in the text, to continue my critical reading of Degot's *Portrait of the Manager as an Artist*, I will merely concentrate on the *counterfactual conditional* statement that management *is* an art and further explore the consequences of Degot's hypothesis.

The creative manager

Degot presents a thematic conclusion that the manager requires talents of a personal nature, not unlike those of an artist (D:21). However, a key critique is that much of what might be referred to under Degot's concept of the *manager-as-artist*, is more accurately a discussion of the "creative manager". For example, in qualifying a creative manager as one with an '*...all embracing view of things which goes beyond the traditional boundaries...*'[42] (D:39), Degot relies on a key premiss that the "good" creative manager is '*...the one whose vision and skills enable him[/her] to achieve maximum exploitation of the corporation's potential within its social and economic environment.*' (D:38). Here writers on creativity in management[43] do not suggest that creativity (and its sometimes partner: innovation) is any more a function of art than a subject in its own right, suitable for the application of empirical observation and objective theory building practice. Furthermore, creativity as a feature of management writing cannot be held to be a recent development within contemporary management thinking – in some way having benefited from the hindsight offered by (say) Degot's artistic insight. As I have observed, Degot's work seems largely overlooked.

As a subject of academic study, creativity can therefore be argued as separate from, but contemporaneous with, Degot's work. As Tierney *et al* (1999:591) observe, creativity is an ever-increasing topic of interest in organizational matters. Indeed to some writers, for example Ford (1999:188), a lack of creativity appears to have overtaken financial constraints as a principal concern facing businesses. Consequently, the discussion of creativity within the context of contemporary management and organizational practice appears divorced from creativity's potential origin in the traditional artistic pursuits. Therefore, although managerial creativity may be argued as desirable, or even necessary, the idea of managerial creativity cannot be sufficiently justified as a premiss for a management artform.[44] Higgs and Hender's (2004:12) abstraction of creativity into a managerial mould characterized by factors such as: openness, drive, energy, unorthodoxy and difference, and experimentation and self-confidence does, I suggest, miss some of the aesthetic "sense" of Degot's Creative Manager.

Higgs and Hender acknowledge three limitations to their work on creativity; these can be critiqued by reference to Degot. Firstly, Higgs and Hender (2004:13) acknowledge that the choice of participants within their enquiry was not on any basis of their being "established" *creative managers*; their analysis simply reflects the participant's "perceptions" of *creative managers*. Thus, there is the real possibility that what might be perceived as characteristic of creative behaviour in management, might be more accurately considered characteristic of "effective management".[45] In contrast, Degot's consideration of the creative manager makes no pretense to identify individual characteristics of creativity. Ultimately, Degot's creative manager simply possesses a range of characteristics, and is engaged in a "personal" project with some envisioned outcome of benefit to the organization. In "managing" their project, Degot's creative manager strives '...*to enhance his[/her] own skills [causing] him[/her]to explore more widely around his[/her] subject, so as to be able to more fully express... personal convictions.*' (D:38). Importantly, no implicit restrictions, by way of labelled characteristics, are evident in Degot's discourse and his creative manager is thus possessed of a personal "space" within which their "artistic" action is, to some extent, sanctioned. Degot's discourse offers a degree of correlation with aspects of the Model II manager outlined in Chapter 2 – specifically the idea of a sanctioned space for managerial exploration.

The association of "space" with Degot's creative manager appears to present a principal difference between the discussion of creativity within an art-related context, and that creativity featured in contemporary management writing. Here the second limitation of Higgs and Hender's work is their acknowledgement that no consideration is given to the organizational context. However, both their theory and research is suggestive of an interaction between the creative individual and their environment. Higgs and Hender conclude that further work is required in this respect and this does suggest that their observations are anything but a long way from providing real insight into creativity in a (non-artistic) management context. Conversely, Degot's management space is a multi-dimensional, environmental consideration, with the overall implication that the creative manager is possessed of the metaphoric space in which to exercise his or her talents as a manager. While these talents invoke a certain requirement for management skills, knowledge and experience, they also include talents in other areas – brought to bear on exploring widely around a subject area.

An ability to exercise freedom of action within a certain "space" is indicative of a certain degree of authority (if not responsibility). Such an authority (and its closely related dimension of power) to exercise personal action might be a function of the self (for example the entrepreneurial owner/manager), the delegated authority of the employee-manager (as agent), or the sponsorship of some champion or patron. The extent to which the creative manager possesses the space for personal action calls into question, as Degot observes, the extent to which she or he might abuse this space in the interests of pursuing their own personal vision, *as artist*, at the expense of the organization's goals. Degot does not, however, dwell on the negative aspect of this "abuse" of artistic space. He simply presents the case of the "good" creative manager, in which all effort is directed to the good of the company (D:39). Therefore, what appears overlooked by both Degot and other contemporary writings on management creativity is art's subversive nature; this is a factor that can clearly be seen in Art's potential to create controversy. It is also a factor within the final limitation of Higgs and Hender's work, where they acknowledge that no attempt was made to link their characteristics of creativity to creative performance.

Adopting Degot's art-centric notion of creativity, the concept of *management art* is only served by virtue of a successful outcome – a "management" *artwork*. Therefore Degot's creative manager achieves his project and, in some form or another,[46] it becomes (critically) recognizable (or, potentially, fails recognition) as a *management artwork*. Any artist – and Degot's management artist is no exception – may see their work presented to a critical audience for acceptance. Given the institutional nature of the organization, the manager's work of management art is (critically) examined in the context of the organization itself. Here the organization is analogous to a form of artworld – a culturally defined, *bounded* space with generally accepted protocols for action. The creative manager must therefore, to an extent, exercise compromise (that is achieve a balance between restraint and freedom) if she or he is to be able to see a project through to fruition.

Given, again, the institutional context – with the manager's task related also to the marshalling of resources – communication becomes an enabling factor. Here, rhetorical and other devices might be called upon, creatively, to manipulate resources to achieve a vision that might not be entirely clear. Only in the case of the entrepreneurial owner/manager is there less of a constraint on the creative process – where the ultimate judge of a successful work is quite likely to be the artist him or herself. We are, perhaps, left with the suggestion that some managers are managers but not just managers. Indeed, Degot's creative manager might be a manager at times and an artistic manager at others. Certainly there is a corresponding theme in art that not everything an artist produces is necessarily worthy of the title of *artwork*.

The work of the manager artist

If we are to assume that there is an argument for management to be seen through the utility of art, then – as held by Degot – implicit within this position is the notion that the "work" of management is the basic creative design that can be attributed to one individual (D:24). Here, the *manager-artist*. This premiss supports Degot's conclusion that the management function has a separate identity – that is it generates outcomes which cannot be attributed to the application, in automatic fashion, of predetermined techniques or rules (D:23). Therefore, central to Degot's theme of the work of the *manager-artist* is the concept of a decision taken on the basis of the "personal initiative" of the manager. He compares such decisions against those arrived at semi-automatically, through following some standardized technique or process of evaluation and action (D:28) – that is, a convention of managerial practice.

Implicit within Degot's argumentation is the fact that: 1) the perception of a need requiring a decision, 2) the evaluation of the right decision, and 3) the implementation of the decision, (argued as the three central parts to a management work) are also to be recognized in much of the decision-making theory that forms '...*a kind of sanctum within the corporation and its theoretical representation...*' (D:28). Here, the concept of the personal space available – within which Degot's (creative) manager enacts an analytical, decision-based course of action – is more indicative of an *emergent* process of work, than of a *highly regulated* or *routine* process. This type of emergence can frequently be seen in the world of the performance arts, such as theatre, as exemplified in the following interview quote in Austin and Devin (2004:49):

> My directing style is based on what the actors are bringing to rehearsal, and on making what you make out of those particular actors then and there. You discover the play throughout the process... sometimes, roughly I know what the journey is. Sometimes I don't... usually we try a scene or a moment so many different ways that the right choice makes itself known. ...We work until we find that.

Yet, as Austin and Devin relate, despite such implied "space for action", plays are managed to some of the strictest schedule constraints imagined. Opening nights are generally immovable. Given such insight, we might therefore argue that in larger commercial organizations, with perhaps many managers, if we are to assume – as Degot does – that an individual manager's role is inclusive of the exercise of personal initiative, then we can only ever (intuitively) expect emergent outcomes that might, indeed be characteristic of a particular manager.

Pragmatically, given the nature of the organization as a cultural space (with defined boundaries and certain accepted protocols), to allow a reliance on emergent outcomes – in some form of managerial anarchy – could be disastrous unless there was a high level of shared vision and empathy between all managers concerned. That is, a strong organizational culture. Therefore, as Degot describes, some managerial outcomes, out of necessity, can best be described as merely the practical application of ideas that were widely current at that time (D:31). This is the following of processes that through trial, adoption, refinement and routine application in reaction to certain antecedent events or requirements, lead to certain desirable outcomes. This is the making of organizational narratives in which outcomes are prescribed by conventions of management practice. Here the manager's role might be said, simply, to ensure the relevant steps of the process are enacted appropriately – making decisions as to resource allocation and so on, and intervening only to correct deviations from the established norm.

Degot likens managerial conventions to administrative practices and their managers to "administrators". I believe that this distinction is too simplistic, it is certainly not supported by even the Argyrian Model I conception of managerial work that I have described in Chapter 2. It is, however, noteworthy that Degot accepts that not all outcomes of managerial work are artworks; non-artworks being those that are a consequence of frequent collective decision-making and implementation using fairly standard procedures and principles (D:32). Degot concludes that only managerial works that imply a basis of an identifiable personal vision are to be implied as management artworks, and that these are, in fact, not the norm. Indeed, Degot's premiss that evidencing the role of the "author" in a managerial work is a task for a (management) "critic" or "historian" – to '...*reconstitute the work from start to finish in a way which focuses on the author*' (D:31) – provides some support for the fact that management works of art are rare. Such rarity, Degot argues, is due to personal vision itself. It might also be argued that it is the lack of an historical or critical perspective that leaves a paucity of such works available for an interested public.

Degot's argument that the profile of major, *prominent*, success hides the success of other managers (D:17) is based on historiographical perspective of "success" that has its roots in the observed output of the major corporations and major business schools. Here we assume that (hitherto) what history has taken account of is the success itself – being the history of a major successful corporation or of a major corporate figurehead. What audience is there for an historical account of minor successes from managers of the less renowned management schools doing outstanding work in less prominent companies? Therefore, those management works that are visible through historical recollection or otherwise, overshadow many more works (that are appropriate from an "artistic" perspective) by virtue of the former's certain appeal to major success. Here, we see the fictitious boundary of "excellent organizations" within Peters & Waterman's *In Search of Excellence* acting to exclude many potentially greater or equally excellent – but smaller – organizations. Degot's conclusion that most management artworks are lost (D:18), acts to rebut his subsequent conclusion that the most "significant" management works are those that best represent the characteristics of the management style at a given time, or are those which mark the greatest innovation compared to preceding works (D:20). Without an *a priori* concept, management Artworks are, in reality, a rarity.

There is duality here. The work of management produces outputs (or consequences) that are representative of the characteristics of a management style at a given time (we might say normalized management practices, or management conventions) – suitable for a Model I management practice. Equally, managerial works may also mark management practice that produces the greatest innovation compared to preceding outcomes (or consequences). Therefore, within the management role there is an identifiable managerial activity that results in management outcomes which cannot be attributed solely to the application, in automatic fashion, of predetermined techniques or rules (D:23). Management may be management or management plus. As I have argued at Chapter 2, it is under conditions of complexity and ambiguity, where the predictivity of extant conventions – that is where narratives of practice becomes unreliable – that there is a call to the innovative capacity offered by a conception of *management art*.

From movement to philosophy

Having established a basis for both the artistic notion of a manager, and of her or his artistic works, Degot moves on to discuss the problematic of how the *artistic manager* comes to be. How is it – given the individual "self's" personal vision, project and the influence of *social factors* on the "self" – that the vocation of the artistic manager is born? (D:34). Premising this, Degot's call to a Weberian *Beruf* (or vocation) appeals to a *social aesthetic* where, to paraphrase Kemple (2005:12–13):

> For Weber and his contemporaries, the relative autonomy… of the sphere of aesthetics emerges as a problem for sociological discussion and analysis not only in view of the social organization of the production and reception of [management] artworks for and by members of a particular social stratum [or organization], but above all with regard to the social conditions within which new aesthetic forms acquire cultural value and significance.[47]

However, Degot does not offer any further insight into this Weberian problematic but, taking it as a given, he leads us to a conclusion that individuals with a true vocation for the *artistic* are more likely to experience *movement* (in general, gain many experiences) within their professional management career, either through their own search for opportunities for self-expression, or seeing their personal projects directed through various (organizational) directions. But what of the manager who's artistic vocation is not identified; who is not provided with (or who has not gained – by virtue of some authority or other) the "space" for such movement and the opportunity to gain varied experience? Is such a manager any the less artistic in nature? Does an artistic manager, by virtue of his/her artistic temperament, necessarily see movement? What of the concept (and implications) of the management class as a social order?

Intuitively, we can reason that an artistic manager is more likely to be able to perform creatively if he or she is able to draw on a greater range of experiences. Therefore, to an artist, *movement* becomes an important factor in their ability to perform (artistically). However, it is not possible to dispense with the counter-example of the non-artistic manager who is more likely to be able to perform in a wide variety of situations if he or she has also had the benefit of wide ranging commercial experiences. The counter position does not invalidate the argument put forward by Degot. Movement (and its corollary of experience) is a factor, but it cannot be a sufficient factor, in determining the vocation of the artistic manager.

Some light is shed by Degot's further discussion on where movement is directed. While, again intuitively, we might reason that the movement of a general (non-artistic) manager is frequently constituted by a *structured* introduction to various functional areas of management within a given organization, Degot concludes that it is '...*hard to foresee which sectors and companies will offer the best opportunities for creative management*' (D:35). In the larger organizations, where many functions are narrowly defined, it is difficult to see where the creative individual can experience the space necessary to function creatively. One might infer from this that the smaller organizations are best for the creative manager. However, even in the smaller firm – with few specific exceptions – space for personal (artistic) expression is only generally met at the top management levels.

With such weak argumentation there are many questions. One can envisage alternative premisses, based on the non-artistic manager, which might equally suggest movement as feature of their professional career. It might, however, be better to take the counter position. Therefore, given that there is the potential for both artistic and non-artistic managers, what would be the consequences of failing to offer a variety of experiences (during their professional life) to those of an artistic nature? And what would be the consequences of offering too many experiences to those who are not? Here there is interesting synergy with the "traditional" concept of the *apprenticeship*, as a passage (or movement) through various skills and/or practices as a route to gaining (craft) knowledge. But, then again, does such apprenticed knowledge an artist make?

With the media coverage of certain corporations and personalities – tending in the main to the "Top 100" list phenomenon – is there (as Degot intimates) a social imperative that dictates directing capable individuals, through fast-track management programs and MBAs, to organizations where their size and complexity offer only narrowly defined functional roles with no space to exercise personal freedom; where any exercise of freedom might well have unintended, and unwelcome consequences? Here, strong cultures and established managerial narratives operating in the relatively "small" spaces of junior management roles appear to offer little scope for the development of the very faculties of managerial practice apparently required of the more senior roles.

There is a dilemma posed by the duality of Degot's argumentation for the formation of the artistic management vocation – an argumentation that appears to hold valid, at some level or another, both for example and counter-example and non-artistic and artistic managers. This does not resolve to a natural conclusion. What is missing, here, is some indication that Degot has identified the value of the artistic manager; specifically, why do we need the *manager-artist*? Here, there is little in Degot's portrait that offers substantive insight into this aspect, beyond the implication that an economic crisis of the mid-70s might have been avoided by encouraging *management talent*, through movement or otherwise (D:19). It is as if Degot is addressing an audience of those that have accepted that there is a *de facto* requirement for management to be understood as an artform, rather than the reality of addressing what, at the time of his writing on the matter, might better be described as a fictitious audience.

By inferring that management talent is to be understood as synonymous with an artistic management ability, Degot concludes that, through enhancing the role of the artistic manager, universities and business schools have a decisive role to play in changing attitudes about management talent and its role in the economy (D:18–19). However, before this can be achieved; before the role of the artistic manager can be properly understood, the clear inference is that it is necessary to develop appropriate historical research. This inference, although not explicit in Degot's work, nevertheless highlights the perception that much of what is generalized about management – through research or other historical processes – is an abstraction of a reality. Such an abstraction removes the individual's influence in the normalization of "favoured" narratives that may then become proffered as prescriptive in the pursuit of "effective" management practice – the development of conventions of managerial practice. If, however, there is to be a value in artistic management, then there is a need to recentre the manager as the "creator", or at least a prime instigator, of a work of management art.

Degot concludes that the compilation of a body of management criticism is to be seen as a study of creativity that involves the reconstruction of past management works (D:27). This implies a working method of retrieving and rearranging facts and so on. It also implies new methods of presentation and procedures for publication. It is therefore, in this context, that Degot argues that the disciplines of aesthetics, history, and criticism sum up possible roads to a management philosophy. Such a philosophy, informed, perhaps, by Weber's *social aesthetic*, should support a history of (management) techniques, of (management) works and their authors, and a critical review of achievements. As Degot suggests, there is a possibility that, in Europe at least, such a management philosophy might have more relevance than the established "sciences" in placing the creative manager and his or her works at the centre of management.

For whom does the critic toll?

My reading of Degot's implicit argumentation has, so far, presented the possibility of a management philosophy centred on the manager. Intuitively, therefore, there is the potential for a variety of plausible takes on any given management scenario. Such a philosophy is the antithesis of any rationalistic sense of a management science (social or otherwise). The basis for this philosophy, contrary to Degot's weak evolutionary parallel between art and management, appears as emergent in a counter-intuitive sense. It is a basis derived from anomalies within an argumentation that appears, in many cases, to support both example (art) and counter-example (non-art). It is within the need to resolve this duality, that there lies a requirement to fully understand an artistic conception of management. However, as Degot has highlighted, there is a paucity of relevant material from within which one might begin to ground an appropriate discourse.

In coming to understand an artistic conception of management, it can be seen that the roles of the (management art) critic and the (management art) historian become one central "means" to an "end" of discovery. As with the areas most associated with the arts,[48] criticism – based on a philosophy of aesthetics – emerges as central to understanding. Degot suggests that the purpose of the management (art) critic is to comment on the works of the artist in formulating an original opinion as to what the artist intended to express (D:42). This suggests the interpretation of a philosophy of artistic management, in order that the values of artistic management are made apparent. However, in order that we can disclose the interpretive nature of this relationship, it is necessary to introduce a further, unstated, audience-related conclusion.

It is to be concluded from Degot's text, that the function and/or usefulness of the management art critic is increasingly to feed the interests of an external, but unspecified, audience. This conclusion arises through the reading of a number of sub-conclusions and premisses that arise within the section of Degot's text on: *the Need for a "criticism" function*. These appear to "hang" without reaching any explicit conclusion. The text at this point becomes "descriptive" of the adjudged need for criticism – based on the suggested parallel between art and management. This descriptive view is set against Degot's effective rebuttal that the role of critic is virtually non-existent – at least at the time of writing (D:44). If the role of management (art) critic was to exist, what would be its purpose, and how would it be manifest? Toward answers to these questions, Degot simply offers a number of cursory observations that, I believe, require resolution to a single conclusion.

As Degot seems to suggest, the interpretive nature of the critic's role arises, at least in part, through acting as the middleman between the manager and a less enlightened public (D:42). The management critic is advanced as an individual qualified to reconstitute the creative process behind any given work and to reward it a place among comparable works (D:43). Over time, therefore, the critic might act as a form of curator of management works, who would place on record the author's intentions and problems and the impact of their works. As Degot also relates, the management critic's role is not restricted to completed works, but it may also include work in progress. Degot further argues that it is the management critic alone who is able to provide timely, '…*relevant and documented comment on work in progress, describing the way a work is perceived from the outside and how it compares with what is being done elsewhere, etc.*'. All of this suggests, as I have observed above, that the function of the management art critic is, increasingly, to feed the interest of an unspecified, but external, audience.

There are two issues with this notion of the audience. Firstly, as with my opening comments, there is the lack of clarity in the targeted readership of Degot's portrait. Secondly, there is the notion of the "external" audience *per se* being the target of Degot's "hinted at" theoretical framework of (artistic) management. As regards the first, Degot's separate appeals to both academic policy makers (in seeking to justify alternative avenues for research) and directly to the practicing manager (through his "anti-neoclassic economics" stance) do not sit naturally – in terms of acceptability, relevance and adequateness – within the overall argumentation. It is axiomatic that the goal of writing is communication with an audience; we must know what audience we are writing for, and write for that audience. Here, as Hughes (1996:258) reflects, we must take into account such factors as the audience's values; their level of education and political sophistication and their level of background knowledge. It is my opinion that Degot's portrait ultimately fails to find an audience through failing to address most of these essential factors. However, in fairness to Degot, it is likely that a clearly defined audience for this work did not then, as perhaps it does not yet, exist.

But for whom would the potential management (art) critic write? If, as Degot infers, a '…*"good" managerial work is that which, during each period, takes the best advantage of the degree of freedom, and adapts best to the constraints, inherent in the social, cultural and political environments...',* (D:41) then what is the value of a critical appraisal, and to what (external) audience might it be directed? Degot's work of management varies between artwork and non-artwork, therefore some management achievements are best described simply as applications of ideas that were widely current at that time. In other words, some purported works of management are merely representational (copies) of some previous work. Other management work, however, seems to subvert conventions; such work requires interpretation. The relationship between description and interpretation is, however, not an easy or clear one, but as Margolis (1961:537) observes, it is one that is central to art criticism's two phases of giving an account of the properties of a work and of evaluating the merit of it. As Margolis (1961:538) continues:

> ...the most characteristic difference between describing and interpreting a work of art lies... in the centre of gravity of the two notions. "Describing" suggests a stable public object available for inspection, the effort of the describer calls for no special notice, differences in description are to be reconciled by a further examination of the object. "Interpreting," on the other hand, suggests virtuosity, an element of performance, a shift from a stable object whose properties however complex are simply enumerable to an object whose properties pose something of a puzzle or challenge – with the emphasis on the solution of the puzzle or on the inventive use of materials, on the added contribution of the interpreter, and with a certain openness toward possible alternate interpretations.

Margolis discusses description and interpretation in relation to the differing classes of art: plastic, performing and literary. However, it is in respect of the performing aspect of interpretation – where Margolis centres the absence of any object prior to interpretation that may pass as the full work of art as antecedent – that I find most congruence with the conception of the interpretation of management art. If we are part of the management artwork by virtue of being part of the performance (whether as artist or not), what is the likelihood that we would be the prime audience for the critic's interpretation? If, as a stakeholder in the organizational sense, our interest lies is the outcome of the performance (for example targets reached, dividends paid, and so on), might we not ponder that a *description* (or narrative) of a successful outcome is more likely to influence succeeding outcomes than some critic's (for example a market analyst) fallible *interpretation* – with which we may, as Margolis (1961:540) comments, be expected to attend to alternate and even incompatible interpretations? Ultimately, I find at this stage no definable audience for Degot's critic of management art.

Resolving the audience

Degot's argumentation appears to resolve toward "the critic", yet his final appeal is to "management practitioners": that is '*...managers could well benefit from informed criticism of their action in an available form.*' (D:45). Is this not where critical management studies has been advanced to offer new insights? The dichotomy between, on the one hand the desirability of a *descriptive* protocol for management that tends to a "positivistic" pre-scription, and on the other hand, the possibility of the multiple "post-modernistic" *interpretations*, is one that is frequently sighted as the *raison d'être* of many critical perspectives; notably "critical realism".[49] Here, rather than any sense of a neatly observed, empirical reality, *the* reality of the management world comprises structures (sets of internally related objects) and mechanisms (ways of acting) that are only contingently related to observable empirical events.[50]

In seeking a centre ground, the critical realist eschews the post-modern. Although it is allowed that *a* knowledge of *a reality* – here the social reality of the management world – is never infallible, Tsang and Kwan (1999:762) observe that it is still possible to acquire a scientific knowledge of it through creative construction and critical theorizing. The academic audience is therefore seen to create ever more inventive ways of resolving the dichotomy; making fallible ontological assump-tions in order to develop new *descriptive* theories about *the* (manage-ment) world we live in. Here I am returned to the Ghoshal's (2005) pathologies of management behaviours, discussed in Chapter 2 and suggested by a surfeit of context-sensitive, functional descriptions of management work. Such behaviours may well inform "styles" of the craft of management, providing a useful set of tools for application to given contexts, but they would appear to offer little to the manager in terms of enhancing their ability to gain closure in the face of ambigu-ity. The manager therefore appears disenfranchised from an academic output that provides a deficit in understanding of the interpretive nature of what much management work appears to be about. The gap between management theory and management practice lives on in Degot's narrative portrait.

In order to conclude my reading of Degot's *Portrait of the Manager as an Artist*, it is necessary to make an assumption about the potential audience for his work. Here I shall simply assert three basic premisses that will inform my own argument:

- **Basic Premiss 1**: there is a deficiency in the practicing manager's ability to internalize extant academic management theories as a constituent element of their sense-making processes;
- **Basic Premiss 2**: extant academic management theories are represented in their language of origin, which may or may not be compatible with the language(s) of its potential audience(s); and
- **Basic Premiss 3**: a manager's ability to make sense of the multitude of informational stimuli he or she receives, and around which his or her cognitive perceptions are constructed is influenced, *inter alia*, by the realm of the aesthetic.

The inclusion of basic premisses allows me to infer that the audience for discussing a *management artform* lies at the conjunction of two seemingly disparate worlds: academia and management. My suggestion, here, is that academics who have a concern for the perceived failure of much management theory to inform practice, and manager's who seek insight from academic theory but are frustrated by its application, might be guided by a new form of interpretive theorizing based on an aesthetic philosophy. Therefore, rather than – as Degot does – merely borrowing from the field of Art, there is the suggestion that a philosophy of social aesthetics might justify valid aspects of management study as: the work of the manager; the concept of managerial "works"; and the need for a critical function in respect of these.

Critically, a "social aesthetic" carries with it its own contemporary concerns. In order to examine these concerns, I return to the historical perspective. Here, as Robinson (1981:5) observes, within the artistic context the historian is in pursuit of matters of fact: who produced a work; when was it produced; and where and under what circumstances? The historian purveys facts. The critic, however, sets out to discover things that may not seem straightforwardly factual; the critic deals chiefly in values, and the distinction between fact and value is deeply entrenched in philosophy. Therefore, if management is to be considered an *artform*, and if there is little evidence of management work that might be characteristic of such *form*, then I argue that we must conclude that the distinction between the facts and values of management is to be developed, at least initially, from philosophical principles. The problematic of the Weberian *social aesthetic* is highlighted in the fact and value dichotomy. My critical reading of Degot's portrait invokes more than simply the concepts of a management art history and of its criticism; it invokes aspects of power, responsibility and authority as well as the organization as an institution of *bounded* cultural space. Inescapably, this amounts to a *politics* of management that I find is absent from Degot's narrative.

Kemple's (2005) observations concerning the problematic of aesthetics' relative autonomy in the context of sociological discussion, arises by virtue of the politics of social organization. These are, in effect, the social conditions within which aesthetic forms acquire cultural value and significance. This is the perceived "value" of artworks held for and by members of a particular social class. A critique of the politics of aesthetics must therefore be addressed within the suggestion that a social aesthetic might offer insight into management. Thus, while critics may suggest that the aesthetic experience afforded by any particular work depends on the backgrounds, education and preferences of a given social class (or audience), they do not argue that the experience does not exist, or that the audience does not find it of a certain value. As Loesberg (2005:2) observes, the argument is, rather, that although a certain work of art and a "taste" for it might exist, its value is specific to a certain social class and thus has no transcendent value. Recalling Booth (2003), it is due to this very lack of transcendentalism within the particularistic and inherently complex nature of the objects and subjects of our social enquiries that requires an historical perspective. But, as Loesberg further suggests, the mere description of a value (as might result from an empiric observation) does not free a work from a critique of social politics. Here Armstrong (2000:58) provides a highly relevant observation: '*An aesthetic needs to be grounded in experience that happens to everybody. Everybody plays. The ceaseless inventiveness of play, which precludes privileged creation, makes an experimental space for living… and this provides a fruitful possibility for exploration.*'

Given the Weberian social problematic, it is necessary to clarify, none-the-least, the roles of historian and critic. Here, Degot's own work appears to blur any distinction. The interpretative judgements required of Degot's critic have an irreducibly evaluative component, they nevertheless rely on judgements of historical fact. As Robinson (1981:6) argues: '*…the art historian in his [sic] turn provides information that is essential to the proper functioning of the art critic.*' In short, the critic cannot be alone, as Degot suggests in his or her ability to restore, effectively, the personal and subjective element of management.

A social aesthetic has been initiated through a careful centring of an historical and critical perspective on the manager and his or her works.

The suggestion is now that – in order to overcome the Weberian problematic of discrete social orders – to find value in an aesthetic of management we again decentre the manager through an interpretive capability that imputes and discovers new "knowledge" features through imaginative play. Therefore, I argue that the ultimate promise of a conception of management art (such as that attempted by Degot) is a promise of a resolution of Chapter 2's call to an *explorative social aesthetic*. However, in order capitalize on the insights from Degot's work, it is necessary to reground his intent through reframing the central, but flawed tenet that management can be considered an artform. This, I argue, requires a conception of art that transcends the specificities of a given craft skill of *the artist*. It requires a definition of what amounts to, in grounded theory terms, the basic social process that is art.

Part II

From the Artworld

4
Transcending Art's Craft

> Without tradition, art is a flock of sheep without a shepherd.
> Without innovation, it is a corpse.
>
> Winston Churchill, 1953[51]

Art in context: 'Art' or 'art'?

Degot's (1987) discourse reveals that valuable insights into organizational management can be attained through the conceptualization of an art of management. However, to realize this potential, a concept of a *management artform* requires a new definition of art that transcends, in a post-disciplinary sense, any mere notion of a specific craft skill base; be that painting, drama, literature, or music and so on. Here, to paraphrase Umberto Eco (1997), *to what do we refer when we talk of art, and with what degree of reliability?* What makes us talk of Art?

Throughout history, but particularly during the 20th century, there has been much debate over the status of art; what art is and why it is so. To illustrate this, Table 4.1 offers a collection of attributed quotations that advance various anecdotal views on the subject of what it is to perceive Art. It is easy, from a non-critical point of view, to intuitively rationalize many of these quotations. But, As E. H. Gombrich (1950:15) noted in the introduction to his popular treatise *The Story of Art*:

...[t]here really is no such thing as Art. There are only artists. Once these were men who took coloured earth and roughed out the forms of bison on the wall of a cave; today some buy their paints, and design posters for hoardings; they did and do many other things. There is no harm in calling all these activities art as long as we keep in mind that such a word may mean very different things in different times and places, and as long as we realize that Art with a capital A has no existence.

Now, alongside understanding the problematic of art's definition, there is also the need to understand the aesthetic experience.[52] As Pepper (1962:201) observed, the problem of defining art, together with the problems of aesthetic evaluation and the artwork (or aesthetic object) itself, are three of the pivotal problems that constitute an aesthetic theory. Therefore, in critical response to Eco, the philosophical question: *"to what do we refer when we talk of art?"* does not, I argue – in following Beardsley (1983:55) – suggest a value in an empirical analysis of what various individuals or populations might come to regard is, or what is not, art. Such an analysis would not appeal to what Weitz (1956:27) suggested was the primary (philosophical) concern of definition: that is, the determination of a set of necessary and sufficient properties (aesthetic or otherwise) of what might constitute a work of art.[53] Any such analysis would be clouded by the subjectivity of its cultural setting.

The philosophical questions, as Beardsley (1983:55) confirmed, are. *'What are the noteworthy features of the phenomena [art].... What are the significant distinctions that need to be marked for... theoretical understanding, and that the word "art"... is most apt... for marking? How does art... differ from closely related things?'* In contrast to the populist expressions of Table 4.1, I outline in Table 4.2 some key philosophical positions on the definition of art and its objects. In reviewing these positions I typify, as example or counter-example, artworks by William Turner, Andy Warhol, and the YBAs Tracy Emin and Damian Hirst. I have selected these artists on the basis of the levels of criticism they either attracted or continue to attract. The defence of Turner was the catalyst for John Ruskin's seminal work *The Modern Painters* and Warhol's *Brillo Boxes* is often cited in philosophical perspectives (for example Danto, 1964; Mathews, 1979; and Lind, 1992). To quote the critic Richard Dorment, writing on the United Kingdom's 1999 Turner Prize,[54] *'[l]ooking at [Tracy] Emin's work, we learn nothing, understand nothing about ourselves. There will be no justice if [she] wins this year's Turner Prize.'* Artists like Emin and her peer, Damian Hirst, continue to attract contemporary audiences who, to this day, react controversially to their work.

But, where to begin to gain a conceptualization of art that might appeal in a management context? As Thurston (1947:131) noted, a

Table 4.1   Some Attributed Quotations Relating to the Perception of Art[55]

Quote	Attributed To
Imagination is more important than knowledge.	Albert Einstein
Art is not what you see, but what you make others see.	Miles Davis
If you don't know where you are going, any road will get you there.	Lewis Carroll
A work of art which did not begin in emotion is not art.	Paul Cézanne
Every child is an artist. The problem is how to remain an artist once he grows up.	Pueblo Picasso
The function of Art is to disturb. Science reassures.	George Braque
An artist is someone who produces things that people don't need to have but that he – for some reason – thinks it would be a good idea to give them.	Andy Warhol
He who works with his hands is a labourer. He who works with his hands and his head is a craftsman. He who works with his hands and his head and his heart is an artist.	St Francis of Assisi
What is art but a way of seeing?	Thomas Berger
Art should not reproduce what we see. It should make us see.	Chinese Proverb
The mere imitation, however accurate, of what is in Nature, entitles no man to the sacred name of 'Artist'.	Edgar Allan Poe
Painting is very easy when you don't know how, but very difficult when you do.	Edgar Degas
We have lost the art of living, and in the most important science of all... the science of behaviour, we are complete ignoramuses.	D.H. Lawrence
Science and art belong to the whole world, and before them vanish the barriers of nationality.	Goethe
To live a creative life, we must lose our fear of being wrong.	Joseph C Pearce
We must remember that art is not a form of propaganda; it is a form of truth.	J F Kennedy
We all know that art is not truth. Art is a lie that makes us realize the truth.	Pablo Picasso
The source of genius is imagination alone, the refinements of the senses that see what others do not see, or sees them differently.	Eugene Delacroix
Art should never try to be popular; the public should try to make itself artistic.	Oscar Wilde

Table 4.2   Key Philosophical Positions on the Definition of Art Objects (derived from Weitz, 1956, & Davies, 1991)

Position	Proponent	Key Aspects
Imitation/ Representation	Plato	Classic view
Expressionist	Croce Collingwood	General category often related to the articulation (to an audience) of expression of emotion; of attitudes and/or beliefs. Can be further developed as Emotionalist, Intuitionist, Institutionalist
Emotionalist	Tolstoy 1896 Ducasse 1928 Knox 1931	Defining property is the expression of emotion in some sensuous public medium
Intuitionist	Croce 1901	Art is a first stage of knowledge achieved through a specific creative, cognitive & spiritual act; an awareness of the unique. It is the putting (expression) forth of purpose, feeling, or thought into a sensuous medium
Institutionalist	Danto 1964, 1973/4 Dickie 1974	Art world. Something is art because of the place it comes to occupy within an art-specific context. The definition of art cannot be understood independently of the institution of art. For Danto, Art is about something; it projects a point of view through rhetorical ellipses; it requires both interpretation and an historical context
Functional	Collingwood <64 Langer <64 Beardsley 1979	Inclusive of Expression; Human Feeling; Affording aesthetic experience. Is more a category of definition rather than a definition per se (c.f. Procedural definitions). Thus many expressionist theories may be seen as being Functional
Aesthetic	Scruton 1974 Beardsley 1983 Mitias 1988 Rowe 1991	Art as aesthetic attitude: a mode of attention (not feeling or emotion) – mode of contemplation through sight, hearing, touch. Imagination directly involved in perception. 'The purpose of giving aesthetic reasons…' (Rowe)
Intentionalism	Hirsch 1967 Saville 1982 Wollheim 1987	The correct interpretation of an artwork is fixed by some subset of actual or possible intentions of the Artist with respect to that work (Gaut, 1993)

Table 4.2 Key Philosophical Positions on the Definition of Art Objects (derived from Weitz, 1956, & Davies, 1991) – *continued*

Position	Proponent	Key Aspects
Formalism	Beardsley Bell Fry	The correct interpretation of an artwork is by reference to significant form; there is no reference to the intent (or otherwise) of the Artist
Non-definable/ Anti-Essentialist	Ziff 1953 Weitz 1956 Gallie 1956 Kennick 1958	Artworks classified by resemblance (family or paradigm classes – a la Wittgenstein) ...that art is amenable to real or any kind of true definition is a false concept. 'A Definition of Art would foreclose on future creativity'
Organicist	Bradley Weitz (earlier work)	Art is a class of organic wholes (comprising a unique complex of distinguishable, albeit inseparable, elements) presented in some sensuous medium
Voluntarist	Parker 1953	Complex definition: art is essentially 3 things – embodiment of wishes and desires imaginatively satisfied, language, and harmony; art is the provision of satisfaction through the imagination, social significance and harmony
Symbolic	Goodman 1969 Langer 1976	Art should aim to capture more absolute truths which could only be accessed by indirect methods. Symbolists employ highly metaphorical and suggestive techniques, endowing particular images or objects with symbolic meaning.
Historical	Levinson 1979 Carroll 1988	Historical (intention – Levinson or narrational – Carroll)
Natural/Cultural	Dickie 1997	Theory classification c.f. Definition; accepting no single definition possible. Art as an expression of emotion (natural kind). Cultural – dependent on an art theory to make art possible (for example Warhol/Emin/Hirst)

multiplicity of conflicting definitions of art – each seeking the key ingredient by which an artwork might be singled out from non-artworks – is reminiscent of the alchemist's search for the philosopher's stone. I might turn to two of the earliest definitions of art. Both imitation (from Plato – who places art as an imitation of an imitation of reality; thus setting up art to be attacked as metaphysically defective) and expression (the predominant 19th-century view – in which art is seen as the expression of emotion) illustrate a marked range of thought and a fertile ground for a debate that continues to confound. However, both of these definitions have subsequently been held lacking. As Dickie noted (1992:109–110), neither presents even a universal characteristic of art.

Defining art as craft

In *The Principles of Art,* Collingwood (1938:6) reflects on the history of the word *art* as largely a derivation of the Ancient Latin <u>Ars</u>; a form of craft or specialized skill. However, recognition of the *art* of Ancient Greece, or of the painted walls of the Lascaux Caves, provides a contemporary dilemma. The concept *Art*, separating as it does the *Fine Arts* (of beauty and taste) from the *useful arts* (craft) did not appear until at least the late 18th century. Therefore, Ancient Greek *art objects* and the Lascaux Cave paintings, while undoubtedly *craft* products, did not hold – for their ancient audiences – the same "art values" as are held by today's "art audience". Certainly, to Plato, the craft of producing art was not to be separated from the representation created; Art was both imitation (*mimesis*) and a craft. But Plato's imitation takes us further from a true understanding of reality. Art is, according to Plato, twice removed from the form – the idea – which is true reality. The artwork is but an imitation of an imitation of reality. So, although Plato thinks art is mimetic, he is critical of artists as imitators (Sartwell, 1992). This ancient critique is of a *Platonic* mimesis that becomes mirror-like: the application of any craft skill so honed to perfection that the craftsperson/artist creates a work that is, to all effect, identical to that which it depicts. There is, then, no value to be gained in contemplation of the one over the other and the exclusion of the mimetic artist from Plato's idealized state is defended.

Beyond the Ancients, there exist many great and acknowledged artworks that cannot be ascribed the classic notion of representation, Platonic or otherwise. As an example of Turner's work, the *Slave Ship* (1840) shows a clear break from the classic basis of Art as representation/ imitation. Warhol's *Brillo Boxes* (1969) could, however, be construed as a return to a more pure form of imitation, in which Warhol's imitation, on first experience, could suggest the ideal example Plato's mirror. Hirst's *Mother and Child Divided* (1993) and Emin's *My Bed* (1998/1999) provide further examples that circumvent the representation/imitation argument; utilizing real objects in often disturbing contexts. Ultimately, Plato's critique provides a narrow conception of the artist's craft; it appears to deny the creative; it denies imaginative ability.

Collingwood (1938:42) also argued against *art* as representation. Unlike *Platonic* art however, for Collingwood the craft skills of the artist are to be excluded from what constitutes art. As representation is unquestionably a practice of craft skill, *representation* cannot therefore be a measure of true art. Collingwood's thesis was developed through his "means"-"ends" argument, in which he provides that there is none of a craft's distinction between "means" and "end" necessarily visible in true *art*.[56] In all, Collingwood presents six qualities of craft; these are each dispensed with by Collingwood in similar fashion – providing his rationale for the separation of craft from art. However, I believe a key weakness of Collingwood's argument is his use of poetry as the core example of art discussed. Of the six qualities presented, the most tenuous is the distinction to be recognized between raw material (as means) and product (as end). Collingwood's thesis may be defendable in considering poetry, but what of *installation art*? What of Andy Warhol's *Brillo Boxes*, which were clearly constructed from a raw material, and yet have gained acceptance as an Artwork?

What is left in representation? It cannot truly be said that art is representation, for representation in the extreme (as Platonic imitation) presents no discernible difference between the artwork and that which it depicts. Arguably, however, some artworks are representational; portraits as a class of artworks are generally representational; Warhol's *Brillo Boxes* may be seen as representational; that Emin's installation of an unmade bed is entitled *My Bed* certainly appears a conscious act of representation. Therefore, in starting to develop my own view of what we might talk of as art, I contemplate Figure 4.1.

I argue that the *Art object* {A} is a product of *art* (the process) {AA}, a conjunction between the process *Craft* {CC} and some *other* process, say {XX}. The *Art object* {A} exhibits qualities of a *craft object* {C}, but it is not solely a craft product. Through this conjunctive schema the *Art object* {A} also exhibits some other set of properties, gained through the process {XX}. *Art objects* may be representational, but they are not *Art objects* because they are representational. Representation requires the exercise of a craft skill, but it cannot be solely a skill. For example, in contemplating Tracey Emin's unmade bed (*My Bed*) – it may appear identical to the object(s) it represents, but I do not see *the* bed. What, then, is the nature of the process {XX}?

Defining art as mimesis

As a candidate for the process {XX}, from representation – rejecting pure imitation – I advance the process of *mimesis*. However I argue that there is a distinction to be made between the Platonic mimesis I have previously described and *mimesis* as an element of my definition of art.[57] Ontologically, mimesis acts to make present unseen elements of the inventory of phenomena, things, concepts and ideas that describe the lived-in world. This requires a richer view of mimesis – one posited in the Aristotelian tradition that provides for *mimesis* as a learning experience. Mimesis is experiential, as Golden (1969:148) observes:

> All art forms... in that they belong to the general category of *mimesis* are essentially learning experiences whose climax or goal is an insight or inference from the individual artistic representation to a universal truth. This is the important role which Aristotle sees for art in human life, the role of deepening our understanding about and insight into the aspects of human existence that are portrayed in artistic *mimesis*.

I argue that, as the Artist seeks to create {A}, a representation of {X}, he or she does so through a learning process that entails the use of all available sensory perceptions. The art object {A} becomes an "expression" of the sense of that object {X} that the Artist both experiences

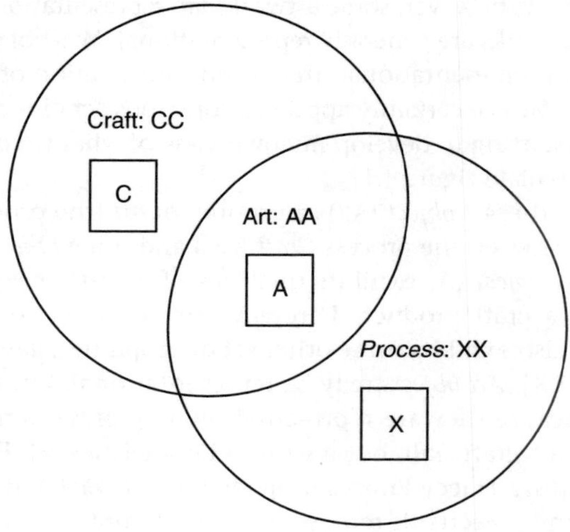

Figure 4.1   Art as Craft

and would have a Spectator or Audience experience. This expression-ism is a functional approach to defining art – *Art* created to realize an end: intending, or giving rise to, an aesthetic experience.

Expressionist theories themselves have come to relate, generally, to those theories that cover the expression of emotion, of attitudes and/or beliefs. Expressionism has come to embrace not only the more tra-ditional *emotionalist* views of say, Tolstoy and Ducasse, but also the *Intuitionist* (Croce) and *Institutionalist* theories (Danto & Dickie). A common thread within expressionism is the notion of a feeling shared between artist and some audience. This shared feeling, in effect, relegates the object *Artwork* as, in someway, inferior to its role as a communications medium.[58] This relegation provides one of the essen-tial criticisms against expressionism. It is also open to criticism through dispelling the relevance of the craft (or technique) of art. Art – as an expression of emotion – can neither be preconceived nor fore-seen and, as such, cannot rely on a craft for its production (Mulhall, 1992).

A further criticism of expressionism is its generally narrow applica-tion. Tolstoy's version of expressionism was developed from moralistic first principles; it used aesthetics as a means to an end; with feelings communicated from the artist to an audience. But, as Jahn (1975:59) noted, while the moralistic[59] component has, itself, attracted criticism, it is the limited nature of those works that Tolstoy thought of as deserv-ing of the status artwork that is problematic. As Whewell (1992:431) notes, Tolstoy failed to acknowledge many accepted works as successful in uniting artist with audience in a common bond of feeling (for example Shakespeare's *King Lear*, Michelangelo's *Last Judgement*, even his own *Anna Karenina*). As Jahn continued, Tolstoy merely concerned himself with a small sub-category of art as a whole. This narrow view of what might constitute Tolstoy's art is reflective of the general nature of expressionist theories. However, to introduce *Art's* epistemic func-tion, my own call on expressionism capitalizes on the relegation of the *object* artwork through the notion of disinterest.

Figure 4.2 shows the process *art* {AA} as the conjunction of both *craft* {CC} and a *mimetic* learning {MM} about the (social) world. Here *art* {AA} acts to create the *Art object* {A}; that is {A} is a representation of the ontological object {M}, an element of an inventory of things, concepts, ideas that describe the social world. The *Art object* {A} therefore exhibits some quality or qualities of the things, concepts, ideas that exist within this social world. Here the *Art object* {A} has a functional quality that expresses some sense of {M}.

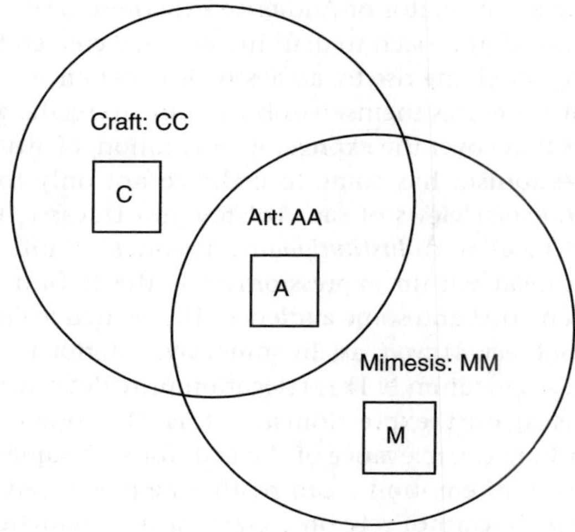

Figure 4.2   Art as Craft & Mimesis (1)

It might be said, as Rowe (1991:286) has, that the *Art object* {A} '*...is intended to support absorbed, disinterested contemplation by either sight, hearing or touch (or some combination of these) on the basis of correctly apprehending it.*' Here, a *disinterestedness* signifies that an *Art object* {A} is not to be contemplated merely as an *end-in-itself.* As Dewey (1934:258) remarked, disinterestedness does not mean uninterestedness. Along with "detachment" and "physical distance", disinterestedness expresses the notion of ideas that apply to '*...raw primitive desire and impulse...*' but are irrelevant to the '*...matter of experience artistically organized.*' This Kantian notion of "disinterest" is one in which the subject is contemplative; it is indifferent as regards the *Art object* itself; it focuses on the represented not the representation *per se.*

The contemplation of the art object – devoid of specific interest in its objective quality – provides Kant with his first explication of the beautiful. To Kant (1987 [1790]:53), '*[t]aste is the ability to judge an object, or a way of presenting it, by means of a liking or disliking devoid of all interest. The object of such a liking is called beautiful.*' I shall go on to explicate beauty as a key aesthetic category within an Art-aesthetic. Here I merely turn to the limited set of artists I feature herein and ask "can such works be subordinated, through the notion of disinterest, to the idea that the *artist* is, through the process of the realization of these works, communicating to the audience in some way?" One critique is that the very nature of works such as Emin's *My Bed* and Hirst's *Mother and Child* provide a "shock" value that obfuscates any meaningful communication. In such a sense, one might question the aesthetic value of an artwork that, intentionally or otherwise, conceals its being an artwork. Such works might, as Gerwen (1996:65) has observed, properly be called *anti-art*. Contemporary artworks therefore prove problematic for the form of the expressionist theory of art that I have so far argued. Can a work be both *anti-art* and *art* simultaneously? Learning to view art in disinterested contemplation may require the learning of new skills within the spectator or audience.

If, epistemically, expressionism is to be understood by the disinterested consideration of its "end" as a new "means", the *Art object* itself cannot, I argue, be divorced from its mode of production.[60] The *Art object* is clearly also "means" related – to the craft skills of the artist. A knowledge of the mode of production therefore becomes essential if, as with much that is contemporary, a disinterested contemplation is not to be facilitated by accepted conventions of interpretation. Here Weitz (1956:32) proposes an inadequacy argument: it is not a question of what art is, but what sort of concept art is:

> ..."Art," itself, is an open concept. New conditions (cases)... will undoubtedly constantly arise; new art forms... will emerge, which will demand decisions on the part of those interested... as to whether the concept [of art] should be extended or not.

While the craft associated with any mode of production is an application of a skill, mimesis calls on a learning process that involves the full extent of the senses. Here character, emotion, experience, learning and pleasure can all be reliably invoked. Therefore a key issue remains in positing *Art* as a conjunction of a craft skill and a mimesis that invites learning through the experience of emotion. Although I argue that an *Art object* is the product of the artist's practice of the *craft-mimetic* conjunction, it is not necessary to explore much further before the conclusion is invited that not all objects resulting from this conjunction are *artworks*. Particularly, there are those works that do not, at their time of inception, attain the status of an *Artwork*, but at some time later are accorded such status. This introduces a temporal facet to the art debate. Certainly, at the time of their initial public showings, Turner's works failed to receive the accolade they enjoy at this present time. Ruskin's great service therefore – as a sympathetic and liberal spectator – was to educate (through the *Modern Painters*) other established, conservative spectators in the interpretive skills required of

Turner's particular (new) language. As Ruskin (1873:MPI) argued in defence of Turner and others, '...*the art is greatest which, conveys to the mind of the spectator, the greatest number of the greatest ideas...*'. It is through the creative expression of ideas about the social lived-in world, and their interpretation, that mimetic learning emerges. I argue, therefore, that there are two further concepts in evidence: 1) there is some other process that, together with the *craft-mimetic* conjunction, acts to distinguish between true art and what might be interpreted as mere *mimetic representation*; and 2) an object of mere representation might – through some additional (institutional) process – be accorded new status as an *Art object* at some subsequent time.

Defining art's innovation

The conjunctive schema of art is now modified by the recognition of a further process; again I temporarily denote this as {XX}. The addition of this further process (Figure 4.3) creates a *complex definition*[61] presenting a range of possible outcomes including, not only the desired framing of the art object *per se* {A}, but also the set of three prime object classes {C, M, X}, and a set of three secondary outcomes {S^1, S^2, S^3}. I shall describe this additional process {XX} as Innovation. In doing so, I invoke the act of introducing something new – in terms of some real (or imaginary) thing, concept or idea. That innovation is associated with artistic activity is a position also supported by Aristotle (see transl. 1996:7), who advanced that mimesis, as natural to us, leads to the development of artistic activity out of improvised activities by a process of gradual innovation.

Let me first deal with the set of prime object classes {C, M, X}. The pure craft object {C}, as any *thing*, concept or idea developed without the benefit of mimesis or innovation can only ever be imitation – it must always be a copy of some other *thing*, concept or idea. The mimetic object {M} is some real (or imaginary) *thing*, concept or idea that populates a social ontology. The pure mimetic object {M}, disclosed without the benefit of either innovation of craft skills, is a realization (or discovery) – an attainment of a knowledge of a *thing*, concept or idea, acquired through either self or social action; a discovery that is neither innovated nor crafted.[62] The class of thing, concept or idea that remains is the product solely of innovation, without the benefit of either craft or mimesis – I label this object {X} an Invention {I}.[63] In doing so I advance the notion that any invention is an instance of a *new* thing, concept or idea. Although invention is sometimes applied, loosely, to the field of artistic endeavour, I specifically exclude such use here, offering a more *pure* form of invention. A pure invention {I} cannot be representational (or possess any characteristics) of any existing thing, concept or idea {M}, since by its nature as an instance of a new type, it does not already exist as an object {M} that can be discovered or copied.

I next turn to consider the three further outcomes labeled $\{S^1, S^2, S^3\}$ in Figure 4.3. In Figure 4.4, I now determine these secondary conjunctions as: Representation {R} – the conjunction of a craft and mimesis; Experimentation {E} – the conjunction of mimesis and innovation; and Design {D} – the conjunction of a craft and innovation. These secondary process conjunctions acknowledge that, if a theory of art (as a conjunction of craft, mimesis and innovation) is to be sustainable, then it must also be possible to arrive at art, independently, through the conjunctions of Design, Experimentation and Representation.

Firstly, the *design* of a thing, concept or idea, is the conjunction of a craft skill exercised with an innovative component. The realization of a *pure design* does not rely on, nor does it invoke, a process of learning or discovery about some existing thing, concept or idea. As a crafted instance of innovation, a design is unique; though clearly the design itself can be imitated (or copied) on successive occasions. Secondly, the *experiment* presents an opportunity to learn and discover further (as yet

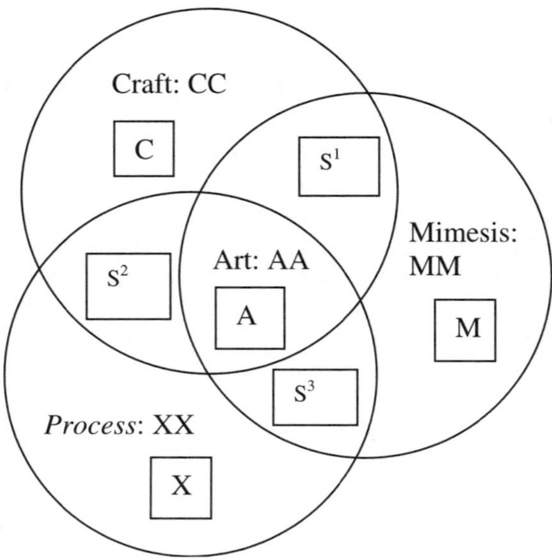

Figure 4.3   Art as Craft & Mimesis (2)

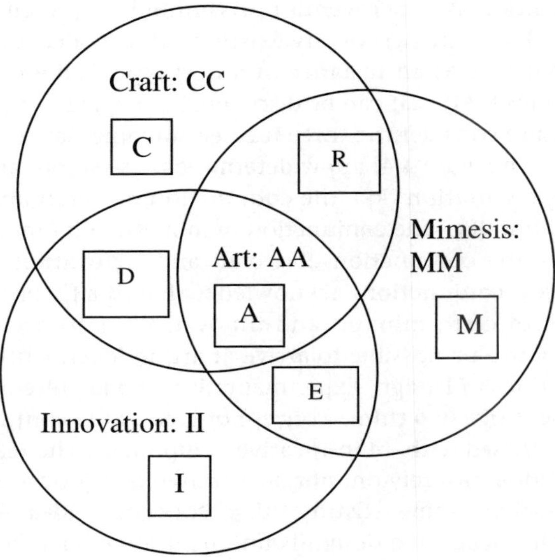

Figure 4.4   Conjunctive Theory of Art (1)

unseen) knowledge and insight into existing things, concept and ideas. However, an experiment does not rely on a craft skill of representation. The *pure experiment*, as a process of discovery through innovative, mimetic expression, appears to satisfy March's (1896) science parallel: a process of embodiment in words, diagrams, mathematical symbols, or other such media (all that is not art), of thoughts with the intention of objectifying human experience. Finally, coming full circle, a *pure representation* is the conjunction of mimesis and craft. Without the consideration of innovation, *representation* cannot be art; it merely tends to a copy of some other object. A *pure representation* acknowledges that there exists a functional capacity for learning within representational objects; that is, as with the outcome of an experiment, the fact that a representational object may not be an artwork does not preclude its role in discovery.

It is now possible to describe the Conjunctive Theory of Art (CTA):

- **Art (the process) is the simultaneous conjunction of the three primary processes of Craft, *Mimesis*, and Innovation.**

At this primary level, *art* is the innovative, mimetic exercise of a craft skill. At a secondary level, however, *art* can also arise from the conjunctions of Experiment, Design and Representation. Within this theoretical model, *art work* is seen to be a consequence of either: 1) all three primary processes acting in simultaneous conjunction, or 2) one of the three secondary processes acting in separate conjunction with the remaining process within some temporal framework.[64] There are, however, a number of dilemmas remaining. What of, for example, *found art*; including Duchamp's Ready-mades (to introduce another often cited artist), Turner's Impressionism, Warhol's Brillo Boxes, and the work of contemporaries such as Emin and Hirst? Why is *Art* to some people and not to others? Why can *Art* be artifact at one time and a treasured, valued and sought-after *Artwork* later? The answer, I argue, lies in the nature of the secondary-level view of art.

At the secondary level, an initial instance of Design, Experiment or Representation is formed through the conjunction of only two primary processes. Rather than a simultaneous conjunction of all three primary processes, the secondary nature of art invokes the remaining third process at some finite time following. Therefore, any instance of Design, Experiment or Representation can, I argue, at any time following its instantiation, be categorized as having the necessary additional characteristics to elevate that instance to an *Artwork*. The Design may be subjected to a subsequent mimetic process in which a new value is found in its use to explain, or discover, some previously unrelated aspect, thing, concept or idea of the social world. The instance of an Experiment may have its basis of instantiation socially accepted as a new representational craft skill, providing a translation of the (first instance of the) Experiment into some unique thing, concept or idea; an *Artwork*. The mere Representation may be re-regarded; played with in new and innovative ways; questioned, seeking new insights and meaning.

The complex nature of *art* unfolds. However, continuing an examination of some of the extant critiques of art theory, the secondary nature of CTA invokes a necessary relationship with an audience. This introduces the *social* element to art. I have stated, at the outset, that this book's thesis is developed from a philosophical position – solely for the interpretation of art within a management and organizational context. That is to say that I seek to define *art* as part of a general requirement to gain insight from an understanding of the role of the artist and the artistic process. This is, necessarily, an epistemological process of coming to know the social world. Therefore, in this context, *art* is firmly posited within the *social*, where a social ontology implies the existence of an inventory of things, concepts and ideas, both real and imaginary that constitute a *worldview*. This social perspective implies – by exclusion of the purely individual view – a normalized (within any given culture or social collective) acceptance of such things, concepts and ideas. Any instance of a mimetic, invented or copied realization; any design, experiment, or representation; any artwork, cannot be so accepted unless it also attains such a normalized acceptance within an appropriately defined social (or institutional) context. Herein lies the notion of the *Artworld.*

Realizing the artworld

Many individual functionalist theories of art fail to adopt some aspect of *art* that another functionalist theory takes as central to its being. Here, the *institutionalist* concept of art has been advanced as addressing this acknowledged failure. Danto's (1964) *Artworld* acknowledges the distinct role of a *public* as spectator/audience. This represents a shift from functionalism to the procedural, in which it is the role of artistic theories themselves that make *Art* possible. As Dickie notes (1997:20), it was Danto's view that something is *art*, not because of what it functions to do, but because of the place it comes to occupy within an *Art*-specific context. As Danto (1964:580) observed:

> Warhol displays facsimiles of Brillo cartons, piled high, in neat stacks... They happen to be made out of wood, painted to look like cardboard... [T]he Brillo people might... make their boxes out of plywood without these becoming artworks, and Warhol might make *his* out of cardboard without their ceasing to be art.

It is Danto's position that such works show that there is no essence of *art*. He continues:

> What in the end makes the difference between a Brillo box and a work of art consisting of a Brillo Box is a certain theory of art. It is the theory that takes it up into the world of art, and keeps it from collapsing into the real object which it is... without the theory, one is unlikely to see it as art.... It is the role of artistic theories... to make the artworld, and art, possible.

In *The New Institutional Theory of Art*, Dickie (1983:50) acknowledges that Danto's argument shows that an artwork exists within some context, but he goes on to argue that the nature of that context is not revealed. He also acknowledges that many different contexts are plausible – as evidenced by the fact that each of the traditional, functional, theories of art may be justified in terms of their own individual Artworld context. However, it is the narrow nature of these specific contexts that make the individual, functional, theories necessarily open to repudiation by counter-examples. But, as Dickie continues, the individual contexts lead in the right direction; they conceive of art as a "human practice":

> Whenever art is created there is, then, an artist who creates it, but an artist always creates for a *public* of some sort. Consequently, [an art theory] must include a role for a *public* to whom art is presented.

As I have argued, Mimesis is a process of discovery – of seeing the social world. In this sense, Figure 4.5 depicts the area (shaded) that is representative of the *social*. As well as the purely mimetic realization, the *social* therefore includes all that is art, experiment and representation; all are mimetic (to some degree) of some real or imaginary thing, concept or idea that is a part of a social ontology. Dickie argues that a primary factor in the *institutional* (or *social*) framework is a "shared" understanding by all, that they are engaged in an activity (that is, *art*). Within this activity, the *Artworld* is constituted by both the variety and totality of roles, from artist, through critic, to public. At this point

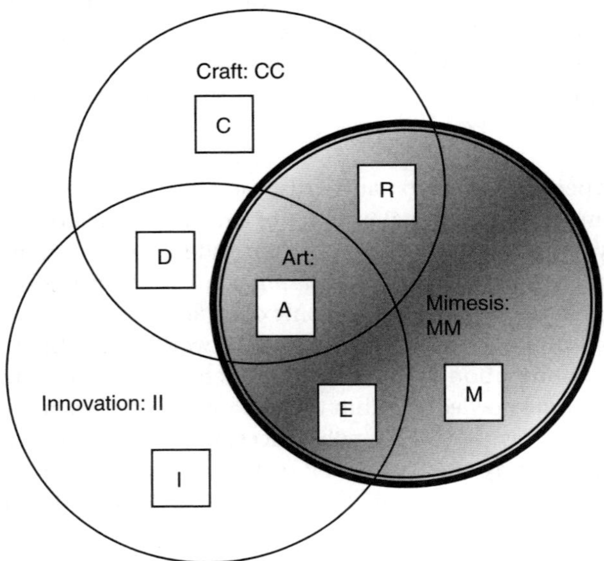

Figure 4.5 Conjunctive Theory of Art (2)

I acknowledge that, by exclusion, pure Innovation {II} and pure Craft {CC} are not, therefore, *social* activities. Neither craft products nor innovations, *per se*, are reliant on the social world (or institution).

As Dickie (1997:21) observes, a remaining issue with the institutional or *Artworld* concept, is that there is a lack of an appropriate notion or process of '...*the conferring of the status of art.*' For the concept of *Art-as-institution* to remain viable and useful it must also address what constitutes *the* Artworld. This is to ask the questions: 1) what distinguishes one *Artworld* from another, and 2) by what authority or through what process are certain classes of things, concepts or ideas granted status as *Art objects* within *the* Artworld. Here Gerwen (1996:58) suggests that '*[p]articipants in the art world who confer art status to new non-art objects must be ready to provide aesthetic reasons for such conferral.*'

Having now argued that art, representation and experimentation are activities carried out and acknowledged within a broader social context, I can now add the process of socialization to the conjunctions contributing to CTA:

- <u>Art</u> (the process) is the innovative conjunction of a craft skill with the mimetic discovery of some aspect (real or imaginary) of the social world.
- An <u>Artwork</u> is any unique tangible realization of a thing, concept or idea resulting from the process of Art, and is accepted as such within a given social context (institution or artworld).
- The <u>Artist</u> is an innovative craftsperson with a propensity for producing artworks.

The Craftsperson, Innovator, and Artist can all participate in the realization of some representational instance of a thing, concept or idea, real or imaginary. What separates Representation and Experiment from Artwork is a lack of an attained status of art as, in some way, furthering of social knowledge. In the social (*Artworld*) context, an artwork must be recognized as such; it must be accepted within the social world as a distinct and indivualistic contribution to the social. Art, therefore, must facilitate a realization of social knowledge within the viewing public; this invokes an act of *interpretation* as part of its public acceptance. Beyond seeing then, *Art* is therefore a way of telling also. It represents a language; a construct of ideas, concepts, signs and symbols. As Ruskin (1873:MP1:74) noted:

[A]rt generally..., with all its technicalities, difficulties, and particular ends, is nothing but a noble and expressive language, invaluable as the vehicle of thought, but by itself nothing. He who has learned what is commonly considered the whole art of painting, that is, the art of representing any natural object faithfully, has as yet only learned the language by which his thoughts are to be expressed.

Embedded within the concept of Art-as-Language is an "act of intent": the artist's *intent* to communicate his or her view of the social world. However, rather than presenting an *Intentionalist* Theory of Art,[65] CTA simply invokes intentionalism as an intent to communicate – even if that intent is only an internalized communication within the artist him or herself.

Art as seeing and telling

Within CTA, the notion of *Art-as-Language* is seen to arise as the corollary of an artwork's process of candidature and acceptance within a given social context of an institution, or *Artworld*. Therefore, the ideas, concepts, signs and symbols that construe art's craft – that is, how these might relate, through innovative practice, to the artist's expression of a world view – must be understood by the *Artworld's* audience. In CTA, *Art* therefore lies beyond a mere language protocol of sign and symbol; it provides a necessary basis in the communication of meaning. It is, I argue, the *craft* element of CTA that is the *language* of Art. This calls on Gaut's (1993:601) observation of the semantic paradigm in *Intentionalism*. It provides for the communication of meaning through the analysis (by artist/audience) of the intended conventions of art's craft. However, how certain craft conventions might be interpreted by an audience is, I argue, *Art's* problematic. As Gaut observes:

> The... thought about art is that the meaning of a work is determined by the conventions under which the artist intends it to be interpreted – one then "decodes" a work by determining what conventions of interpretation are applicable to it.

Collingwood (1938:273–275) also argues that *Art* is a *language*. He advances the notion that art "creates" language as it goes along. However, there is no suggestion, by Gaut, that the artist must have in mind some new convention(s). Neither is accepted that artistic activity necessarily employs a *ready-made* language. Therefore, I argue for a modification of Collingwood's concept by advancing the notion that, in CTA, craft merely has the facility to either recreate or modify itself as it goes along; craft, as the language of art is malleable.[66] Craft skills are therefore seen to be employed in the artist's interpretation of a reality; a knowledge of the craft skills used by the artist therefore becomes necessary in the interpretation of that view of reality by an other. *Art*, itself, presents a dialogue; it exists as a form of narrative interpretation of a reality set up for its own interpretation as narrative. Here, As Lind (1992:118) comments:

> Clearly, art is able to communicate a wide variety of nonverbal meanings that become intersubjectively "interpretable" in virtue of the shared associations of a knowledgeable art community. Such meanings are "interpreted" by those familiar with the particular style, school, or tradition of the work.

Within CTA it is allowed that, in the development of *art's* craft, any new or modified style, school or tradition, is itself required to be socially accepted as a valid convention of interpretation, before a candidate work of *art* can become accepted as an *Artwork*. Such a normalized means of interpretation facilitates an audience's understanding of the necessary qualities of craft, mimesis and innovation that constitute an object's claim to being an *Artwork*, and of the meaning that *Artwork* might communicate. An artist's particular innovative use of the ideas, concepts, signs and symbols that construe the conventions of his or her particular craft need to be understood by an audience. But, importantly, it might well be that it is not the artist that chooses to ensure such understanding.

The craft object {C} or the design {D} that results from a craft process {CC} (or its techniques) and that has not yet been adopted by an Artworld, cannot claim to be mimetic of a social reality. Such a claim can only arise through the ability of the Artworld to perform the same mimetic process of discovery in contemplation of the artwork as did the artist in its production. The Artworld requires to understand the craft (that is, language) in use by the artist. Here, again, I return to Turner. As noted earlier, Ruskin's *Modern Painters* acted as instruction to many in the existing Artworld of the time, in the craft techniques (that is, the *art-language*) employed by Turner and his contemporaries: collectively *The Modern Painters*. Prior to Ruskin's intervention, I argue that Turner's craftskills evidenced in, say, *The Slave Ship*, were originally contemplated as no more than mere *designs*. Using CTA as a basis for understanding the socialization of artistic method, there is a plausible argument that a large number of what we now know as *Artworks* are, in reality, reassessments of earlier artistic designs. This is to say that, at some point since their inception, certain designs have undergone, or been subjected to, a reassessment in the light of their originating craft being subsequently accepted as having a mimetic value by an existing, adapted or new Artworld. As Lind noted (1992:126):

> All that is needed for a work to satisfy this [Art-as-Language] function, then, is that there be a "reference class" of past present or future individuals in a position to interpret and appreciate it as a significant aesthetic object.

Lind (1992:117) also noted that as new artworks are accepted, theorists have attempted to capitalize on what are seen as their salient features in defence of some new theory. Additional new works are therefore often seen to act to dislodge each new theory. Paradoxically however, as Dewey (1934:3) observed, the mere existence of works of art upon which art theories are formed becomes an obstruction to theories about them. Extant theories of art can tend to isolate art by placing the artworks they reference into individual, *institutionalized*, Artworlds. As Davies (1991:64) has argued:

> A definition of art... foreclose[s] on future creativity. If art has some immutable essence [as implied by many extant theories], then the art of the future could not... challenge, alter, subvert, or depart from the art of the past. But... art is the history of such a process [of change].

As an art theory, CTA does not fall victim to Davies' critique; CTA recognizes that art is a complex concept and an artwork itself arises through the primary conjunction of a number of essential processes. It also allows that certain objects, arising through a *secondary conjunction* might, at some future point in time, be accorded artwork status. Within CTA, the concept of art as a communicative process provides for the *artwork* as a medium that allows the artist, or audience, an ability to gain insight into some aspect of the social world though a process of mimetic discovery.

The art installations of Emin and Hirst provide a contemporary example of CTA in operation. That both individuals have been accorded a public status of artist, in the mould of the YBAs, is without doubt. That their individual works have been accepted into certain Galleries or Collections as *Artworks* is indicative only of their adoption as artworks by a certain *Artworld*. To requote the critic Richard Dorment, '*Looking at Emin's work, we learn nothing, understand nothing about ourselves.*' Under CTA however, *art's* problematic is the craftskill by which such artworks are realized. Criticism such as Dorment's is invalidated through a characteristic failure to comprehend any craft component to Emin's *art*. If such a component is not comprehended, then it is not possible to complete the set of conjunctions required in contemplation of the art object. This is not to say that this or that component might not be present – simply that it is not yet comprehended. However, it remains a valid "reading" of Emin's installation to make a critical comment on an *Artworld* that chooses to accord such an installation the status of art![67]

As an art theory, CTA sits well with Gerwen's thesis, as a recursive definition in which art itself must conform to an acknowledged artistic process. But, this is not an Artworld process *per se*. As Gerwen (1996:60) notes, Art processes are (or should be) acknowledged as *artistic* by those within an Artworld who are certain that their typical instantiations occasion a specifiable experience. To this I would add that the specifiable experience must be of a mimetic nature, an *aesthetic* process that entails the use of all available sensory perceptions.

5
The Aesthetic of Art: a Mediation of the Sublime

> He who has not felt that there may be beauty without little-
> ness, and that such beauty is a source of the sublime, is yet
> ignorant of the meaning of the ideal in art.
>
> John Ruskin, 1873

On the object of art

The process of art that I have advanced in defining CTA is simply one method by which we might begin make sense of the work of a certain type of individual, *the artist*, in reaching a plausible knowledge of their view of our social world. In a general sense, the social world becomes the *object* of the Artist's *art*.[68] Here I make the broad assumption that the social world exists as a complex set of phenomena (for example real and imaginary things, concepts and ideas and their inter-relationships) and that CTA allows for the portraying of a plausible knowledge of it through an aesthetic realization of social facts concerning these phenomena. However, in a particular sense, I am also concerned with gaining an Art-aesthetic understanding of specific phenomena that represent the subset of the social world delineated as the sub-universe of management and organization. Within this subset, I have posited a key premiss that the totality of the phenomena and their relationships constitutes a manager-ial burden of complexity and ambiguity. Intuitively, the totality of this burden is great enough so that it tends to the axiomatic that – to an indi-vidual's contemplation – many phenomena and relationships remain unknown or even unknowable. I therefore argue that many social facts lie outside an individual's primary modes of perception. Here, in its totality, I label the sub-universe of management and organization as a *sublime* environment.

The conceptualization of the sublime environment allows me to employ an aesthetic understanding which refuses any seduction by what Chia and Morgan (1996:37) have termed "the dominant signifying systems" that characterize contemporary thinking. Here, in the *aesthetic* context of a sublime environment of management and organization, judgement is exercised on issues beyond the limits of true comprehension. However, as Strati (1992:568) noted, even here the discipline of Aesthetics was, itself, founded as part of a rationalist paradigm; where Aesthetics facilitated the institutionalization of art and made possible the discipline's autonomous development. But Strati also observed that the aesthetic within the life of organizations is not to be observable in some pure form. Therefore, in order to avoid the autonomous nature of a "rational" aesthetic discourse, I look to the sublime itself as it is representable within a *paradigm* of art; the *work* of art as an *interpretation* of the object of Art. The challenge here is the explication of an *Art aesthetic* of the work of an artist that concerns aspects of the object – the sublime of management and organization. Such an explication is to be elicited as a basis for the acquisition of a plausible knowledge concerning the sublime. To achieve such a discourse key actors – that is the market, the competitors and consumers – are all to be considered as the product of processes whereby they are invented, negotiated and redefined, using the entire complex of the actors' knowledge creating faculties (for example see Strati, 2000:13).

I have argued that CTA's *art* is a communicative process through which the Artist exercises a faculty to present a mediation between the positive and negative affects of, say, the feelings of awe, anguish and pleasure present in the sublime experience. Here I adopt a Kantian (1790 [1987])[69] position on the sublime; it is an *experience* of awe-inspiring extremes, invoking (*inter alia*) mental or physical anguish. The sublime provides a category in which the complex and/or the unknown within the social world induce a certain feeling of astonishment; of a certain degree of horror in scale. In an epistemic sense, I argue that art allows the artist to disclose (for universal assent) a nascent knowledge: a *truth* content about some experiential aspect of the sublime that lies beyond a primary sensibility. In the aesthetic dimension, such universal assent is, I argue, initiated by the concept of beauty.

An aesthetic discourse – Part I: on the sublime...

To Strati (2000:21), the sublime[70] is an aesthetic category distinct from beauty; but is always interacting or merging with it.[71] The sublime involves the mysterious pleasure aroused by contemplation of tragic events or representations of terror and anguish. This account of sublimity – based on entities of events or representations – follows Burke's empirical account. Kantian philosophy, however, rejects this empiricism in favour of a pure sublimity that calls for a universality of feeling; it distinguishes between the two categories of the *dynamic* and the *mathematic*.[72] The *mathematically sublime* is a category of scale and is one that is not explicitly reflected in Strati's concept of the sublime. However, Strati does use the term "grandeur", evoking feelings of majesty and splendour.

Parallels can be drawn here to Ruskin's (1873:[MP1]107) discussion of the sublime, in which '*[a]nything which elevates the mind is sublime, and elevation of the mind is produced by the contemplation of greatness of any kind… Sublimity is… another word for the effect of greatness upon the feelings.*' Preziosi (1998:582) describes a more general meaning of the sublime, in which he notes it as a term gaining philosophic and aesthetic currency during the Enlightenment. He refers to the sublime as that which exceeds rational understanding either through "awesome or extraordinary qualities", or through a "massiveness of scale". By the mid-18th century, the term *sublime* had gained frequent use, both as an adjective and a noun. As Mothersill (1992:407) commented, every individual of taste had a catalogue of examples: for example volcanoes, raging seas, towering cliffs, the pyramids, ruined castles and blasted heaths. Consider the following passage by William Wordsworth (1770–1850); taken from the Thirteen-Book Prelude (1799–1806): Book Two, *School-Time (continued)*:[73]

Which, but for this most watchful power of love,	310
Had been neglected – left a register	
Of permanent relations, else unknown.	
Hence life, and change, and beauty, solitude	
More active even than 'best society',	
Society made sweet as solitude	315
By silent inobtrusive sympathies,	
And gentle agitations of the mind	
From manifold distinctions (difference	
Perceived in things where to the common eye	
No difference is) – and hence, from the same source,	320
Sublimer joy. *For I would walk alone*	
In storm and tempest, or in starlight nights	
Beneath the quiet heavens, and at that time	
Have felt whate'er there is of power in sound	
To breathe an elevated mood, by form	325
Or image unprofaned. And I would stand	

> *Beneath some rock, listening to sounds that are*
> *The ghostly language of the ancient earth*
> *Or make their dim abode in distant winds:*
> *Thence did I drink the visionary power.*   330
> I deem not profitless those fleeting moods
> Of shadowy exultation – not for this,
> That they are kindred to our purer mind
> And intellectual life, but that the soul,
> Remembering how she felt, but what she felt   335
> Remembering not, retains an obscure sense
> Of possible sublimity, to which
> With growing faculties she doth aspire,
> **With faculties still growing, feeling still**
> **That whatsoever point they gain they still**   340
> **Have something to pursue. And not alone**
> **In grandeur and in tumult, but no less**
> **In tranquil scenes, that universal power**
> **And fitness in the latent qualities**
> **And essences of things, by which the mind**   345
> **Is moved with feelings of delight, to me**
> **Came strengthened with a superadded soul,**
> A virtue not its own.

The emphasis in this extract (**Bold** – mine, *italic* – Sircello) mirrors what Sircello (1993:542) baptizes as *"the theme of epistemological transcendence"*. The suggestion in 313–321 of, for example, *'difference Perceived in things where to the common eye no difference is'* and the *'visionary power'* in 330 support the conception of the sublime as question of the *absent other*. The sublime, in this sense, indicates a reality that extends beyond the natural (or immediately knowable) world and includes "other" aspects that defy (at least on initial contemplation) the ability of "human mental powers" to perceive them. Our reality is necessarily bounded by our *a priori* knowledge of it; within this, the *absent other* is formless. The contemplation of any ontology in its totality (the Aristotelian universe) therefore presents an "unboundedness" that Kant (CJ:98) used to justify the conception of the sublime as the "presentation of quantity". As Kant (CJ:103) continues, 'We call *sublime* what is *absolutely large*'.

I argue that contemplation of the social world as a whole; the scale of it and, necessarily, the scale of the unknown within it, and of the complexity of its construction, provides a workable definition of the sublime as the "object" of this work. Even in the subset of the social world that I choose to label *the management world,* there is still an enormity of scale and complexity that suggests an appropriateness of a sublime discourse. This mirrors the Aristotelian concept of *Scala Universi* (for example see Mure, 1932:177) and renders the social world as a *universe* in which our knowledge of it must be incomplete. This invites Aristotle's view that knowledge arises as *emerging states of consciousness* and provides the environment in which CTA has a role in facilitating this *emergence* through the mimetic experience.

To suggest the use of the aesthetic category of the sublime to develop an epistemological position is to invoke, in some way, a background *theory of the sublime*. Although an over generalization, Mothersill (1992: 407) makes a point that 19th- and 20th-century scholastic writing is not replete with a sublime discourse on which a theory might be established. The sublime appears to survive only in mock literary writing – in restaurant guides, for example. Is the world (social, management or otherwise) in any sense sublime, and in what sense can the concept of the sublime be truly understood? Philosophically, this invites (*inter alia*) a classic dualistic response on two fronts: both realist/non-realist, and rational/ irrational. Firstly, the sublime world is a world view that is inclusive of the *absent other*. The view of *the idealist*, as a non-realist, that the essence of *objects* within the world exist by virtue of their mind and spirit (as subject), is not subverted by the concept of the sublime. Neither is *the ontological-realist* undermined by a sublimity in which facts about the world will continue to exist independently of their discovery. Faced with contemplation of the world in its entirety – the *Scala Universi* – both the realist and idealist cannot help but acknowledge a limit to their knowledge of it. I therefore argue that the inclusion of *the absent other* cannot strictly be refuted by either. The concept of the sublime simply provides a "descriptive category" in an aesthetic discourse on reality.

Secondly, the concept of the sublime – as sensory experience – precedes a complete knowledge of the world it describes. This of course can be taken to be a wholly irrational standpoint. The rationalist would have us believe that genuine knowledge of the world can only be acquired by starting at a state of certain knowledge and proceeding, carefully, by "certainty-preserving" deductive steps (for example see Curley, 1992:411). To suggest that knowledge might be acquired through a discourse of the sublime attracts an instant challenge from both the rationalist who rejects the value of experience, and the empiricist who rejects all but experience. However, through a paradigm of art, such irrationality cannot, I argue, be invalidated.

The sublime experience motivates the sublime discourse. Furthermore, as Sircello (1993:541) advances, the sublime experience can and does occur in a large variety of personal, cultural, social and historical contexts; all such contexts also inevitably involve experience that is not specifically sublime. As the basis for an epistemology of the *absent other*, the sublime concerns not an object of our senses *per se* – open, as it were, to empiric reflection – but represents our sensory experience of an object (or reality) that cannot be synthesized as a unity within our mind. Knowledge in this context is a personal (or tacit) knowledge – it is not necessarily normalized within a general (social) context; through it may exist as a candidate for normalization. This represents an ability to think the unthinkable; it reflects the Kantian conception of an individual's faculty to transcend experience. The sublime experience reflects a state of subjectivity brought about by an individual's (super)sensible[74] encounter with certain "objects" (in a social reality) that require a synthesis, through reflection, in order to approach a unity of comprehension; such unitary synthesis being generally beyond normal comprehension owing to "a greatness beyond all comparison".

...on the sublime: as experiential phenomena

Even conceptualized as above, the sublime is problematic. As White (1997:126) would observe, the whole theoretical discourse is predicated upon the belief that there really is such a thing as an experience of sublimity and that it is a continual possibility of human existence. Here, for Kant (CJ:123–127), the sublime was not '*...in any thing of nature, but only in the mind.*'. It is what, '*...by its resistance to the interest of the senses, we like directly.*' To summarize Kant's position on the sublime experience, it is what '*...determines the mind to think of nature's inability to attain to an exhibition of ideas.*' Or, as White (1997:130) argues, '*[i]n the experience of the sublime, the individual is confronted by the power and immensity of the [Scala Universi] in so far as this is made manifest by an exceptional part of the [Scala Universi] itself.*' It is on this basis, therefore, that I argue that *the Sublime* is more properly considered phenomenologically.

In striving for an epistemological approach to considering, in essence, the possibilities for perception forming at the boundary of social knowledge, it is the domain of our immediate experience of the world we live in, as opposed to the possible scientific or philosophical reconstructions of it, that is of interest. Here, As Merleau-Ponty ([1945] 1993:64–66) relates:

> We see things; we agree about them; we are anchored in them; and it is with "nature" as our base that we construct our sciences. ...We

live in the midst of man-made objects, among tools, in houses, streets, cities, and most of the time we see them only through the human actions which put them to use. We become used to thinking that all of this exists necessarily and unshakeably.

As I have argued, the dominant paradigm of rationalism and its traditional mode of enquiry (for example empiricism) assume the domain of our social reality to be both "fully determinate" and "totally objective". However, in contemplating the sublime experience – an experience of the *Scala Universi:* the *absent other* and a reality that extends beyond our immediately knowable world – we may presume, as Gutting (2001:188) notes, a general inadequacy of both empiricism and rationalism. Here, Merleau-Ponty's *primacy of perception* (cited in Johnson, 1993:8) suggests how we might perceive the sublime, and thus how a plausible knowledge of the sublime environment might arise, as an Aristotelian *"emerging state of consciousness"*. Thus:

> [b]y… "the primacy of perception," we mean that the experience of perception is our presence at the moment when things, truths, values are constituted for us, that perception is a nascent *logos*; that it teaches us, outside all dogmatism the true conditions of objectivity itself; that it summons us to the tasks of knowledge and action. It is not a question of reducing human knowledge to sensation, but of assisting at the birth of this knowledge, to make it as sensible as the sensible, to recover the consciousness of rationality.

To take this further we need to understand the phenomenological stress placed upon what had, prior to the acceptance of phenomenology, been determined an "object's" *secondary qualities*; specifically the sensible properties of the world – that is: colour, taste, sound, odour, and touch. In the rationalist, empirical world, such *sensible properties* are generally subordinated to what Locke named the *primary qualities* of point, line, plane, and ratio.[75] These *primary qualities* provide epistemic repeatability and reliability and were deemed superior to the subjective, sensible, properties. As Johnson (1993:12) continues:

> Since [sensible properties] are the ones more closely connected with the emotional and valuing tone of our experience, emotions and values were also relegated… resulting in an arid and sterile rationalism that Husserl called the "crisis of European sciences."

> ...[in phenomenology] Merleau-Ponty sought to restore the solidity
> of the lived-qualities of the world.

There is an almost total futility in any proposition that the sublime
might be understood by reference to Lockean primary qualities. I
argue, therefore, that as the basis of an epistemological theory of Art
that seeks – as Merleau-Ponty advocated – a restoration of a primacy of
sensibility, the sublime with CTA provides a viable concept in which to
frame an individualistic experience of the world in which we live. Such
a world is a world in which, in the end, it is not possible (because of,
inter alia, its scale and complexity) to say anything of, save as the
object of knowledge. The sublime experience then, in comparison to
any other worldly experience, acts to draw in the individual through a
Lockean admiration of their own ignorance concerning that experience. This promotes (within an appropriate thinking body) a desire for
rationalization – a desire to attempt to resolve the sublime experience
through a (super)sensible contemplation beyond its "visible" elements –
into components of pleasure, anguish or whatever; arguably in the birth
of a knowledge concerning it. To paraphrase Burke (1759 [1998]:110):

> [We] are bound by the condition of our nature to ascend to [such]
> pure and intellectual ideas [of the sublime experience], through the
> medium of sensible images, and to judge of these qualities by their
> evident acts and exertions, it becomes extremely hard to disentangle
> our idea of the cause from the effect by which we are led to know
> [the sublime experience].

...and of the sublime in management and organizations

Having explicated both the concept and the experiential nature of the
sublime, I reintroduce the concepts of art, artist and management. This
is appropriate in terms of retaining the context of management and
organization studies. It is reasonable to assume that not every individual may possess the same faculty of aesthetic sensibility. Therefore,
to submit something as "individualistic" as nascent knowledge – gained
through an aesthetic sensibility to the sublime – to a wider audience
in seeking some form of social acceptance, becomes the *raison d'être* of
the process of socialization within CTA. I am thus concerned with the
social emergence of a new plausible knowledge, arising out of an individualistic realization of *the absent other* within the sub-universe of
management and organizations. This is a response to the perceived

inability of the dominant paradigm of rationalism in coming to understand what remains, in essence, unknown.

In CTA's positioning of *the sublime* as the "object" of art – rather than it being "autonomously" subjective of art – I argue that the status of the aesthetic of *the sublime* changes from a device for aesthetic critique, to a device which is valued for the development of the cognitive process. However, for a (plausible) individualistic nascent knowledge to become an "admitted" candidate to a set of universally accepted knowledge, some form of normalization (or process of social acceptance) is required. The sublime experience must therefore play its part in the "communication game". As Lyotard (1982:77) suggests:

> The sublime sentiment… [is] a strong and equivocal emotion: …in it pleasure derives from pain. Within the tradition of the subject, which comes from Augustine and Descartes and which Kant does not radically challenge, this [pain/pleasure] contradiction …develops as a conflict between the faculties of a subject, the faculty to conceive of something and the faculty to "present" something.

The epistemological nature of art lies within the "social" process of the ascension of a nascent, individualized *artist's* knowledge to a universal consensus. For *Art* to provide an epistemological contribution in this manner, it must therefore communicate something of the artist's *sublime* experience. In doing so, and assuming that not every individual may possess the same faculty of a sensibility to the sublime, the work of *art* itself – as an "end" – must facilitate the mediation of that experience within the wider *social* audience. Here I return to the linked concept of beauty. As Lyotard continues:

> Knowledge exists if, first, the statement is intelligible, and second if "cases" can be derived from the experience which "corresponds" to it. Beauty exists if a certain "case" (the work of art), given first by the sensibility without any conceptual determination, the sentiment of pleasure independent of any interest the work may elicit, appeals to the principle of a universal consensus (which may never be attained).

Art then, as an epistemic device, should mediate the individualism of the sublime experience through the universal appeal of beauty. While this is clearly a generalization that appeals to all social knowledge, in the sub-universe of management and organization, the development of knowledge is no less relevant. Although we might therefore ask of the manager, as Pelzer (2002:414) does (and, in general, of any audience), an undisputed acceptance of the *artist* as a mediator of the sublime – a communicator of *the absent other* – the *artist* becomes implicitly bound by his or her responsibility as a translator. As Merleau-Ponty ([1945] 1993:70) relates:

> It is not enough for [the artist] ...to create and express an idea; they must also awaken the experiences which will make their idea take root in the consciousness of others. If ...[the work of the artist] is successful, it has the strange power of being self-teaching.

In the context of management and organizational practice, the role of the *manager-artist* within CTA is to practice mediating the sublimity of this or that (complex or ambiguous) management or organizational situation, gained through their sublime experience of it. This is a responsibility to deliver, to his or her audience, that which cannot be explained; that which remains a secret. For example, if we presuppose the existence of complexity within global organizations (that is, through a greatness of either scale or the dynamics of organizational relationships), we might comment that the achievement of a universality of aesthetic feeling with regard to such organizations is beyond a rational understanding (for example Microsoft, Enron, and the Disney Corporation and so on). In exercising a monopolistic desire for totality of market share, the notion that a global corporation invokes the sublime and feelings of anguish is not unrealistic. It is certainly reasonable to assume that there would be, in many relationships within (and without) the global corporation, an individualistic desire, within some section of the audience, to rationalize any feeling of anguish faced as they contemplate that which appears beyond contemplation.

Following the above line, the mediation of the sublime experience through CTA provides a route for the mimetic externalization of the (tacit) knowledge of the artist. It is this tacit knowledge that Sumpf (2002) argues is mandatory in influencing decision-making processes; the externalization of which leads to learning and the transferability on innate knowledge and expertise. Sumpf relates this externalization to the process and use of *images* to alleviate the familiarization of objects and situations which would otherwise remain unclear and remote. In this way, Sumpf argues, metaphors can be invoked that develop perspectives that may never normally be taken into account by managers. The externalization of tacit knowledge is a goal of the appeal of a universal consent to the translation of the sublime experience by the artist. But, it is the linked concept of beauty that, alone, creates, in both artist and audience, the necessary preconditions for a disinterested engagement with art's *object*.

An aesthetic discourse – Part II: on the beautiful...

Although Burke (1759) argued a conception of beauty that was based on the characteristics of the observed object (such as line, smoothness, and so on) this is again an empirical conception rejected by Kant (CJ:79) who argued that:

> [t]here can be no objective rule of taste, no rule of taste that deter-mines by concepts what is beautiful. For any judgement from this source [that is, taste] is aesthetic, i.e., the basis determining it is the subject's feeling and not the concept of an object.

The Kantian problematic is that an objective sense of beauty – as some measurable quality – is, in effect, not material in forming an aesthetic judgement of a work of art. However, this is not to say that some other concept of beauty might not be useful. Kantian beauty can be seen as an experiential phenomenon; one experienced between *object* and con-templative *subject*. As Sircello (1975:4) notes, the Kantian notion of beauty is not determined by concepts: no criteria of beauty can be given in terms of the features of the translation of the sublime experi-ence to which the judgement of beauty is then applied. This is *the* problematic in the appeal to universality of any concept of beauty. If we cannot determine universal concepts of beauty in relation to a work of art, how would it be possible to acknowledge beauty as a contribu-tion to the universal assent required for the transference of knowledge?

Beauty is an essential form of attraction between an *object* and its con-templative *subject*; one that is essential in the process of contemplative engagement between the two. In CTA's process of the mimetic objectification of the sublime experience into an *object* of *art* – a candidate *Artwork* – the artist is called upon, *inter alia*, to employ his or her craft skill in the innovative translation of the "beauty" he or she finds engag-ing within the sublime experience, into a beauty that will assist their audience's engagement with their work. Here, as Zangwill (2001) notes:

> [b]eauty does not stand alone. ...Things are beautiful because of the way things are in other respects. ...What then is this beauty, which is so closely tied to other features? ...It is uncontroversial that

beauty is an object of human thought and experience. We think about beauty and we experience it… [it] is something we value and desire; and we take our judgements about it seriously, in that we think some judgements are better than others.

The challenge to determine the attributes of beauty can therefore be seen to have continued – from the origins of the problem posed by Kant – through to more contemporary studies of the concept. Here, Brand (1999) notes that such contemporary studies place beauty at the intersection of aesthetics, ethics, social-political philosophy and cultural criticism. Beauty is a significant matter to artists and critics alike. However, contemporary beauty appears bereft of references to, say, Plato, Burke, Hume or Kant; therefore denying any philosophical importance to the concept. As Brand (1999:5) observes:

> [the] institutionalization of beauty has spawned an entire industry devoted to beauty *matters* where "matters" designates the noun… Thus beauty… [is] tied to women's mental health, physical well-being, and decoration.

The institutionalization of beauty is contemporaneous with the institutionalization of other aspects of aesthetics. Therefore we have autonomous art, in a commercial sense, becoming increasingly associated with brand management and collections of paintings adorning the walls of institutions (for example see Pelzer, 2002 and Sumpf, 2002). Here, the sublime has subverted the concept of beauty, where to revere (Hirst's) "dead sharks" as beautiful invites a new "dark" critique (see Brand, 1999:7).[76] Therefore we are faced with what Eaton (1999:11) concludes is the simplistic version of Kantian beauty – that if something is beautiful "one just sees it" – becoming juxtaposed with non-traditional views such as a conception of beauty that is '*…related to [our] beliefs or moral judgements.*'

While contemporary accounts of beauty invite the critique I have outlined, beauty's problematic is also apparent in a historical context. Tolstoy believed that pleasure alone – as inferred by the *pure beauty* of Kantian theory – cannot fully account for the tremendous value that art has in society.[77] To Eaton (1999:12), few people in her experience seem to agree that beauty is either universal or necessary. Her acceptance that an ecologist friend '*sees ugliness*' in the guise of the "Purple Loose Strife" flower where she sees "*beauty*" calls for an illuminating discussion in the context of beauty as I apply it to CTA.

Let me suppose, for the sake of argument, that at some point in time no person had knowledge of the *purple loose strife*; that it lay undiscovered in its native habitat. Certainly, person A possesses no knowledge of the plant. Person B happens, through discovery, to encounter the *purple loose strife*. In its discovery, person B is sensible to the plant, its environment and a great many other things. B is drawn to the plant but "senses" an element of danger. We might say that B (knowingly or otherwise) cognizes this element of danger through the sublime experience of having discovered the plant in a particular contextual setting. Person B is also an artist and, rather than take a cutting of the plant, paints two pictures of it, one *a representation* in highly detailed (almost photographic) relief against a plain background, the other *an impression* set in the context of a decaying ecosystem, in which the plant is depicted as dominating its environment to the exclusion of other living things.

When B shows the two pictures to person A, A remarks on the beauty of the tall, vibrant, purple blossom. The first painting, *the representation*, elicits no more than a comment of the apparent beauty of the object, the *purple loose strife*. A's judgement of this painting is a *verdictive* judgement of beauty in the traditional aesthetic sense. It is a judgement based on the *object* itself – the painting. To A, with no prior conception of *the* plant, the representation provides nothing more than a depiction of form and of colour. It says nothing; it teaches nothing of the absent other – the embryonic tacit knowledge sensed by B on that person's encounter with the plant in its natural environment. While the *representation* might exhibit beauty, it does not, I argue, represent *Art* – despite the mastery of the craft of painting practised by the B. The *impression*, however, can inform A of the potential danger of introducing the *purple loose strife* to an alien ecology – of the potential for the plant to "rapidly destroy the delicate eco-system". As an element of the painting, the plant itself may still exhibit a quality of beauty similar to that encountered by the *representational* painting; I argue that it is this beauty that attracts us to a study of the painting and a more concrete learning experience. Here beauty becomes a factor in establishing the relationship between the audience (B) and the real (the plant itself).

...on the two faces of the beautiful

Zangwill (2001) argues that beauty – a verdictive property of a "thing" – is determined by that thing's substantive properties (for example: dainty, dumpy, graceful, garish, delicate, balanced, warm, passionate, brooding, and so on). This may be a reasonable argument in terms of the critique of art objects *per se*.[78] However, to move away from the consideration of beauty as verdictive, I am no longer concerned with beauty expressed primarily as a judgement of taste. Beauty, I argue, is to be understood in its aesthetic sense of being used to explore a living historical situation; that is, in its relation to problems of existence. This is an epistemic mode of understanding beauty, one that seeks to reconnect an artwork with the lived experience. It relates to the *Art aesthetic* of CTA in respect of Beauty's effect of assisting the subject to *engage* with experience – *Art* as a "means" to an epistemic "end". Here, to reflect on Van Gogh's famous Sunflower paintings, what is beauty in the context of a sensible category? Why should the beauty of something, for example a sunflower, figure in the exercise of taste – a formation of a judgement about that thing?

Beauty imbibes the sensible-*self* with "good" and "pleasurable" feelings – but what are these feelings and how might they be described or otherwise explained? Is beauty purely pleasurable or are there other aspects to this aesthetic category? What do other cultures have to say about beauty and its defining signs or symbols? Is there a broader concept of beauty that can offer some form of universal, holistic sense of good feeling? Is beauty what we strive to identify in order for the "self" to be at ease with its environment? When we see, touch, hear, smell or taste some *beautiful* "thing", we are using our senses and forming a judgement that the "thing" we see, touch or hear (and so on) *is* beautiful. We make a sensible judgement that – in accordance with an *a priori* concept of beautiful – this or that "thing" is, in fact, beautiful. We make a judgement that is based on our own existence. A painting of a sunflower may exist without our own existence, but it is only in our own individual contemplation of it, that the sunflower can be judged as beautiful (or not) since it is only at the time of contemplation, at the point of our engagement with it, that the sunflower, itself, assaults our sensibility.

Do we, when we view Van Gogh's 1889 painting *Still Life: Vase with Fourteen Sunflowers,* simply note the painting as "beautiful" when viewed on a gallery wall? Do we see a *representation* of the sunflower as depicted by the "acknowledged" craft skill of the *Artist* Van Gogh; marvelling in the quality of the brushwork, the form, colour and the setting of light versus shade? Do we merely regard the painting *Still Life: Vase with Fourteen Sunflowers* as an object of desire and value? Do we compare the "Sunflowers" with other great works, as we stroll through the gallery's space, making comparative judgements of taste based on our sensible attitude; perhaps sharing our opinions with others? Or do we look past the beauty and engage with the painting as a "means" of understanding that the "Sunflowers" is the fruit of an idea Van Gogh held at the time of its painting? Do we question *why this something*?

Van Gogh's painting provides one of his interpretations of sunflowers; it is an "end" of his process of artistic endeavour, representing his engagement with the sunflowers as "objects" within *his* ontological perspective of *his* reality. The painting represents a synthesis of *his* knowledge (both tacit and explicit) concerning sunflowers. However, while we may make an individual judgement of the beauty of Van Gogh's painting, in actually experiencing *judgemental beauty* we have, *de facto,* engaged with the painting itself. I shall refer to *judgemental beauty* as the "first mode of beauty". However, this *de facto* engagement with the painting itself infers some other visible essence of beauty. This "second mode of beauty" – that I shall refer to as *attractive beauty* – precedes *Judgemental beauty*. Attractive beauty is a condition of *social visibility*. *Judgemental* and *Attractive* therefore present two faces of beauty; it is this second mode that attracts the mind to contemplate what is before it. Beauty in this mode is not a condition of the existence of the work (see, for example, Ducasse, 1928:181). Therefore, to understand the work of *art* in an epistemological context, I argue that we must look beyond the condition of social visibility, to consider the "work of *art*" in its *subjective* relationship to the *object* of which the work is a mimetic realization – that is, the sublime experience. Contemplating an *Artwork* as a process of mimetic discovery obviates any need for a judgement of the beauty of the *Artwork* as object itself, since we do not objectify the *Artwork* as subject. We must take a disinterested view of what it is that we behold.

If, beyond an *attractive* beauty, we find there is little more than form and colour then we are not subjected to a learning experience. However, if we perceive – as the artist perceived in the creation of the *Artwork* – something of the *absent other*, we may add to our body of tacit knowledge of *arts* object. Judgemental Beauty does not concern us; Attractive Beauty matters – but only insofar as we must learn to be disinterested in it. Judgemental Beauty is subjective whereas Attractive Beauty can appeal to a universality. This conceptualization can be used to reconcile Tolstoy's rejection of beauty, where he believed that art's importance in human lives depends upon seeing how it is tied to interests and beliefs that contribute to a community's sustainability. As

Eaton (1999:13) observes: '*[a] concept (poem, horse, dynamo, proof) leads one to notice things (rhythm, muscle structure, organization of parts, organization of evidence), and the noticing is pleasurable.*' As Knox (1931:486) argued, Tolstoy suggests that the function of art is not merely a manifestation of the beautiful. It expresses a very cogent and efficacious human activity whose function it is to enrich and intensify the comprehension of life through the infectious communication of emotions.

...and of the beautiful in management and organizations

In an experience of the sublime, a nascent knowledge of that experience – the result of a lived experience shared – is achievable through CTA's process as a mediator of the sublime. Beauty, rather than a concept to be applied in judgement, becomes a necessary condition of engagement with the communicative process within CTA. In the context of management and organizations, the feeling of beauty is one of the factors that, Strati (2000 and 1992) argues, structures organizational life. To Strati, beauty may be seen in the combination of qualities that please the senses of the actors. Here we see beauty in a judgement of the organization as a member of the class of "objects" called organizations. This is, I argue, beauty in the first mode – judgemental beauty; it is a function of an autonomous aesthetic of beauty. Such a judgemental concept of beauty is not invalid. Intuitively, for actors within organizational life, there may be a combination of qualities that tie them (as employee or manager) to the organization (as employer). "This is a good (that is, beautiful) organization to work for." From shareholder and others perspectives, strategies adopted in pursuit of organizational development may achieve a status of "beautiful"; as may individual products and policies. But, for each of these cases in which some actors might perceive "beauty", it is not difficult to counter with examples of actors for whom "beauty" is not present to the same degree. As Strati (2000:20) might concur, *judgemental* beauty highlights the "conflictual dynamics" operating within businesses and other groups of actors.

The autonomous rationalization of organizational beauty presupposes that the boundary of the organizational dynamics lies within the limits of the subject's comprehensibility. Judgemental beauty is not, I argue, a concept relative to the sublime. In a judgemental mode, beauty – as a basis for a management judgement – would drive a comprehension of the organization through the identification of *the beautiful* within it. Such a judgement either assumes or seeks (a certain) uniformity, within which generalizations concerning the organization, as a whole, are made. In identifying the beautiful aspects of the organization, a judgement of liking appeals to a universal prescription by which other, similar, aspects are also to be judged (or prescribed). Organizational narratives become modelled on the judged "beauty" of success. Here, any attempt at a comprehension of the (potentially sublime) organization on the basis of Judgemental beauty is, I argue, symptomatic of the postmodern condition. The modelling of an organization on the replication of *the beautiful* – an absolute, flanking the notion of truth – can be seen in the following of management *fashions*. Here, as Baudrillard (1983:8) has observed:

> [j]ust as the model is truer than the true (being the quintessence of the significant features of a situation), and thus procures a vertiginous sensation of truth, fashion has the fabulous character of the more beautiful than beautiful [the sublime]... The seduction it exerts is independent of all value judgement. It surpasses the esthetic *[sic]* form in the ecstatic form of unconditional metamorphosis.

The implication, here, is that at the boundary of comprehensibility concerning the potentially sublime organization, the replication of the apparently "beautiful" features of the organization may lead, in itself, to the condition of the sublime. Therefore, within CTA, my concern is with a process that communicates knowledge about the organization through an engagement with, and a consequential disinterest in, that which is merely *attractively beautiful* about that organization. Here the potential of the *manager-artist* lies in highlighting beauty in this "second mode"; in identifying the conditions of social visibility that will engage the organizational audience within a mimetic learning process that communicates the unknown, the absent other, that is the sublimity of the organizational reality.

An aesthetic discourse – Part III: on art and communication

The *Art-aesthetic* of sublimity and beauty provides, I argue, a constructive basis for the non-autonomous application of aesthetics within management and organizational practice. Here, in the formulation of CTA, *Art* is a form of communication that employs its craft as a language with the intent to transfer meaning. The reception of meaning occurs through the act of interpretation of the language in use. Therefore, without an understanding of the language-in-use, there can be no communication of meaning. A recipient's shared understanding of a language's signs, symbols and protocols thus provides for their faculty to interpret meaning. Here, as Gaut (1993:597) argues, the interpretation a work of art is to give it meaning. However, this presupposes that we understand "meaning" as a concept far wider than "linguistic" meaning.

In positing artistic communication as the intent to promote, in some "audience", the same sensual meaning perceived by the artist, then there is an implicit reliance on the use of all sensual faculties for the interpretation of that meaning. This view of intent goes beyond the concept of 'simple intent' noted by Gaut (1993). Any view that there might be a correct interpretation begins to fade with the lack of a literalist defence. A further issue is what of the artist that fails in his or her intent? Within CTA, failed intent is characterized by way of a 'design', 'experiment' or mere 'representation'; it would not result in an 'artwork'. The meaning within an artwork – that which is the communication – is therefore understood as a complex structure of properties that invoke, within the sensible audience, certain sensual perceptions. While Gaut goes on to develop a Patchwork Theory of Interpretation, I argue that this sense perception is an *aesthetic attitude* of disinterestedness, where Rowe (1991:272) notes that:

> [an *aesthetic attitude*] …is not a feeling or an emotion (although it might give rise to either of these) but it is rather a mode of attention or contemplation of an object of sight, hearing or… touch. We regard these as the "aesthetic senses" because their objects have *parts* and an element of internal complexity.

The concept of an *aesthetic attitude*, practiced with disinterest, is both compatible with the concept of a language, and acknowledges the internal complexity of properties that construe meaning. In *Art-as-Communication*, artworks are the medium of transmission of some aspect of the sublime (social) world that the artist, through the artistic process of CTA, is translating for communication. Epistemically, I generalize this as the mimetic process of CTA acting to mediate, through the communication of a sublime discourse, a knowledge concerning the sublime experience.

Two main counter arguments affect this position. Firstly, as Zangwill (1999:316) observes, it can be argued that some art might not be intended for the process of communication; that is, art that was not meant for an audience. Such examples are: 1) *Private Poetry* and

2) *Working Sketches*. However, as Collingwood (1938:247) points out, in its most elemental form language is not necessarily addressed to an audience. One can communicate with one's self, without attracting the observation that language is not being used. Therefore the artist, practicing art in relation to his or her own translation of a sublime experience into a desired art medium (be it paint, music, poetry and so on) for his or her own "self"-interpretation, is still exercising the concept of *Art-as-Communication*. Working sketches are communicated notes of reference to the sublime. The simple fact that, as functioning, reasoning individuals, we think in terms of the ideas, concepts, signs and symbols that represent our own language, is illustrative of a concept of "self"-communication.

The second counter argument is that if art is communication, then art must be about something. But, although many artworks are about something, there are – as Dickie (1997:21) observes – many *Artworks* that appear not to be about any "thing" at all. My own counter to this critique is that the social-world, in which CTA is exercised, legitimately includes things, concepts or ideas, real and imaginary. Certainly, within the argument for attaining knowledge through the concept of the sublime experience, a "work of *art*" may result as the translation of an imaginary concept (or idea) held by the artist. Until universally accepted, a new concept or idea might well appear as no (accepted) "thing". But, if accepted *as Artwork* in any context, a work at least becomes about its "self" and is a commentary on the *Artworld* that recognizes it as such.

I therefore argue that CTA, as an epistemic device, mediates the individualism of the sublime experience through a communication of the sublime discourse. It provides for the externalization (and potential universalization) of an experience of the sublime (as knowledge – tacit or otherwise) through the engagement of the individual with the communication process that is *art*. This is an engagement that results from the (universal) appeal of *Attractive beauty* within an *Artwork*. This conception of the epistemic role of art further underpins Pelzer's (2002) commentary on both Velasquez' Las Meninas and the 1957 Picasso rendition of the same. The *artist* poses as the *intermediary* to the *sublime*, to that which cannot be readily explained. This highlights the individuality of the lived experience – a phenomenon that gives rise, in the *sensible* individual's mind, to some new conception or nascent knowledge.

6
A Portrait of the Artist

> What is the popular conception of the Artist? Gather a thousand descriptions: the resulting composite is the portrait of a moron. He is held to be childish, irresponsible, and ignorant and stupid in everyday affairs.
>
> Mark Rothko[79]

Conceptualizing the artist

There are many public conceptions of what an *Artist* might be, as there are many – generally accepted – fine *Artworks* populating our museums and galleries. That a "work" of the process *art* might become accepted by an appropriate *Artworld* as (*inter alia*): poetry, text, painting, sculpture, or performance and so on, suggests that it is an almost futile task to attempt to produce a generic "portrait" of the artist. For that matter, what of the *faux artiste* also? However, in leaving aside such pragmatics, the approach in deriving CTA and its *Art-aesthetic* precepts of the sublime and attractive beauty has been necessarily theoretic. Thus, in considering the role of the artist in the process of art I do not, therefore, refer to the aesthetic categories of the sublime and beauty in their generally perceived autonomous sense, but in the sense that *the sublime* is the object of an *art* that allows – through a disinterested engagement with an *attractive beauty* – the meaning of an absent "other" to be communicated. This prompts the question *"what can we learn about the real work of the Artist engaged in CTA?"*

Art, in general, is a constitutive force; it creates a particular view of a reality. This is as true of writing, drawing, painting, sculpture, and so on, as it is of speaking; and as true of science as it is of poetry. As Richardson (1991:174) observes, producing artworks – as with producing other "things" – involves value judgements: what to produce, what to name the productions, and what the relationship(s) between artist, named artwork and audience (if any) will be. Art is a *socio-historical* construct invoking accepted craft devices (for example, in writing: narrative, metaphor, and so on, and in painting: line, form, colour and so on) not only for adornment, but also emergent, cognitive meaning. Although there are many accepted forms of *Art*, here I shall offer some focus on the disciplines of *Fine Art* and *Installation Art* as illustrative of the artistic process in general. However, I acknowledge the limitation of what might, to some, appear a potentially narrow, and overly specific, cross-section of the possible "artistic" population. But, the concept of CTA is transcendent of the specific craft skill(s) of the artist. Therefore, as art transcends its craft, the apparent futility of the task of producing a generic "portrait" of the artist is mitigated, and the *Artist* tends merely to CTA's definition of an innovative craftsperson with a propensity for producing *Artworks* through a mimetic (learning) process. Here, the application of craft skills is the language tool for communicating the mimetic discovery of some aspect (real or imaginary) of the social world. *Art* may, in some circumstances, even be seen as accidental; it certainly evolves as a meditation between the known/knowable and the unknown/unknowable elements of the *Artist's* experience. The process of *art* results in a potential *Artwork* as a unique and (objectively) tangible realization of a subjective experience of some phenomena of the sublime.

I have argued, under CTA, that the capacity for a "work" of *art* to be acknowledged as an *Artwork* is a function of "social" acceptance. This requires, as antecedent, an engagement with the *work* by an observing *Artworld*. In order to achieve this engagement, there must, about the potential artwork, be some *Art-aesthetic* quality of *attractive beauty*. However, while essential, an attractive beauty is not a sufficient premiss for conferring a status of *Artwork*. Social acceptance is not merely the achievement of a universality of liking – such liking is only likely to lead to an expression of judgemental beauty. Therefore, I am not concerned, here, with *faux art* or the *faux artiste*. A candidate *Artwork* must communicate some meaning that is only mimetically knowable about the *Artist's* worldview. However, a candidate *Artwork* may require additional interpretation (for example by some other artist, critic, audience, or patron[80]) before its meaning is communicable, and its candidacy is accepted. A knowledge and skill-of-hand in the practice of the *craft* of, say, painting (including an affinity with one or more of the acknowledged schools: for example classicism, realism, surrealism and so on) does not confer on a person the status of *Artist*. Under CTA, not all the works of, say, Picasso, should automatically be conferred with the status *Artwork,* just because they are "Picassos".

The problem posed of the artist is the application of their craft in striving to attain a goal of a unitary synthesis of their *worldview*. Art is, by CTA definition, of the very highest <u>order-of-application</u> of a craft skill. But this is not the same as the practice of an accepted craft skill to the highest order. The painter, painting decoratively or merely representationally, to the highest standards of their craft is not necessarily engaged in art.[81] This is Plato's criticism of a mirror-like *mimesis*. The painter, acknowledged for their craft skill, accepting a commission to produce an "artwork" cannot be guaranteed to produce one – though their work may prove perfectly acceptable and *art like* to their patron. Epistemically then, while an Artwork might be an acceptable "end" in its own right, it is not reliant on its representation as object. In a sense, an Artwork need not be representational of anything other than an artist's imaginary idea. It is an allowable candidacy for knowledge therefore, that some artists advance the concept that their art need not be "of" any "thing" at all. The surrealist and abstract natures of, say, Dali and Rothko's work, evidences art's potential to subvert its own objectivity.

Ars Poetica to Tolstoy: on art's nature

As a "frame" for my portrait of the artist I draw on Aristotle's four themes (or corner-stones) of the artistic process. These themes are: (A) the situation which supplied a stimulus to the artist, (B) the artist, (C) the work of art, and (D) the observer. This framework is consistent with CTA. As Tracy (1941) describes these themes, "A" represents Nature: the '*...mass of unorganized and discontinuous situations, the gross data of environment, some parts of which through special features tend to produce a special response in people of artistic temper.*' This description is not inconsistent with CTA's positioning of the sublime as the *object* of art. To paraphrase Tracy (1941:500–504) therefore:

> From the sublime environment, some thing (notionally an experience of the sublime) has happened (or been caused to happen – for example even a request or commission might act as a stimulus) to arrest the notice of the artist. It may be that experience of a phenomenon, or object (real or imaginary), or group of such experiences has presented itself that attracts the artist's eye, and induces him/her to make a symbol of it by some manner of application of

their craft (for example picture or statue). These objects or experiences as they occur are unorganized and shapeless. They need to be patterned and modified [mediated] by an organizing mind sensible to their relationship with the lived experience (by the artist), so that they might become incongruous with the form they will subsequently take as a (potential) work of art. In such a manner, the artist is seen to be concerned with the rehabilitation of his/her (lived) experiences in the form of units (artworks), through their particular medium.

The question arises that some art is simply about the artist expressing emotion and/or feeling, or that the stimulus to the artist in his or her work is at least something that is neither objective nor experience as such. However, I have already noted that an artwork need not be representational of anything other than an idea of the artist's imagination. In deriving CTA, the common thread within this *expressionist* critique is the notion that the artwork itself is, in someway, relegated as inferior to its role as a medium of communication. While this advances expressionism as 'means'-related, it can only be understood by a disinterested engagement with art's "end": the *Artwork* itself. The artwork becomes the window through which the artist may be in a process of communicating emotions, but that these emotions are related, phenomenologically, to his or her existence in the world. Here, Tolstoy's *Anna Karenina* provides some contextual relevance. As Geiger (1961:82) relates: '*...it is Tolstoy's assumption that art, however inviolate, functions to present insight into and vision of the forms and objects of reality... [Art] serves as an insight into the "characteristic" or fundamental nature of an object...*'.[82] Art acts to strip off the wrappings which hinder the object, *a sublime world*, from being seen directly.

To add to the frame of my artist's portrait, Tolstoy's insight is worthy of further consideration. Geiger provides an analytic of Chapters 7–13, Volume Two, Part V of *Anna Karenina*. In essence, this is a narrative dealing with the relationships existing between the Aristotelian cornerstones: (A) the subject (Karenina), (B) the Artist (Mihailov), (C) the objects (artworks by Mihailov including that of Karenina's portrait), and (D) the would-be observer/critic (Golenishtchev) and *faux artiste* (Vronsky). The relationships between these four Aristotelian cornerstones are seen by Geiger as contributing to the artistic debate in five themes: 1) the nature of art, 2) the psychology of the artist and the creative process, 3) the education and technical achievement of the artist, 4) communication and responsibility, and 5) the interpretation and evaluation of artworks. Again, these are themes consistent with my argumentation and an Aristotelian frame-of-reference; each of which, I argue, will become an essential element of reference in understanding the significance of art in relationship to the practice of a craft of management.

There are two particular aspects of Tolstoy's narrative that I wish to introduce as illustrative of the nature of art's cornerstone relationship between Subject (A) and Object (C). These are the concept of *faux art* and the content (or subject) of art. Given the definition of CTA, the nature of art is perhaps most easily represented by illustrating its negative form – the concept of a *faux art*. Consider the following passage from the text of *Anna Karenina* in which Tolstoy (1877:463), as narrator, provides a prescient commentary on the nature of art as I argue it:

> [Vronsky] had a talent for understanding art and for imitating it with accuracy and good taste, and he imagined that he possessed the real power an artist needs. After wavering for some time between various kinds of art – religious, historical, genre or realistic – he began to paint. He understood all the different kinds and was able to draw inspiration from all, but he could not imagine that it is possible to be quite ignorant of the different kinds of art and to be inspired directly by what is in one's own soul, regardless of whether what one paints belongs to any particular school. As he did not know this, and was not inspired directly by life but indirectly by life already embodied in art, he found inspiration very readily and easily, and equally readily and easily produced paintings very similar to the school of art he wished to imitate.
>
> He liked the graceful and effective French School of painting best, and in that style began painting a portrait of Anna dressed as an Italian, and he, as well as every one else who saw it, considered the portrait to be a great success....

Firstly, the basic conception of *faux art* and the *faux artiste* is "easy and imitative". In the character of Vronsky, Tolstoy exposes the nature of the *faux artiste* as drawing inspiration not *directly* from life but *indirectly* from life embodied in art. The *faux artiste* is merely seen to produce the sort of art he or she is trying to imitate. By way of CTA, *Art* is neither objective of an object of nature, nor is it objective of another art object; art must, through innovation and mimetic representation, include something of the absent other. Therefore all Art is unique, since once disclosed an absent other is no longer absent and cannot feature as such in another work. All "works" of *art* therefore have a subjective nature that legitimates a perceptive, mimetic, discovery of a reality's absent *other* and, as Geiger (1961:84) observes, '...there is nothing quite so good for an artist as the largely ineducible capacity to *perceive* something.'

As a creative process, innovation and mimetic perception cannot be denied; they are the drivers to the construction of plausible boundaries in the unbounded space of a sublime experience. Therefore, as Geiger continues:

> [the Artist's] creative state of mind implies… unceasing labor [sic] of a frequently agonizing sort. …[we see] Tolstoy's picture of the true artist, …as intuitive, carrying his own kind of emotional burden, frequently a heavy one. His interest [is] in accomplishing rather than in the thing accomplished, he is different in every major respect from the imitative… weakly creative pseudo-artist.

The *Artist* patterns and modifies his or her lived experience through an application of his or her own craft medium – so that such experiences might become incongruous with the *form* they will subsequently take as a candidate *Artwork* for an audience "approval". The nature of *art* is therefore seen in the *Artist's* application of a craft medium to organize the unorganized; it is analogous to the bounding of the unbounded.

Psychology and the creative process (after Cézanne)

The nature of *art* concerns, also, an application of the *Artist's* sensible faculties. Art arises from the *Artist's* sensible perception of their world. This introduces the notion of the *psychology* of the Artist. As Rothko (1940/41:24, 83) notes, this deals with both the mechanics of the Artist's sensual apparatus, and the notion of his or her subjectivity. The very relevance of this psychological theme is reflected in the following anonymous quote from the *Journal of Political Economy* (1916):[83]

> It is being recognized more and more that psychological study is a pre-requisite of an adequate understanding of those sciences that deal with a phase of human experience. The educator, the doctor, the political scientist, the historian, the lawyer, the artist… are all awaking to this fact.

This is not to suggest the requirement for an explicit study of key psychological elements in the context of this text, but to accept that – as a psychological phenomenon – the make-up of the individual artist is as complex (and varied) as the phenomenon of *art* itself. Here a fine illustration of the relevance of the psyche of the artist is cited in Merleau-Ponty's (1945:59) essay *Cézanne's Doubt*. In 1906, aged 67, and shortly before his death, Cézanne wrote:

> I was in such a state of mental agitation [in early life], in such great confusion that for a time I feared my weak reason would not survive. … Now it seems I am better and that I see more clearly the direction my studies are taking. Will I ever arrive at my goal, so intensely sought and so long pursued? I am still working from nature, and it seems to me I am making slow progress.

The link between art and psychology has been established around, not only the traditional themes of perception, cognition and personality, but also the theme of developmental psychology. Here, as Bornstein (1984:131) describes, *the Artist*, as an individual, is contemplated in the context of his or her "life-span" interaction with their own "lived-environment". As Cézanne intimated, a lifetime in the development of studies towards a long sought goal clearly led to "*…so much uncertainty, so much labor [sic], so many failures, and suddenly, the greatest success….*" As Merleau-Ponty continues in the essay, '*…the "hereditary traits," the "influences" – the accidents in Cézanne 's life – are the text which nature gave him to decipher.*'

Cézanne's *works*, as a consequence of the "free" decisions taken in the exercise of his craft skills, are characteristic of his psyche. As Merleau-Ponty notes, '*[i]f Cézanne 's life seems to… carry the seeds of his work within it, it is because we get to know his work first and see the circumstances of his life through it….*' But, for artists to truly exercise free decisions within the practice of their craft – within a psyche governed by a form of *continuity-of-existence* – they must do so within their life-span by going beyond their original situation yet not ceasing to be themselves. To paraphrase Merleau-Ponty:

> Two things are certain about artists: that they are never determined and yet that they never change, since, looking back on what they were, we can always find hints of what they have become.

It is the paradox of the Artist's simultaneous exercise of "free" choice in the process of *art*, while at the same time maintaining the credible bonds of their work with the *lived-world*, which we must come to understand. That, to Merleau-Ponty, Artists might never change is not to suggest that, from time to time, their mode of expression or style does not change. As Bornstein (1984:132) notes, such change may be subtle or magnificent, gradual or discreet, seldom or frequent. Therefore we see that Cézanne, as with many other recognized Artists, experienced different phases within his artistic endeavours. As Merleau-Ponty describes in *Cézanne's Doubt,* up until about 1870, Cézanne's first pictures were painted fantasies; incantations of imagined scenes. There then followed impressionism, quickly giving way to the pursuit of reality. Such changes of style are clearly evidential amongst artists in general; they relate to the development of the artist's craft; they may be picked up and used by others (for example Tolstoy's Vronsky). What does not change – at least in terms of identifiable classifications, schools, classes or categories – is the *continuity-of-existence* that is the *psyche* of the artist. I argue that it is this "unchanging" aspect of the artist's psyche – an innate ability to exercise free decisions in the exercise of aesthetic judgement – that contributes to the artistic process.

The psyche of the artist contributes to *art* on two levels: a regard for the "lived-experience" and a contribution to an innate capacity to exercise their craft without constraint. There are, within the psyche of the artist therefore, questions arising with regard to (*inter alia*) imagination and genius; in the past, both defining features of an artist. Within CTA imagination is embraced within the concept of innovation, as the exercise of the artist's ability conjure up new approaches to their craft. However I argue that the concept of genius is not relevant. I simply argue that genius is a relative term that might well be used in some comparative analytic of, for example, *this* Artist versus *that* Artist. However, in the context of CTA, what is relevant is the acquisition of the artist's craft as an essential component of the *art* process.

Education and technical achievement (after Rothko)

The psyche of the artist determines his or her *sensibility* to an experience of the sublime, and a propensity to employ their craft skills in a mimetic realization of their own particular perspective. Here, both Schopenhauer's and Geiger's artist is someone who just happens to look at the world in a certain way. If this is the case, can an artist learn about how to represent his or her unique perspective in order to create a work of art? Geiger (1961:84) argues that if nothing else, the artist may learn '...*in struggles with his [sic] medium*' – meaning that he or she may learn "efficient habits" of composition. Therefore, given any craft, there are the norms of that craft's commonly accepted skills and its medium to be learnt and/or developed. However, given the following premises: 1) the absence of an appreciation of the conjunctive nature of CTA's art; 2) the cloud of obscurity between products of art and pseudo-art (*faux art*); and 3) the wide range of differing opinions on art and its definition; there is little to point to a conclusive "how-to" for the production of an artwork. Consequentially, if there is no "how-to", how can we attempt to "learn"? In respect of such an observation, all *Artworks* (certainly in an historical sense) are *a posteriori* socially accepted conceptualizations and, as such, cannot (or at least their production cannot) be taught as an *a priori* concept. To be able to "teach" *how-to* produce *Artworks*, "art's" *a priori* process needs to be understood independently of its *a posteriori* objects.

Within CTA, the *a priori* and *a posteriori* distinctions are, I suggest, explicit. There is the craft skill requirement – about which, I argue, there can be no issue that such skills, properly identified, can be taught; with which no individual can actually be born with.[84] Here, there are those that might be taught and go on to practice a craft skill, but who do so other than in the artistic process, such as "media" and "advertising" executives, the "illustrator", the "portraitist" and so on. These roles all employ the craft skills of the artist but, as Rothko (1940/41:19) argues, such applications of "craft" are generally other than in the process of *art*.[85] The inference is that, with innovation and mimetic perception being the remaining drivers of the *art* process, what is required of the artist is the aesthetic sensibility inherent within his or her psyche. Thus any individual might, arguably, be born with a greater sensibility than another and, rather than any notion of teaching "sensibility", such sensibilities might be identified and encouraged through the living process. Again, this is congruent with CTA.

Although the psyche of the artist is a key separator in identifying artist from non-artist, the education and technical achievement of the artist is a necessary consideration within CTA. Here the education of the artist relates to his or her attainment of a craft skill, while the technical achievement however, may be related to the practice of that skill in producing *Artworks*. This distinction allows that varying Artists may possess and utilize craft skills in varying degrees. Although the YBA Tracy Emin received some formal training in painting, her installation *My Bed* does not display the high degree of artistic education evident in the work of other accepted artists, yet it was this work that brought her much of her recognition as an Artist.

Technical achievement is a function of the process of art. This process is, to Rothko (1940/41:47), the manipulation of *the plastic elements* of art; these elements impart a sensation of reality through the sensation of movement of things in space. Rothko is, however, unclear as to what "plastic elements" are in particular. The suggestion is that they are, in essence, the intangible stimuli created by the artist in inviting his or her spectator or audience into taking a journey of discovery within the realm of the artwork. This is analogous to my conception of *attractive beauty* as a necessary antecedent of the social visibility of an Artwork. The technical achievement of the artist, in the context CTA, can therefore be argued, at least in part, as the artist's ability to permeate their artwork with a quality of attractive beauty; thereby stimulating the observer to engage with the work, towards a journey of mimetic understanding. This consideration of the technical achievement of the artist presents the possibility that if, for example, we consider Rothko's conception of space as not only volumetric, but also extended it to include the temporal, there is – in the artistic sense – a multi-dimensional (holistic) space in which things (or an experiential knowledge of things) exist in a state of fluid realization. Here also, an artwork can take a multitude of different representations dependent, not only on the journey of the spectator, but also on the relevance of the temporal context (both relative and historical) in which (through the concept of attractive beauty) their engagement with the artwork is enacted. Such fluidity, as a context in which an *Artwork* can manifest itself, may indeed be plastic.

The malleable nature of experiential knowledge does not conflict with the conception that art's *epistemic* purpose is the facilitation of the mimetic discovery of some new aspect of the artist's worldview; that is to say facilitating the birth of a nascent knowledge concerning some new insight or thing (real or imaginary). The technical achievement of the artist, as opposed to the technical achievement of a pure craftsperson, is ultimately therefore, related to their ability to apply a craft in assisting the birth of this nascent knowledge within the mind(s) of the spectator(s) by first engaging them with the *artwork*. This view of the technical achievement (of the artist) is therefore separate from, and again transcends, the specific craft skills of the artist that may, in fact, be taught or gained through education.

Responsibility (after Ruskin and Merleau-Ponty)

The reliance of art on the concept of an artist's *sensibility* lies at the heart of the aesthetic dimension. Here, the complex relationship between the nature of *art*, the *Artist* and the *Artwork* as a mediation of the sublime experience (a problem also of communication and interpretation by an audience) is resolved to one of the exercise of aesthetic judgement. This provides a return to my argument for an (epistemological) Art aesthetic that provides for disclosure, through experience, as a route to understanding. This is aesthetic interpretation – from artistic vision through aesthetic response to an ontology. As the *Artist*, through his or her technical achievement, manipulates the intangible stimuli within their work (Art's *attractive beauty*), he or she invites the spectator/audience to take a mimetic journey of discovery into the Artwork's subjectivity. As Merleau-Ponty (1952:93) describes:

> [t]he painter can paint while he is looking at the world because it seems to him that that he finds in appearances themselves the style which will define him in the eyes of others, and because he thinks he is spelling out nature at the moment he is recreating it.

Communicating something of a sublime experience is the responsibility of the artist. Although Ruskin's commentary on "truth" (in *Modern Painters*) is principally directed at the landscape painter, its relevance to the concept of an artist's responsibility is easy to extrapolate. To paraphrase Ruskin (MP1:110):

> ...the artist must always have two great and distinct ends (or responsibilities); the first, to induce in the spectator's mind (including the artist him/herself), a faithful conception of their artistic vision (as a mediation of the sublime); the second, to guide the spectator's mind to those aspects of their vision most worthy of its contemplation, and to inform him/her of the thoughts and feelings with which these are regarded by the artist him/herself.

Towards the first end, the artist simply presents his or her work for consideration by the spectator without the benefit of translation. Here the spectator is alone with the work and is expected to make of it what he or she can; to engage with it or reject it as might be the case. The success of an audience's engagement with an Artwork relates back to the technical achievement of the artist. To the second end, Ruskin identifies the artist's responsibility to communicate the sublime discourse to the spectator in a manner that is, at least, guided by the artist. As Ruskin continues:

> ...the artist talks to [the spectator]; makes him a sharer in his own strong feelings... under the sense of having... been endowed for a

time with the keen perception and the impetuous emotion of a nobler and more penetrating intelligence.

In the artist's exercise of a freedom of choice in the process of art – in deciding the value judgements of: what to produce; what to name the productions; and what the relationship(s) between himself or herself, the named artwork and the spectator will be – the artist has a responsibility to maintain a credible bond between their work and their *lived-world*. However, this freedom is seemingly bound by the *a priori* conditions established as the currently accepted norms of their *Artworld* (or their aspirations to an *artworld*). The artist therefore exercises freedom in using, adapting, developing or even breaking the conventions of their craft (as by definition they must do through innovation). However, the paradox of Ruskin's challenge in maintaining the dual "ends" of artistic responsibility poses an artistic dilemma if a truth of perception is to be realized. As Stallknecht (1936:709–710) observed:

> [t]he successful [observer] may be said to reveal the conscience of an artist by answering questions which the artist's responsibility has rendered answerable... When no answer can be offered, when we can not after long acquaintance tell why... this or that line is drawn, we must admit that the artist was irresponsible.

As with Cézanne, Turner, Emin and others, many *Artists* are seen to address Ruskin's artistic dilemma with a tendency to their responsibility to communicate a truth of perception. This favours less the responsibility for a truthful application of the accepted norms of their craft, or any accepted school of, for example: classicism, pointillism, realism, surrealism and so on. It is not that that artist always works in ignorance of a potential audience (for the accolade of critical praise is, in general, well received by any individual) but in CTA's epistemological nature – when faced with Ruskin's imposed dilemma – the "true" artist might be said to favour a "truth of perception".

In seeking an audience critique, or the acceptance of an *Artworld*, the artist must operate in a full knowledge of the bonds with the lived experience that he or she may have broken. This is so that – to achieve the communication of meaning related to the lived-world, and to fulfil a complete responsibility to the communication of their perceived truth – at some future point in time, the justification for his or her action can be provided as part of an acceptance of their *candidate Artwork*. The reconstitution of the bonds between any *candidate Artwork* and a lived experience may, as I have argued, require arbitration or mediation within a given *Artworld* context. For Turner we have Ruskin, and for Cézanne, Merleau-Ponty. Paraphrasing Merleau-Ponty (1952:93):

> [Art]…always says something. It is a new system of equivalences which demands precisely [such a breaking of bonds], and it is in the name of a truer relation between things that their ordinary ties are broken.

It is not sufficient for the artist to be seen merely as a rule breaker, and perhaps as Rothko observed: *"childish, irresponsible, and ignorant"*. The artist must be fully cognizant of their responsibilities, and of the artistic process that they are engaged in. The importance of a craft knowledge as an element of this process is verified, if only so that the artist understands the current boundaries marking their own freedom.

The concept of the Artist's responsibilities also leads to the question of interpretation. Therefore, coming full circle, I reintroduce my protagonist, Heidegger, and his note on Van Gogh's painting *Old Shoes With Laces*. In transcendent form, Heidegger provides his audience with a "nascent" knowledge concerning a peasant derived from his interpretation of the painting's subjectivity. Epistemically, that this knowledge "arises", is an efficacious "end" – regardless of Van Gogh's initial intent. As a generalization, Heidegger's comment confirms one function of Art and, therefore, one of the Artist's responsibilities. As previously noted, Art serves the disclosure of a truth of being, placing ontology as a legitimate (though not exclusive) function of the aesthetic experience.

The epistemological nature of CTA provides that an *Artwork* should promote, encourage or otherwise give rise to nascent knowledge. In these terms, the interpretation and evaluation of a new, candidate work of art – as an exercise of subjective realization – creates a new, lived-situation in which the candidate Artwork is passed for ascension as a new (bounded) element within the holistic (unbounded) space that is the nature of Art. Having argued that not every individual may possess the same faculty of a sensibility to the sublime and, therefore, the ability to learn form the sublime experience, it becomes the *raison d'être* of, and the responsibility of, an individual with any claim to the title *Artist* to facilitate the engagement of a wider audience through a mode of cognitive understanding.

The form of an artist

My conception of the work of the Artist is a *socio* and *ahistorical* constructive phenomenon that transcends the notion that art might solely depend on accepted conventions of craft (for example, in writing: narrative, metaphor and so on, and in painting: line, form, colour and so on). I have argued that CTA's innovation suggests that the responsibility of the artist is to explore, bend or otherwise disregard traditional boundaries and conventions but, at the same time, maintaining a *continuity-of-existence* that is their sensibility to their lived-environment. By the same token, if CTA is to prove useful in the context of extrapolating a discourse of an *Art of Management* then it should, ultimately, also provide a framework within which empirical evidence may be examined and found to support a general case.[86] Here, my preceding discussion of the five key thematic relationships – namely: art's nature, the artist's psyche, the artist's technical achievement, the artist's responsibility, and art's interpretation – in terms of the four Aristotelian corner-stones of the concept of art – namely: subject, artist, object and spectator – provides CTA with such an empirical framework. I have reproduced this framework at Table 6.1. To briefly illustrate its application, I turn to a review of a series of archive interviews that cover general perspectives on the working lives of the following artists (with interview dates):[87]

Salvador Dali (7 January 1962)	Francis Bacon (23 March 1963)
Andy Warhol (7 March 1981)	Howard Hodgkin (2 January 1981)
Bridget Riley (25 January 1988)	Lucien Freud (7 February 1988)
Helen Chadwick (11 February 1982)	Paula Rego (21 October 1988)

Firstly, I consider the corner-stone of the artist's situation. Of the eight Artists featured there is no discernible, privileged ontology (or worldly view-point) from which an individual *Artist's* work is to be viewed. As with Salvador Dali (1906–1989) and Bridget Riley (b1931), individuals may be predisposed to a view of reality in which they might reflect on their relationship with the external world. As Dali – whose imagination is seen to be projected onto an external environment – commented: *'One of the more characteristic things of [my]... personality... is [its] complete... connection with... the geology; [the] landscape.'*. Riley, on the other hand, observes the features of nature as stimulus: *'...[the] sparkle in a cut glass bowl... colours in the sea... [and the] shadows that the clouds [throw] ...over water.'* Alternatively, views of the world might be bounded in some way, as with Andy Warhol (1928–1987) who appeared as an observer of a commercial world or, say, Francis Bacon (1909–1992) who is to be seen as an observer of a reality that comprised of social interactions. Warhol, however, appears to strive for a

Table 6.1　The Derivation of a Framework for CTA Analysis of Artists

Corner Posts of Art	Key Relationships		CTA	
(A) Situation	Nature of Art – the unbounded (holistic) space	The Sublime Environment	Subject	Artist's (Subjective) Reality
	Psyche of Artist – a sensibility to the situation; the Artist's existence in the world	Subject – Perception (A particular view of Reality)	Sublime Experience	
(B) Artist	Education	/Medium /Skill/ Technique /Devices etc.	Craft	Artistic Process – Constructive Disclosure
	Creative Process – Psyche of Artist (Free Decision)	Aesthetic Perception & Judgement		
(C) Work	Interpretation & Evaluation (Instantiation)		Innovation	
	Technical. Achievement – Attractive Beauty		Mimesis	
	Communication & Responsibility			
(D) Observer	Interpretation & Evaluation	Social Mimesis	Object	Social (Objective) Construction
(A) Situation			Subject	

view devoid of emotion in order to reach an uncomplicated, simple perspective – as he commented: ' *...[I] have [feelings] I wish I didn't... [it] would be a good idea [to get rid of them altogether]...'*. Bacon, conversely, sought to reawake culturally suppressed emotions such as the emotion of terror – displaying a sensibility to that which is desensitized in many: pain and terror with (perhaps) a focus on the uniqueness of a situation.

Each Artist is seen to have his or her own unique perspective within which they act out their lived-existence. They may be (*inter alia*) imaginative, minimalistic, fluid, emotional, accidental, or simply overly subjective or, indeed, any combination of these and/or other traits. Their views, conceivably, may vary over time. It is a sensibility to the possibilities of (or existence of) an aesthetic response to certain phenomena – resulting from their individual, psychological make-up – that determines, at any point, what the artist senses, sees or believes about the world they live in. Their thoughts and ideas are not constrained or suppressed by norms of culture or expectation.

The framework of Table 6.1 separates the artist's ontological reality from the artistic process of constructive disclosure; a separation of the process of art from the vision that precedes it. It is therefore possible to also note the variety and range of potential indicators to be interpreted within the process itself. Accepted classifications of various artforms feature, and can clearly coexist within the definition of CTA. This generic approach provides a latitude to accept and develop new, as yet to be discovered, techniques and schools of art; it allows the invention of different spaces within which the artforms produced have a credible relationship with the overall artistic space they are presented in. As Bridget Riley noted:

> The great painters move in a little, and deny [;] they close the plains and open them up in a loosely fluctuating space, which promises more but never actually, ruthlessly, paints it out. So it, so to speak, drops hints [;] it's an invented space. But it is a credible space, because that [is] it can only be successful if it is credible [;] it's credible through the relationship of the forms to the place therein [;] even if they're fictional.

It becomes apparent, from the small sample of Artists featured, that there is little discussion attributable to mimetic learning as a concern of the individual artist's endeavors. Although the interviews were only reviewed phenomenologically, and were not directed to this specific factor, the absence, even implicitly, of any mimetic reference provokes a critique of CTA. However, the framework itself presents two levels of *mimesis*, one within the artistic process (at the individual level of the artist) the other as a form of *social mimesis* in terms of an objective construction. The separation of the individual from the social within the *mimesis* of CTA occurs by virtue of CTA's primary and secondary levels of conjunction, in which the nature of art's mimetic value is resolved through a temporal connectivity between the "work" of the artist's endeavor, and its subsequent social acceptance as "artwork".

While the (theoretical) mimetic case within CTA does not preclude the form taken in the analytic framework, empirically it does suggest that further explication is necessary in relation to the artist's practice of *mimesis*. At the level of the individual artist then, *mimesis* (as a learning experience) might legitimately be interpreted as a discovery of the necessary elements to be communicated as the artist's interpretation of their perception. The concept of attractive beauty is clearly invoked as the artist must discover what, within his or her vision will help an audience in the process of their engagement with a work. Here, Howard Hodgkin (b1932) relates that his intention is to achieve, within the observer, a direct communication of the "same kind of emotion" as he himself perceived in first conceptualizing a work. Hodgkin attempts to achieve this through making a picture that '*...would look desirable enough... that [the observer]... would begin [their mimetic engagement with it].*' In a similar process, exploring the means of facilitating communication, Paula Rego (b1935) practices a distancing of reality by substituting an alternative (more attractive) reality – for example, through the injection of subversive humour and story-telling by way of fictionalized characters – in which menace and danger are made approachable, and thus more knowable, by removing emotional threat and fear. Therefore, implicitly, the Artist appears concerned with the facilitation of *mimesis* – accepting that, as observer, the artist himself or herself may undergo an actual mimetic experience in his or her own right – either as part of a Hodgkinesque socialization or in an apparent denial of such, in the manner of Lucien Freud (b1922).

Mapping the artistic space

Empirically, the lack of an Artist's dialogue directly relevant to the theoretical process of socialization is not a major concern here. In making certain assumptions concerning Artists whose work has already been accepted there is, I argue, sufficient logic within the framework of

CTA to suggest that the basic conception of the theory holds valid across a sufficiently large number of cases. This, I argue, allows the CTA framework to be used as a basis for further exploratory work. Here, the temporal gap related to the process of the socialization of a *candidate* Artwork it is not to be seen as a necessary feature of the process of art *per se*; it arises as a consequence of the communication from artistic vision, through artistic process, to a new (objective) reality.

Within CTA, *art* exists in a fluid state bounded by the four dimensions of craft, innovation, mimetic facilitation and mimetic learning. The process of socialization of an artwork becomes the temporal connectivity between mimetic facilitation and a social mimetic learning. In this way CTA provides a capacity to describe, at least pictorially, relative spatial positions for all *Artists* and their *Artworks*, within a single conceptual definition. Such a conception of the artistic process therefore has the capacity to include even those artists who might otherwise be sidelined, or even rejected in accord with other traditional or contemporary *Artworld* specific theories. Through a process of the evaluation of an artist and their works against the framework of CTA, it is possible to attempt a visualization of artistic space. Arbitrary values may be assigned to the "key relationship" elements (Table 6.1) of the *Artistic Process* of *Constructive Disclosure* (*mimesis*, innovation and craft). This process is illustrated in Figure 6.1 through the assignment of subjective values from 1 to 5 on the following basis:

1. *Craft*: 1 (low) to 5 (high), dependent on the extent to which either a taught (or acquired) skill was evident within the work of the artist, or of the complexity (or technicality) of the creative process involved.
2. *Innovation*: 1 (low) to 5 (high), dependent on the extent to which an innovative, imaginative or novel approach to the application of craft skill was evident; for example Dali's integration of a surreal imagination within traditions of classicism was rated as highly innovative (5).
3. *Mimesis*: 1 (low) to 5 (high), dependent on the extent to which the artists work appears to address the unknown and facilitate a contribution to an understanding of their particular world view. Here, 1 would represent a realistic or naturalistic approach, with little attempt by the artist to obviate Ruskin's artistic responsibility of maintaining a credible bond between a work and the *lived-world*. The "hallucinatory decay" of Dali's images is seen at the opposite end of the spectrum, as surreal, with the risk of breaking the bonds with an observer's lived-world.

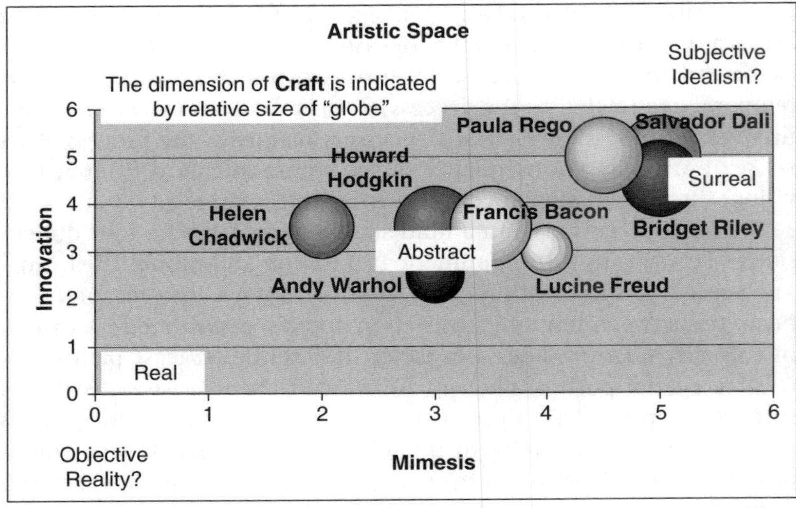

Figure 6.1   Mapping the Artistic Space

The arbitrary values used are, I acknowledge, wholly subjective and both temporally and contextually sensitive. The assignment of a value to the dimensions of Table 6.1 merely affords me the capability of generating a conceptual map of the fluid space in which the artist typically functions. In acknowledging this limitation, I merely offer Figure 6.1 an example of the *concept* of a spatial Map of Art. Following Riley, I am simply advancing a single conceptual space in which *Artists* and their artistic approaches, hitherto subject to a multitude of alternative definitions, can retain a credible relationship with each other. In this respect CTA, its *Art-aesthetic* – an engagement with (and mediation of) a sublime object – and a disinterested contemplation through the attractive beauty of art, provides a useful framework for conceptualizing the process of art. The relative positions of *Artists* will vary, both in cognizance of the problem of artistic change – as the artist's style responds to changes in technique, craft and other influences – and in the temporal dimension. The fluid nature of the space may be represented by a series of maps covering a range of differing temporal or *Artworld* perspectives. The value of this mapping lies, therefore, not in a single view, but in coming to understand how *Art*, *Artists* and their *Artworks*, move in relation to the total artistic space.

Ultimately, the "end" of art may be said to justify the "means". However, where the "end" of art initially fails to be seen as art by an observer within this artistic space, there exists the opportunity for a subsequent (re)interpretation and (re)evaluation of the art object. This may permit (or benefit from) the establishment of new, accepted norms of craft skill, or alternatively new, accepted norms of what might (or might not) amount to innovation. This brings out the fourth (temporal) dimension to that of innovation, *mimesis*, and craft. Mimesis will not fully occur until there is a closing of the temporal gap between mimetic facilitation (by the artist) and mimetic experience (both individual and social) – this calls for the transference of meaning within the broad aspect of artistic communication.

7
A Negotiated Existence

> The desert will give you an understanding of the world; in fact, anything on the face of the earth will do that. You don't even have to understand the desert: all you have to do is contemplate a simple grain of sand, and you will see in it all the marvels of creation.
>
> The Alchemist, Paulo Coelho

The dichotomy of language

Although CTA's temporal disconnect – between the mimetic facilitation of the artist and the mimetic learning of art's audience – is theoretically dealt with by CTA's process of the socialization of a candidate artwork as *Artwork* proper, this process is theoretically problematic in its indeterminacy. To overcome this problematic it is necessary to introduce a further, meta-theoretical, justification which is at least cognizant of the temporal nature of the transference of meaning. I am, in essence, looking to add back the historical to an *ahistoric* conceptualization of art. Temporality however – and, indeed, the malleability of meaning as it is transferred between social actors – complicates the suggestion that an *Art of management* might be a useful concept for future empiric study. Here also, traditional empiricism assumes a specific ontological position; this is further complicated by the argument that the nature of CTA, rooted as it is in an *Art aesthetic* of the sublime and beauty, is an idea that is antecedent to a given ontology.

Within a social theorizing, the *communication of acquired meaning* is reliant on the concept of language. Reextending the present art-world discussion to the realm of management and organizational practice we can, for example, relate to the research process of academe as culminating in the production, in the language of academe, of an externalized SK. Such knowledge is (generally) in published form; it is implicitly monologic. As Cunliffe (2002:128–129) argues, the process of theorizing is a cognitive act in which, through the use of abstract theoretical frameworks or models, the meaning and significance of actions are to be understood separately from the actions themselves. Language becomes the means by which we model, theorize or otherwise describe the realities of others, from within the status of expert. However the manager, as an *embodied self* in the social context of his or her role in an organization, is engaged with other individuals and is, therefore, participating in a practice that is rooted in everyday discourse; this is a dialogic[88] practice. As Cunliffe continues, this dialogic notion draws on postmodern and social-constructionist perspectives, in which language itself is used to constitute, rather than describe, reality.

In the *postmodern*, much is being done by researchers who eschew the modern in favour of dismantling the "grand narrative" of functionalism. In the *postmodern* few explicit claims are now made for the "truth". In this *postmodern* era Carter (2000:58) surmises, that:

> ...science is not so much about the truth (or its approximation) determined by some existential reality, but is more an issue of social consensus... [within] a set of normative philosophical commitments. [By implication] there may be more than one set of normative commitments and more than one community of scholars that calls its collection of commitments and practices, science.

However, even now, where the sciences of the "social" allow for theories of *representation-in-experience* – that is to say a body of theory that conceives of a primacy of empirically founded SK embodied in the (human) mental acts of perceiving, remembering, talking, writing, imagining, playing, thinking, exploring and other forms of acting – we can see what Cussins (1992:651) argues is a failure of such theories "in their own terms". From the academic world view, the *end* of research – be it: modern or postmodern; quantitative or qualitative; objective or subjective, and so on – remains the exteriorized *publication* of a base of SK, within a community of scholars with a predefined set of commitments characterized by its own (defined) language. We might safely "sign" such publication as Mode 1 knowledge production.

In the postmodern, the publication of SK simply tends to the phenomenon of a fragmented, but nonetheless monologic form of knowledge that serves the unrelenting dismantling of any form of dialogic narrative. I argue, here, that all knowledge of an academic nature – whether it is based on the philosophical primacy of *thought-over-experience* or its converse of *experience-over-thought* – is monologic; SK is thus inherently problematic in terms of its application in practice. As Cunliffe argues, any presumption of a primacy of a monologic language acts to deny the possibility of *learning-through-experience* and the construction of social experiences. As I have argued in my introduction, this is the trap of the Enlightenment paradigm of rationalistic thought that – even *post*-Enlightenment – continues to constrain postmodern moral, legal and aesthetic discourse in an autonomy of monologic form. However, Cunliffe goes on to advance a dialogic approach to communicating, in which the premisses are that: 1) language is metaphorical, 2) language and meaning are an embodied practice, and 3) language is indeterminate. Dialogic language presumes nothing and denies nothing. Here, as antecedent to dialogic communication, perception enters the realm of communication as simply prescient to the notion of a truth of any given situation in which the individual is embodied; perceptions form a representation of an individual's *ontology-of-the-moment*. As Cussins (1992:653) advances:

> [i]f we can understand how to start our theorizing without truth and the other denizens of the realm of reference, *but nevertheless with a genuine notion of significant representation*, then we will be able to survive [outside the circle of intentionality] for long enough to tell whether truth can be recovered.

I reason, therefore, that the concepts of "artistic" or even "managerial" perception" are all-inclusive of the individual artist's or manager's social-cognitive skills, including (*inter alia*) their ability to make sense of information from a wide variety of sources.

In *practice*, the individual gathers, processes, disseminates, judges and acts on information received. He or she performs mental acts of perceiving, remembering, talking, writing, imagining, playing, thinking, exploring and other forms of acting. In this respect, the idea of art or management as being both embodied practice and sense-making is more than just the reception of sense data. It also exceeds a mere pluralism of perspectives. Therefore, within this non-autonomous, dialogic idea of *practice*, the realm of the aesthetic (aesthetic senses and aesthetic judgement) is legitimized. Returning to the *Art aesthetic* of the sublime and attractive beauty, we can see that such an *aesthetic* has as an important part to play in understanding management and organizations as do the concepts of precognition, recipes, formulae, legends, folk tales, intuition and monologic knowledge. The aesthetic precedes ontology; an *Art aesthetic* therefore provides a legitimate device with which to describe a dialogic notion of an individual's own ontological perspective. Therefore, through a dialogic notion of thinking about the process of art, the temporal disconnect within CTA, a function of the transference of meaning between the mimetic facilitation engaged in by the artist and the mimetic learning of art's audience becomes a dialogic realization of a shared ontological reality between artist and audience.

Ontology: from a grain of sand

A monologic priority presupposes the importance of the production and accumulation of autonomous SK. Within the UK's academic environment, the existence of Research Assessment Exercises (RAEs) – the idea that the quality of academic research might be assessed on the basis of its published output – certainly appeals to Chia's (2003) "epistemological priority". At the same time, such a priority disenfranchises the attainment of a "direct unmediated knowing". This is in contrast to what Chia observes is the *oral-aural* cognition typified by the cultures of East Asia – where knowledge is often acquired through practice. This contrast makes explicit the potential conflict between a manager engaged in a direct relationship with an ontology – the manager's *organizational world* – and the manager engaged in a practice mediated through an epistemological reflection on an alternate (academic) ontology. It is a reflection of the cultural paradox of management's theory-practice divide.

Chia's observation of both direct and mediated ontological relationships points to there being two conceptual modes of abstraction of importance to this text; abstractions may be of either an ontological or an epistemological nature. Furthermore, I argue that each mode of abstraction is characterized by its own form of language. Ontological abstraction is characterized by a dialogic language of negotiated practice, while epistemological abstraction is characterized by a monologic language of representation. For example, while an ontological abstraction could conceivably describe an intrinsically impossible object, an epistemological abstraction could not. Epistemically, it is difficult to rationalize the existence of an object until at least an "abstract idea" of it had, itself, been through a process of socialization, that is accepted as a legitimate (*a priori*) object in its own right – a fiction,[89] no longer a mere representation of an idea. Such a process of socialization is the central tenet of what I have previously introduced is the philosophy SNA; SNA is an essential theoretical aspect in considering the socialization from candidate *work* of art to *Artwork*.

Within the varied ways of thinking about the world, ontological perspectives assume a primacy of function; they frame a knowledge of the world. As Fleetwood (2005) observes:

> [t]he way we think the world is (ontology), influences: what we think can be known about it (epistemology); how we think it can be investigated (methodology and research techniques); the kinds of theories we think can be constructed about it; and the political and policy stances we are prepared to take.

Such perspectives, as Dixon and Dogan (2003:460) note, encompass both structure (in its many guises, *inter alia*: anthropological, functional, linguistic and post-structuralism; historical materialism; hermeneutic phenomenology; symbolic interactionalism; language games; and post-modernism) and agency (embracing, *inter alia*: rational choice; social phenomenology; dramaturgical analysis and ethnomethodology). Therefore, while many legitimate fields of inquiry are clearly evident, there appears little consensus concerning what might, or might not, present a unified set of philosophical traditions. As Mason (2002:14) argues, the need for the social researcher to understand and set his or her "own" ontological view of the world becomes a necessity – rather than assume the acceptance of an *obvious and universal truth*. The potential for hiding philosophical problems, such as the practical application of autonomously developed thought, becomes prone to an ever-increasing variety of realities. Here other views of science (for example phenomenology and post-modernism in its various forms) have been offered at various times in dualistic opposition to a tradition of positivism. In such cases the ontology is not realism, rather there is a process of *social construction* that permits a *range* of ontological perspectives; each perspective realizing a view of the world that is constructed on the basis of concepts that we, ourselves, hold. For example, as Searle (1995) observes:

> [h]ow… can there be states of consciousness or meaningful speech acts as parts of the physical [realist] world? …How does a mental reality, a world of consciousness, intentionality, and other mental phenomena, fit into a world consisting entirely of physical particles in fields of force?

However, Searle's observation can be reversed against such unitary *anti-realism*. Popper (1963:102) himself remarked that some regard science (and thus, by extension, realism) as '*...very useful... [but] It cannot... reveal to us new worlds behind our everyday world of appearance; for the physical world is just surface: it has no depth.*' Therefore how can a piano be considered – in a "socially constructed" sense – "real", as Popper continues, '*...while its alleged molecules and atoms are mere "logical constructions" (or whatever else may be indicative of their unreality)...*'. How is a desert in any sense real if a mere grain of sand is a social construction?

Hands (1998:712–713) notes several features common to social constructionist studies – and I note that Hands appears to use the terms construction and constructive interchangeably – they: 1) appear to be primarily studies about practice, rather than method; 2) are very local and very specific; 3) do not start from tight priors – implying a negotiated theoretical framework; 4) view very little as fixed – everything appears up for grabs (or, again, negotiation); and 5) they infer that nature plays little or no role in socially constructed science. My own reading of Hands' summary is that *social construction* may be viewed as the construction of localized ontologies through a practice in which local "knowledge" is negotiated between practitioners of social construction. I do however make a distinction between construction and constructive, in order to suggest *constructive* as a more conceptual activity. However, as a *localized* activity, social construction does not offer an easy route to understand a non-local ontology – as suggested by an inquiry into generic issues; that is, in the context of this text, using social constructionism to develop an understanding of the *character* of the manager.

A philosophy of socially negotiated alternativism

Our ontological position determines our epistemology; that is, what we think can be known about our world. Can we safely reject positivism and its empirical realism? This is often a starting point within post-modernist and/or post-structuralist studies – where socially constructed ontologies underpin and inform much contemporary social theorizing. But, as I have argued, even where social science has moved to socially constructed theories of *representation-in-experience*, the empiricism of an observed (localized) social has led others to a critique (and in some cases rejection) of social constructionism. Here, Bhaskar's (1975) critical realist project has found contemporary favour in a rejection of both positivist and social-constructionist ontologies; where *critical realism* seeks to present both a fallible interpretation of reality, and to suggest that such fallibility can provide a reference for "scientific" research. As Cruickshank (2004) notes, this Bhaskanian project seeks a unity of both natural and social science epistemologies. However, while this project has much to offer the study of the social, negatively – for example see Fleetwood (2004:27) – critical realism condemns both positivism and social-construction as "mistaken".

I argue that critical realism is no more than another socially constructed ontology. It provides a worldview adopted by a certain population of researchers as a position which should be established and understood as "their" basis for empirical study. Critical realists adopt a natural science or "real" ontology as a fallible contribution to an ongoing critical dialogue about the social world. They argue a *transitory*[90] notion of a reality as a basis for a *non-transitory* epistemology. This, as Cruickshank (2004:568) observes, is an epistemic fallacy. However, I argue that the hegemony evident in critical realism does not invalidate its project. A critical realist ontology provides a "useful" *view-of-the-world* which would, perhaps, be better served by ceasing any hegemonic claim to a perceived – even if fallible – "correctness". My own view is that critical realism should embody the critical realist in a dialogic relationship with others about the "possible" nature of the world – a distinctly pluralistic notion. In this sense, as Cruickshank (2004:582) argues:

> [ontological] presuppositions may be recognized as being situated within the transitory domain, [where] social scientists... draw upon the most useful ontological definitions that currently prevail.... We may accept that is fallacious to define reality in terms of a foundationalist epistemology, but still locate ontology within an anti-foundationalist epistemology.... In contrast to [foundationalism]... [we] may instead hold that our beliefs are engaged with the world and that we need to revise and replace our theories in the course of [that] engagement.... Theories would, on this reading, be intrinsic to practice, [they] would mediate our interaction with our environment.

I argue that all ontologies have a value in contributing to a dialogic critique. They all present a contribution to a negotiated understanding of what a social reality *might* be – a reality where there is, in fact, no perceived primacy of any ontological position. This creative pluralism presents the possibility of a variety of ontologies competing to influence an individual's *worldview*. Here Kelly's (1955) philosophy of Constructive Alternativism (CA) provides some insight.[91] Anderson (2001:3) describes CA as introducing the notion that each person perceives the world differently, but that that person is also able to alter their ontological interpretation of it by revision; that is, by development or replacement through adopting another alternate construction or part of one. A fundamental tenet of CA is, however, the idea of the *"individual-as-scientist"*. It is at this point that I make a departure from the strict application of Kelly's philosophy. At the ontological level, there is much to commend Kelly's pluralism. Constructive Alternativism is an excellent device for the explanation of certain observations of personally and socially constructed behaviour and, therefore, for providing insights into an individual's ontology. However, the suggestion that an individual always behaves as a scientist – seeking to predict and control his or her environment – does not provide a satisfactory device for explaining the future behaviour of a social group (such as an organization) or of an individual (such as a manager) within that group.[92]

As Anderson notes, Kelly's *CA individual* is given to play a large part in determining his or her own behaviour. However, as I have already discussed in reference to *the manager*, in a social context the individual does largely what is expected of them as they enact their role within the "norms" of some defined socio-cultural framework. To continue to draw from MacIntyre (1981), in the abstract, I merely advance the notion that certain *characters* – the manager, the headmaster, the therapist, and now (for example) the *scientist* and the *artist* – will be possessed of a certain predisposition as to the malleability of their worldview.[93] While CA permits a description of *how* the individual might internalize their own reality through pluralism, I argue that CA itself remains a monologic notion, in that it concentrates on the individual's view. Indeed the research methodology (personal construct theory) and method (repatory gird analysis) traditionally associated with CA leads to yet another monologic language of representation.

I argue that in order to fully embrace a dialogic ontology, an extension of CA is required to embrace the idea that our worldview is a result of a constant process of negotiation as we live our lives in social discourse. In the context of developing a meta-theory of CTA's application to management and organization, a socially negotiated ontology would underpin the shared experience gained as a manager goes about his or her role, directing and influencing the actions of others. As Carter (2000:66) notes, the addition of *social influence* provides a natural extension of Kelly's work; it is a prominent conception in the field of social psychology. For example, as Moscovici (1988:214) observes, a *Theory of Social Representations*:

> ...makes it possible for us to classify persons and objects, to compare and explain behaviours and to objectify them as parts of our social setting. ...Representations that shape our relations with society are in turn a component of social organization.

While not an ontology *per se*, Social Representation allows the theorizing of representations of worldly phenomena, rather than the phenomena themselves. Moscovici describes representations as often located in the minds of individuals, but that they may just as often be found "in-the-world" and, as such, examined separately. Here I advance the idea that a theory and language of Social Representation is a corollary of the language of ontological abstraction itself. It allows that an ontology of infinitely variable nature might exist. In a sense, this does not require the precursive adoption of any specific ontological position – one simply needs to accept some existing "set" of representations (or abstractions) merely as a basis for commencing the exploration of a particular social setting.

Moscovici (1988:215) describes the theory of Social Representation as being developed from within the field of social psychology to investigate a specific problem. That problem was how the many forms of knowledge and beliefs – with which we deal every day – can be understood by reimmersing them in the actual social laboratory where they take shape, namely the social setting of communication. I therefore argue that a theory of social representation is a useful device through which we can conceptualize how the infinitely malleable ontology of the "one world", which we as human individuals occupy, is negotiated. This negotiation is a continuous, dialogic process in which we may alter our own interpretation of the world by some reference to another's alternative interpretation – revising and replacing elements of our interpretation as required. Here I explicitly define CA, as extended by a theory of social representation, as the theory of Socially Negotiated Alternativism (SNA).

A non-foundational epistemology

Socially Negotiated Alternativism presents a philosophy; it is not founded on an single ontological position – rather it implies an infinitely malleable ontology. It presents a view of the social world that is open to various legitimate interpretations. The world is one world that may be viewed from different perspectives. It is constantly subject to change; that is, the nature of the social world is transitory, as elements of it and other associated phenomena are added, negotiated, revised and subtracted or replaced as required. Therefore SNA legitimizes not only theories of *representations in thought* and *representations in experience*, but it also legitimizes theories of *representations in ideas and fictions*. As a basis for an ontology, SNA is not, itself, fallible – as is the case in critical realism – however individual (or groups of) elements and phenomena within it may be. The implication is that a philosophy of SNA permits the concurrent existence of multiple *ontological subsets* (for example positivism, social construction, critical realism *and so on*); each subset may provide for a "limited", context sensitive, ontology.

Unlike critical realism, there is no suggestion of hegemony within SNA, since any such suggestion is precluded by virtue of the process of negotiation itself. However, if I am to argue that my thinking about the world is a continuous dialogic process of negotiation with various alternative ontological perspectives – some local, some non-local, some mine and some of an *other's* – in which I can freely initiate ideas and fictions as a basis for negotiation, what do I think can be known about the world? What, in essence, is to be my epistemological position? Here, I am stepping beyond the dualistic separation of polarized beliefs. While I might reject critical realism – with its implication that I accept something as true (a conjecture) until it is proved otherwise (a refutation) – I can accept both aspects of traditional realism and the existence of socially constructed concepts. All concepts may be considered as legitimate candidates to a (negotiated) knowledge of the world.

Importantly, SNA allows me to include many candidate explanations of a reality, including my own *ideas* of how the world might be. To paraphrase Searle (1995:149) *I presuppose the existence of both facts dependent on me and those that exist independently of me.* Facts independent of me may be *natural* facts or, indeed, facts that are dependent on another individual. On the basis of this presupposition, I therefore precipitate – through a dialogic relationship between me and an *other* – a pluralistic *ontology-of-the-moment*. Here, the pendulum of thinking and theorizing about the world around us is allowed, in a transitory fashion, to swing freely between the more traditionally accepted poles of thought – seeking to avoid any notion of an idealized order of things. This favours neither a preferred construct nor deliberately seeks an absent other to the exclusion of a reality present.

Clearly, as suggested by Cruickshank, I cannot seek to adopt the pluralistic and transitory ontology of SNA as a precursor to an epistemology that embraces the traditional objective-subjective relationship. Such a foundational epistemology would be based, as Dixon and Dogan (2003: 459) argue, in either naturalism (*inter alia*: empiricism, logical positivism, verificationism and falsificationism) or hermeneutics (*inter alia*, epistemological hermeneutics, existentialism and transcendental phenomenology). A foundational epistemology provides its own set of terms within which SK is, I have argued, presented in monologic form. Rather, I allow a dialogic form of knowledge to "emerge". This is an anti-foundationalist premiss in which what I think can be known about a transitory ontology can legitimated, in transitory form, as NK; that is to say the emergence of a plausible narrative *knowledge-of-the-moment*.

Theorizing on an anti-foundationalist epistemology is, by its dialogic and transitory nature, intrinsic to practice. It provides theories that mediate action with environment – be that environment the social world or a part of it, such as an organization or its management. In one sense, such theories are inferably "reuseable"; their output – as *knowledge-of-the-moment* – possesses only an instantaneous use-value as a precursor to some action (or event) within the social context that precipitated its emergence and use. In this sense, it is the theory itself that is of relevance to *generic practice,* rather than the NK it produces. In essence, a theory of interpretation provides the "means" by which a monologic "end" – an epistemological abstraction – might be translated into a component of a negotiated ontology as a new ontological abstraction; for example that learning achievable within Heidegger's commentary on Van Gogh's "*Old Shoes With Laces*".

Both the pluralistic, fluid ontology, and the non-foundational, interpretative epistemology of SNA, are based on dialogic principles. Their transitory nature presupposes non-specific concepts such as abstractions.[94] Abstraction, and specifically the language of ontological abstraction, is a central tenet of this text. If, in a traditional foundationalist epistemology, the assumption is made that the majority of abstraction occurs in an epistemological sense – as abstractions of a given ontological position – abstractions, as "ends", can only ever be fictions; that is abstractions become "truths" in their own right. Here Baudrillard's (1981:1) discussion in the opening to his treatise on postmodernism: *Simulacra and Simulation* is insightful:

[t]oday abstraction is no longer that of the map, the double, the mirror, or the concept. ...It is the generation by models of a real without origin or reality: a hyperreal. The territory no longer pre-

cedes the map, nor does it survive it. It is nevertheless the map that precedes the territory.

If all rational (empiric) social science is by its very nature a form of epistemological abstraction, then the postmodern may be seen as the ultimate conclusion of the social's epistemological abstraction – an accumulation of fragmentation. In applying Baudrillard's metaphor to the social studies environment, we might then argue that academe's *social construction* of a map of epistemic "fictions", leads to "a truth" that is unrepresentative of the "real". In striving to follow the map we create a new territory that supersedes the real and we live Baudrillard's hyperreal. Such an argument precedes Giddens' (1984) *double hermeneutic*.

If I now reframe empiric fictions within an interpretative epistemology, the resultant "truths" become reclassified as transitory; that is, empiric fictions are open to revision and replacement and their "free" (re)use as further abstractions in a pluralistic, dialogic ontology. With such interpretative theorizing, I may begin to consider survival outside Cussins' *circle of intentionality* long enough to judge whether a plausible, if transitory, truth can be recovered – at least in so far as we might be able to provide a new map of relevance to the practicing manager. However, the new map is one of accepted ontological abstractions in which, I suggest, the importance is in the method – that is "the means" – of map reading. Extending Baudrillard's metaphor yet further, the *character* of the manager or artist as *"an explorer"* must first understand the theorizing behind a map's construction. It is not the territory that is fallible; it is the map. The *explorer* accepts any existing map's inherent fallibility as a basis for their own journey.

Within CTA, the abstracted concept of *mimesis* provides an aesthetic process of discovery about an ontology. It allows that new objects – things, concepts, ideas, and so on – may be discovered, introduced or otherwise included within an existing ontological inventory of things. This is consistent with a philosophy of SNA. I argue, therefore, that CTA's process of art presupposes a transitory ontology. Art thus provides *one* method for coming to terms with *an* ontology. Art, with its aesthetic root precedes a specific ontological state, but it is always a result of a preceding ontological state.

Romancing the stone: creative pluralism

The autonomous thought processes that I have argued are a corollary of the enlightenment project are generally observed in dualistic opposition. In such opposition, distinctions are transformed from heuristic devices into reified ontological realities. Examples include: Action and Structure (within Organizational Studies); the Individual and Society (within Social Studies); Individualism v Holism (within methodology); and the distinction between ideal and material reality (within philosophy). But dualistic theorizing through an episteme of representation commits what Knights (1997:3–4) refers to as *fallacy of misplaced concreteness*. Here theorizing results in the belief that the distinctions made as part of the ordering of "reality", or of organizing the world, are accurate or true representations of a reality beyond – and independent of – the theorist. But, as Hart (1998:51) observes:

> [w]e might begin by noting that all [theorizing] originates from some view of reality, which means that there are different ways of gaining an understanding of some aspects of the world and different ways of confirming our understanding (i.e. knowledge).

Let me consider the "paperweight". I might reasonably surmise that early versions of this "object" were little more than stones of an appropriate size and shape. The paperweight does not exist independently of me; yet a stone of appropriate proportions (perhaps the first ever paperweight), can well be understood to have a natural *(real)* independent existence. The "stone" therefore exists only as a paperweight due it sharing certain of the attributes of the "concept" of a paperweight that have been determined within a society that accepts, and has use for, the *socially constructed* object: a paperweight. That what I shall refer to as *the original paperweight* arguably can exist, as both "real" object and "social construct", negates any suggested use of dualism's traditional alternative – a unitary perspective. I am therefore left with the alternatives of the *pluralist* attempt to *reconcile* the contest and antagonism between polarized dualisms, or the *deconstructionist* perspective that focuses upon that which is "other", "marginalized" or "disavowed" in any construction or representation of reality.

Although Knights accepts a *certain* attractiveness in reconciliatory pluralism, the integration of the best analyses of any pole under consideration is ultimately seen to fall victim to a tendency to reproduce the dualisms it seeks to reconcile. This failure is seen in respect of a lack of critique of the *enlightenment epistemology* upon which Knight's suggests reconciliatory pluralism is based. As an example, Knights cites Barglow's (1994:202) questioning of the *Global Village*, on the grounds that it may represent nothing more than '...*the construction of a network of tunnel visions: a world totally compartmentalized along lines of social class and professional specialization.'* In comparison with the deconstructionist project however, SNA offers the further alternative of an argumentation that retains a level of abstraction embracing, rather than focusing on, the *absent other*.

Returning to the paperweight metaphor, I am therefore presented with an ontology that suggests my *one world* consists of both entities that have a physical existence independent of me (for example, stones – I shall refer to these as Independent Entities, IE) and entities that are dependent on concepts held by me (for example, paperweights – I shall call these Dependent Entities, DE). As outlined in my introduction, the aesthetic interpretation that is central to this book's core thesis is generally unmediated by knowledge. Aesthetic interpretation is enhanced by an imagination that offers a capacity to experience mental images and a capacity to engage in creative thought. In making my own interpretation of the sense of the one world in which I live (that is, my own ontological reality), a pluralistic view permits me to experiment and play creatively with the set of IE and DE classes. Such "play" is now seen as conducted within a framework of SNA.

Further extrapolation of SNA into CTA now provides a correspondence to an *Ontology of Artworks*. In a general sense, an ontology – as an inventory of a reality – provides an inventory of entities that circumscribe and describe *a* world; *our* reality. An ontology of artworks (in essence a subset of the general ontological inventory) describes an artworld; it importantly also admits (to that world – through a process of social negotiation) entities as *fictional* or *non-fictional*. Here, non-fictional entities relate to both to IE and DE classes of entity. Both stones and paperweights might equally be construed within some artistic context. However, the acceptance of the class of DE itself presupposes the existence of Fictional Entities (FE). A DE can only be possible through its relation to one or more concepts (or abstract ideas) held by us – these concepts may be individual or socially accepted. A new class of DE may be '*unreal* (or *non-existent)*' or '*possible* (or *non-actual)*'.

I, as my "self", may introduce a new "candidate" class of DE (for example, in the terms of CTA's experiment, invention or design), a form of self-dependent abstraction, either unreal or possible. Such a candidate "self-dependent" DE (DE_{sf}) is based on some, as yet socially unaccepted concept. Through a process of SNA, such unreal or possible ontological abstractions gradually take on their own concrete nature (or are rejected) as fictions. I therefore argue that, unless a pluralistic ontology embraces not only the *naturally* and *socially* real, but also (through an inherent malleability) accepts the existence of both the *unreal* and the *possible* objects as candidate fictions, then the first (original) paperweight did not exist and, therefore, by inference, neither do subsequent paperweights exist. In order to move from the *stone* to the *paperweight*, the first such object must have been held by at least one individual (let me say the inventor of the paperweight) against an initial conceptual idea (of the paperweight) that she or he had formed – an abstract of the eventual class of DE objects to become known as *paperweights*.

At this stage, the concept of the paperweight had no general acceptance and thus the original paperweight would have been unreal – in its place a mere stone. Only in the "mind" of the inventor, with both the capacity and facility to play creatively with concepts (including the development of new ones) could the paperweight therefore actually emerge as a candidate DE_{sf}. A gradual acceptance of the concept of the paperweight therefore leads to the *possibility* of its existence and finally, through a process of social negotiation, to a *universal* acceptance of the concept and its actual existence and status as a DE. Yet the original paperweight would always be open to classification in an IE form as a mere stone. Furthermore, I, as an individual, am free to develop a further self-dependent concept that presupposes the class of paperweight as an entirely new DE_{sf}; I may invent another, altogether innovative use for the object that is a paperweight. The new object may therefore inherit attributes of a now absent other; that is, the paperweight has some similar characteristics to a rock. The paperweight possesses density, weight, hardness, and so on, but it is no-longer characterized by its "rockness".

Exploring management

I have argued that the creative pluralism of a philosophy of SNA, exercised through CTA, will allow for the creativity associated with an interpretivistic epistemology. Therefore, a theorizing of social abstraction that is intrinsic to *practice* can be practiced as a basis of a mimetic engagement with the world. I am now, therefore, concerned with how – through this notion of an interpretivistic epistemology – it is possible to investigate a world that embraces entities that are both real and fictional; including newly developed ideas and abstractions. Clearly my argument eschews traditional forms of management study – for example pure, applied and action research. How does, for example, one embrace the research of non-real FEs?[95]

Positivism sees only that our world exists externally. Positivistically then, I would investigate my world by focusing on facts concerning the entities within my ontology, looking for causality and/or fundamental laws. How, then, do I reconcile positivism with the study of one or more entities that are accepted, at the outset, as fictional and/or non-existent? Here, positivism seeks to render fictions (for example hypotheses) as non-fictions (that is, objective truths), or else obviate their value as fiction. Phenomenology, however, may be argued to allow such value. I, an *observer-in-the-world*, am part of the world observed – my observational focus is on meanings attributed to the world. Phenomenology accepts that whatever the world may be, I can only come to grips with it by forming my own interpretation of it.

Phenomenology and its closely related partner of existentialism are however traditionally associated with the foundational epistemology of hermeneutics. I have already argued that, within the management domain that provides the context for this text, even the "experiential-based" NK of organizations and managers falls to a Cartesian-based causal analysis that is symptomatic of positivism's dominance. Such analysis perpetuates a view of management "science", providing a (Mode 1) causal analysis of experiences – proposing a scientific know-ledge (SK) that purports to explain the functioning of management and organizations. Prescriptive practices are both developed from, and ascribed to, SK; and from such practices predictive outcomes are sought. However, while the strict positivism of the early 20th century might be argued to have been superseded, an early pluralistic social world – in which the management and organizational domain is seen as a subset of all entities and relationships – fails to permit entities for which no causal analysis can be developed. That is, there is a failure to permit specifically fictional entities, for example those that might be *unreal* and *possible*. Let me illustrate this point by taking one specific management environment as an example, that of the retail sector and the response of consumers to certain phenomena. As Kotler *et al* (1999:253) observe, most large companies research consumer buying decisions in great detail seeking predictors in the buyer-decision process. However, '*...learning about the whys of consumer buying behaviour and the buying-decision process is not so easy – the answers are often locked within the consumer's head.*' The perceived need to translate such a subjective and individualistic experiential phenomenon as a person's buying behaviour into a rule-based objective rationality, as a basis for determining marketing strategy, represents a dualistic separation of both the mental and physical worlds.

As Cruickshank argues (2004:582), Cartesian rationalism can not rejoin the mind and world by suggesting that the buying world equates to the *rational idea* of the buying world. Neither can empiricism suffice with its argument that the *buying mind* can directly experience the *buying world*. I suggest that it is perhaps axiomatic that there will remain scenarios where a consumer makes a purchase decision based, not on the universally held (use) concept of a specific object, but on the basis of a fictional (use) concept to which that particular consumer believes can be applied to the said object. How often do we see examples of objects in use for purposes one imagines the object was not designed for? I, the inventor, might buy a paperweight to be included as part of a new invention that just so happened to require a part that shared similar attributes to the abstract idea of the part I envisioned in my design. By rejecting a method embodied in foundational epistemology I can be encouraged to experience entities within some new context, for which new concepts are revealed as possessing a plausible truth value. Through interpretive theorizing I can move to translate from epistemological abstraction back to an ontological abstraction.

Within this text I borrow from existential phenomenology only in so far that it seeks to describe experiences as they *emerge* within some context. Therefore, as a generalization, I argue that management strategies that advocate the use of a *science* of customer relationship management to understand which customers are truly profitable, and how best to change the behaviour of the rest, are symptomatic of the systematic and objective decontextualizing of knowledge. While such theories tend to work within the context of their origin, they are not so efficacious in the complex and ambiguous scenarios often faced in management and organizational practice. The generalization of any theory in an application *out-of-context* – that is, in an application beyond the bounds of a theory's origin – epitomizes, perhaps, the perception of a potential gap between theory and practice. The study of management and organizational practice as an existential phenomenon suggests, as Thompson *et al* (1989:137) argue, a world-view that is a *contextualist* view in which:

> …experience is seen as a pattern that emerges from a context… The research focus is on *experience* as described from a *first-person* view… The research logic is *apodictic* meaning that researchers seek to apprehend a pattern as it emerges… The research strategy is *holistic* and seeks to relate descriptions of specific experiences to each other… The research goal is to give a *thematic description* of experience.

Where, then, is the point of departure that gives rise to the cultural paradox of the "Management Gap"? To draw an appropriate empirical insight, we need to examine the emergent experiences (of "the gap") that arise from two sets of entities (managers and researchers). Clearly any such supraset will still only represent a subset of the total ontological inventory. For a representative set with the ability, in its own right, to provide an emergent pattern of experience representative of the root cause of the gap, the sample size would be beyond the scope of the resources available to most researchers; thus laying open any presentation of further "truth" claims concerning *the gap* to the principals of falsification.[96] But, having noted a particular pattern emerging from the context of a study, we could be guided towards the selection of respondents who might provide a greater possibility of obtaining "disconfirmatory" empirical evidence and arrive at "answers" much more quickly. It is, however, not difficult to intuitively arrive at a conclusion that the falsification of any empirically derived "truth" can be socially engineered – particularly if based on limited sample size. Certainly, at the limits of current knowledge, investigating what can be known about the world of management and organizational practice under complexity and ambiguity (a pluralistic ontology) and, in particular, the phenomenon of the *Management Gap* – a socially negotiated DE concept, or fiction – is problematic. I therefore argue against a premature empirical view of experience. Such a view would merely characterize the gap within some limited contextual setting.

Thinking a potential phenomenon

In contrast to merely framing some form of empirical theorizing, I will conclude Part II of this text by positioning my phenomenological argument, a conjunction of CTA and SNA, as a legitimate basis for an analytic of the concept – a potential phenomenon – of an *Art of Management*. Here I shall call on a paraphrasing from Sartre's (1943: 252) *Being and Nothingness* in which I seek to illustrate two things. Firstly, in reversing two sections of Sartre's text, I highlight what I shall refer to as the *paradox of social construction* as further support for a philosophy of SNA. Secondly, in contrasting "*the* individual" with an "*other* individual", SNA's fundamental requirement for negotiation is made explicit. Therefore:

I, as an individual, exist within a social system (or framework) of meanings and experiences that are distinct from my own. As I go through my existence (my understanding of) this framework which is external to my own experience (but nonetheless influences it) is gradually "filled in".

To the extent that I strive to determine the concrete nature of the (social system) and my place therein I transcend the field of my own experience. I am concerned with a series of phenomena which on principle can never be (fully) accessible to my intuition, and consequently I exceed the lawful limits of my own [narrative] knowledge. I seek to bind together experiences that will never be my experiences and consequently this work of construction and unification can in no way serve for the unification of my own experience.

Within this social system, the other person is indeterminate. The other is, in a certain sense, the negative of my own experience – since s/he is the one for whom I am no longer subject, but an object in their own system. Therefore, as the subject of knowledge, I strive to determine as object, the subject who denies my own character as subject and who determines me as an object.

Sartre's passage exemplifies the monologic nature of "*the* individual" coming to terms with a reality in which a knowledge of certain aspects of the "social situation" (for example *the self*) is denied. This is the paradox of a socially constructed knowledge; one that is determined by the conflicting languages of origination and interpretation. Therefore:

I can never apprehend the relationship between *an other*… and *myself* and such *an other* is never (a) given, but gradually I may constitute *an other*… as a "concrete" person. But the other person is not an instrument who might serve to predict an aspect of my own experience, but there are aspects in my experience which might serve to constitute this other person as concrete. What I constantly aim at across my own experiences are the feelings, ideas and volitions of the other because the other (person) is not only the one whom I see, but the one *who sees me (emphasis added)*.

In this reading of Sartre, I exist in both social and pluralistic ontologies – each describable in potentially diverse, monologic languages of thought. The removal of the paradox of a monologic social construction is therefore realized – through an engagement with *the other* – in a dialogue that might reveal a richness of information with the potential to contribute to a better understanding of a social situation – be it, for example, the presentation of this book or the gaining of an understanding of a managerial issue. The method of gaining this understanding is, I argue, embedded in the dialogic process of communication. This presupposes either a common language of dialogic exchange (that is, an ontological abstraction), or an effective means of translation.[97]

Finally, if the interpretivistic limitations of *management-the-science* are to be avoided, the phenomenological approach suggests a value in the concept of *management-the-artform*, in which many interpretations of a phenomenon are to be encouraged. Here, I argue that the framework of CTA/SNA provides a more erudite premiss for arguing this concept of *management art,* than does Degot's (1987) own correlation between both management and art's evolutionary nature. Since CTA does not specify any given craft as the basis of the process of art, or of the social acceptance of any artform, it is therefore open to the substitution, *inter alia*, of a craft of management and organizational practice. This is not to suggest that management and organizational practice is an artform *per se* – simply that it might be *practiced* as an artform. Neither does CTA/SNA suggest that a work of management and organizational practice is necessarily a *de facto* work of art. It simply suggests that, given the possibilities of a manager's innovative application of his or her managerial craft skills in a mimetic discovery of certain aspects of their organizational reality, then there is a case that a process of socialization – that is, SNA – might lead to an element of a manager's efforts having the characteristics of a entity that some *body-of-an-audience* might accept as a work of *management art.*

Empirically, theorizing about potential management artworks cannot suggest some theory of unified knowledge concerning management and organizational practice – one that might be relayed to managers for their future prescriptive guidance and, therefore, allaying concerns over the value of academe's potential to contribute to such practice. Rather, the suggestion is that thinking about the potentiality of a phenomenon of management as an artform – that is, theorizing about the process rather than its potential products – makes explicit certain features of management and organizational practice. Such features could provide the insights necessary – for the audiences of both academe and practice – to relate to the nature of knowledge in what is a shared environment of interest.

Part III

On an Art of Management

8
A Portrait of the Manager-Artist (after Degot)

We must cease once and for all to describe the effects of power in negative terms: it "excludes," it "represses," it "censors," it "abstracts," it "masks," it "conceals." In fact, power produces; it produces reality; it produces domains of objects and rituals of myth.

Foucault, The History of Sexuality[98]

Reframing Degot's portrait

At the close of Part I, I presented a critical reading of Degot's 1987 article: *Portrait of the Manager as an Artist*. Although I argued that Degot elicited useful insights into management and organizational practice, his basic premiss of an evolutionary parallel between both art and management was, at best, dubious. However, in recognizing the value of Degot's work as a potential contribution to the debate over management theory and its practice, I argued that it was necessary to explicate a new premiss for considering management as an artform – one that was rooted in an understanding of what the concept *art* might, in fact, be. Part II of this text presented a comprehensive argument for such a new premiss. It is a premiss for an *art of management* that is based on conceptualizing a Conjunctive Theory of Art (CTA), together with a philosophy of Socially Negotiated Alternativism (SNA). I therefore advance the idea that *management art* is an epistemic *practice* of plausible knowledge development, in which:

- **<u>Management Art</u>**, as a process, is the innovative conjunction of the acknowledged craftskills of management with the mimetic discovery of some aspect (real or imaginary) of the management world, and:

- **<u>A Management Artwork</u>** is any unique tangible realization of a thing, concept or idea resulting from the process of Management Art, and is accepted – through a process of SNA – as such within a given management context (an organizational institution or management world), also:
- **<u>The Manager-Artist</u>** is an innovative manager with a propensity for producing management artworks.

In contrast to *management art*, and as a reprise from Part I, the rationalistic paradigm represented a *poietic* bringing forth of management knowledge, within the *self* as a manager (see Figure 1.1). Under rationalism, I argued that a desired consequence (**C1**) of effective management practice was that: through generating and applying new, plausible narrative knowledge, a manager is better able to resolve ambiguity and complexity within management situations, and to manage to successful outcomes. It is now possible to add a fourth premiss (**P4**), where management is best practiced on the basis of an artistic process, in which the acknowledged craftskills of management are applied innovatively within the mimetic discovery of some aspect (real or imaginary) of the management world. The central thesis of this book is therefore given by the guiding hypothesis, **H4** {P4 → C1}. Simply stated, hypothesis **H4** suggests that management, practiced as an artform, is likely to lead to a manager being better able to resolve ambiguity and complexity within management situations, and to manage to successful outcomes.

In a critical context, there are now four plausible alternatives of management practice {**H1**, **H2**, **H3**, **H4**}, representing the two competing paradigms of rationalism and art. The notion that there might exist a "most plausible" hypothesis suggests that, from the point of view of academic theorizing about management and organizational practice, there should be some realizable form of *management skill(s)* that could be identified, empirically rationalized and generalized into some "theory" or other – to be taught to prospective managers, enabling them to better cope with complex and ambiguous management challenges. However, the paradox of these competing hypotheses is that, while empiricism is a *de facto* feature of a rationalist viewpoint, an empirically-based study of potential *management artists* and their *artworks* cannot yet be achieved, since there has, hitherto, been no generally accepted *a priori* concept of what might constitute a management artwork.

The achievement of some unified theory of knowledge concerning an art of management and organizational practice is, I suggest, not yet realizable. Rather, I have suggested that theorizing about the possibilities of management as an artform can only presently be achieved at a process level. Reframing Degot's *Portrait of the Manager as an Artist* – in terms of the processes of CTA/SNA – will allow me to explicate a paradigmatic view of *management art* that, not only provides an answer to *"what"* Degot's *art of management* might be, but also – critically – contributes a philosophy of *"why"* a *management art.*

The historicity of the manager-artist

The *manager-artist* is engaged, above all else, in a process of mimetic learning. This is an aesthetic *bringing-forth* of a plausible knowledge of some aspect of a management reality, as a means to overcoming an inherent ambiguity and/or complexity. The *manager-artist* is seen to possess a certain aesthetic sensibility to their lived-situation. But, a "non-artist" may also possess a certain aesthetic sensibility to their own lived-situation; this is problematic. Thoughts and ideas may originate, aesthetically, within both the *manager-artist* and the non-artistic but aesthetic individual. However, it is an individual's ability to facilitate the hypostatization of those thoughts and ideas – as a plausible contribution to an organizational (narrative) knowledge – that offers the critical differentiation. It is, I argue, evidence of an individual's "sensible" capacity to facilitate a communicated meaning that marks the *manager-artist*. However, there is a paucity of relevant *management art* material to empirically support this view of the *manager-artist*. Degot's (1987:18) narrative is cognizant of this problematic, in that he observes that most management artwork is lost. Following Booth (2003), and also Lamond (2006), the historicity of my own *manager-artist* starts with a distinct call to the importance of an historical perspective of management as a basis of aesthetically informed enquiry. As Degot (1987:45) concedes, because of the lack of relevant material "systematically compiled" it is hard to press such views further.

The problematic of identifying the management *aesthete* is evidence of an *aesthetic gap* in which I argue that the socially contrived specificities of culture, space and temporality, prevent a hypostatized, plausible *aesthetic* knowledge from transcending its boundaries.[99] Here, rather than seek empirical support for my own characterization of the *manager-artist*, I intuitively note that the specificities of the "contrived" organization – the essential *object* of management – provide a bounded space in which *management art* might either be encouraged or repressed. Such a space, in a highly complex and/or ambiguous organization, presents no less a sublime environment than that beheld by other artists. It is the complex and ambiguous nature of the specificities and boundaries that delineate the sublime – the artistic space. In this respect, the notion of the sublime is a "sign" to identify the boundary between the far-field of our own individual space and the unknown that we might sense lies beyond it. It is the sublime nature of complexity and ambiguity associated with organizational life that offers the "object" of *management art*.[100] Here I have argued that the mimetic learning required within the context of management and organizational practice is a function of the temporal gap between the mimetic facilitation of the *manager-artist,* and the mimetic experience of the organization – as an audience – for whom the *manager-artist* practices (or performs). The separation of the *manager-artist* from the organization becomes a corollary of the temporal mimetic separation between the primary and secondary nature of CTA. The resolution of this temporal disconnect, as a process of social negotiation, is the epistemic challenge faced in understanding the nature of a *manager-artist's* work and its subsequent organizational acceptance.

Mimesis – as a learning experience – can be legitimately interpreted as an aesthetic bringing-forth, within the "self" as manager, of the necessary elements of a plausible knowledge to be communicated as "their" *interpretation* of the complex and/or ambiguous management situation they find themselves in. Here the aesthetic concept of *attractive beauty* is invoked as the *manager-artist* (or indeed patron, champion or critic) must discover what, within such an interpretation, will help the organizational audience in the process of engagement with the reality of the "work". This Hodgkinesque notion sees the *manager-artist* (or an other) possessed of an intent to achieve, within the observing audience, a direct communication of the same kind of aesthetic response as was achieved in first conceptualizing a work. The step from the individual mimetic experience to the organizational aesthetic response is unquestionably embedded in the power and politics of management. This observation is firmly echoed by Rancière (2000:12–13) who argues that:

> Having a particular "occupation"... determines the ability or inability to take charge of what is common to the community; it defines what is visible or not in a common space, endowed with a common language, etc. There is thus an aesthetics at the core of politics... This aesthetics should not be understood as the perverse commandeering of politics by a will to art... [but] in the Kantian sense...

as the system of *a priori* forms determining what presents itself to sense experience. It is a delineation of spaces and times, of the visible and invisible, of speech and noise, that simultaneously determines the place and the stakes of politics as a form of experience. Politics revolves around what is seen and what can be said about it, around who has the ability to see and the talent to speak, around the properties of spaces and the possibilities of time.

Having regard, therefore, for the factions and dissidence that also lie at the root of any community's politics, while the *manager-artist* is an individual who may have the ability to "take charge" of the organization's community, they nevertheless are a potential catalyst to its adoption of a shared, common and plausible knowledge as a basis for action. Therefore, if the "end" of *management art* may be said to justify its "means", where that "means" might initially be seen to fail, there must exist the opportunity for a subsequent interpretation and evaluation of its object. This reinterpretation may permit (or benefit from) the establishment of new, accepted norms of craft skill common to the management community. The historicity of managerial artworks becomes evidence of the process of SNA, the fourth (temporal) dimension to that of art's innovation, *mimesis*, and craft.

Organizationally, mimetic learning will not fully occur until there is a closing of the aesthetic gap between the mimetic facilitation of the *manager-artist* and a shared mimetic experience – an aesthetic gap that is also, ultimately, a function of the power and politics of the organization. The notion of the "aesthetic gap" strengthens Degot's historical theme of a gap between management practice and management theory, and it offers some insight into that gap's potential closure.

Creativity and management artworks

For Degot, it is only the "good" creative[101] manager, successful in achieving maximum exploitation of the commercial organization's potential, who is of central interest. However, Degot does discuss the creative manager with a resistance to any attempt to define specific characteristics of the *creative individual*.[102] While this resistance is a strength in his work, he does however fail to make explicit his assumptions about *creativity* before he uses it as a device to explain how the "good" *manager-artist* is able to achieve his or her objective. By failing to highlight the aesthetic sense of creativity, Degot's discourse obscures the *aesthetic gap* while inferring that the "good" creative manager possesses all that is required to succeed in managing towards his or her vision. While Degot's discourse on the creative manager is highly suggestive of the relationship between power and politics within management, it fails to make this explicit and, fundamentally therefore, misses the aesthetic nature of this relationship.

Creativity involves the use of the imagination or original ideas in order to create something. This definition underpins my use of the term *innovation* within CTA. Taking both of these two basic terms together, my own "creative" *manager-artist* is someone with an ability to employ their *imagination* – applying new thoughts and ideas – in the process of creating a new (or enhanced) level of plausible management knowledge. There is no presumption, here, that the *aesthetic-creative* is necessarily invoked in the successful completion of some management project.[103] After all, many painters may have strived with their craft for years, perhaps only being recognized as an artist posthumously, when some critic, historian or patron managed to persuade an artworld of the value of the artist's work. Indeed, making explicit an aesthetic creativity highlights rather than obscures the problematic of the aesthetic gap as a historio-social phenomenon. As Rogers (2004), the daughter of Carl Rogers[104] writes:

> [c]reativity threatens those who demand conformity. ...[C]reativity is subversive to those who demand conformity to a political system. ...[The creative person] stays open to options, is flexible, and values individual differences. The conformist, on the other hand, is closed, rigid in his/her thinking, and follows the leader without using his/her self-knowledge or ability to discriminate.

Degot's "good" creative manager appears prepossessed of the personal space within which he or she is able to exercise creativity in the practice of his or her work of management art. It is this presupposition that constrains Degot's conception of *managerial art* – it leads to a blurring of the possibilities of a management art's history and of its criticism. However, my own conceptualization of *managerial art* is as an epistemic function. Here an "end" of plausible knowledge generation is made available to the management decision-making process. Therefore, unlike Degot's position, this reconceptualization precludes any subsequent decision act and its outcome. I argue that to understand *managerial art* is to engage with the epistemic process of SNA itself – that is, to come to understand how and why a plausible knowledge is internalized within a process of organizational learning. The utility of a *managerial artwork* lies in its ability to invoke, within the observing audience, a comprehension of a plausible knowledge. This notion is fully cognizant of an Art-aesthetic broadening of the creative discourse into one of interpretation, as has been suggested by Guillet de Monthoux (2000). An engagement with the epistemic process of *managerial art* is an engagement with its work's *aesthetic*; and it is on such an aesthetic basis that Rancière (2000:14) comments:

> … it is possible to raise the question of "aesthetic practices"… that is forms of visibility that disclose artistic practices, the place they occupy, what they "do" or "make" from the standpoint of what is common to the community. Artistic practices are "ways of doing and making" that intervene in the general distribution of ways of doing and making as well as in the relationships they maintain to modes of being and forms of visibility.

I argue that CTA's concept of a *managerial artwork* is thus some "thing" that makes visible to the organization, the process of a mimetic bringing forth of a plausible, management knowledge. The *management artwork* itself becomes a visible representation that stands apart from the norms of visible representation within the organization. I argue that such artworks are not to be found in the norms of organizational convention, process and presentation. Legislative constraints, compliance requirements, strategies, policies, procedures, and so on, are all normalized presentations of the "sensible" shared (or imposed) in common across an organization's community.

What, then, are the forms of visibility, *the management artworks* that disclose the practices of the *manager-artist*? What place do such *works* occupy within the organization, and what difference do they do or make from the standpoint of what is common to the organization? If we are to look for management *artworks*, then the implication is that they must be sought from amongst the non-standard forms of representation within the organization – from within *the unique*. We may, for example, seek the stories, the narratives, the histories, the metaphors and the biographies that characterize, not only the individualistic nature of the organization, but that also characterize the *manager-artist's* contributions to it. However, why look for such unique works?

If the utility of *management art* concerns the development of management *knowledge*, it is necessary to establish the potential value of *managerial art* when set against the other forms of organizational knowledge development. It is therefore necessary to resolve the set of hypotheses {H1, H2, H3, H4} competing for the growth of management knowledge. This is, as I have already indicated, problematic – there is, as yet, no accepted *a priori* explication of managerial art. Consequently there is, as yet, no empirical basis for an examination of the hypothesis **H4**. How then is it to be demonstrated that a premiss (**P4**) of *management art* practice might be the most favourable antecedent to the desired consequent (**C1**). In the commercial organization this is a problem of economics, in which as Cowan and Foray (2002: 542) observe, the traditional theoretical approach is based in comparative statistical analysis. We can, for the time being, go no further.[105]

The audience and the aesthetic of power

In accepting the limitation of a lack of any evidence of *management artworks*, I argue that CTA/SNA at least justifies the establishment of a place for the "concept" of *management artworks* within the organizational context. However, I also now need to clarify the concept of an *audience* within which the discussion of management as an *artform* is relevant. Here I return to my conceptual distinction of the Art aesthetic. The *manager-artist* acts to mediate the *sublime*; sensing and presenting something of the absent other as a mode of externalizing their aesthetically sensed knowledge. This mediation appeals to a universal consent for the translation of the sublime experience through the concept of *attractive beauty*. This attraction signifies an engagement with the process of SNA that communicates the unknown, the *absent other*, within the potential (or actual) sublime organizational setting.

As an intermediary, the *manager-artist* is an "agent" of the organization, and is thus also subject to the ubiquitous agency relationship. Here, the principal (the organization) requires the performance of the agent (the *manager-artist*) in a particular organizational role (as manager). The inference of such agency, as Eisenhardt (1989) surmises, now introduces a need to resolve two problematics of agency theory. The first problematic occurs when there is both a conflict between the desires and/or goals of both the principal and agent, and there is a difficulty in the principal verifying the agent's effectiveness. In this case, the organization is – certainly at this conceptual stage – ill-prepared to comprehend the nature of the *manager-artist's* work and is thus unable to verify the plausibility of the management knowledge presented as a basis for some management action.

The second problematic of agency lies within the distribution of risk[106] between the organization and the *manager-artist*. Both the organization and the *manager-artist*, through the existence of the aesthetic gap, may hold different preferences for subsequent action by virtue of their differing interpretations of a plausible knowledge and its attendant risks. In the first instance, the audience of the *manager-artist* is undoubtedly the organization[107] as "principal" over the work of *management art*. Here, the imperative of the *organization-as-audience* is a necessity to accept, on trust[108] the work of the *manager-artist* as both plausible and relevant. A resolution of the *aesthetic gap*, the problematic of the Weberian social aesthetic, might therefore be sought from within the twin agential conflicts of desire and interpretation. This is a resolution that infers a negotiation between two parties, each with their respective power bases. Figure 8.1 provides a schematic depiction of the resolution of three simplified power-relations between two parties: the organizational *principal* and the managerial *agent*. The resulting balance of power represents a "force" towards a negotiated position – in this case a negotiated interpretation of a plausible knowledge.

Within Figure 8.1, cases (1) and (2) provide examples of an unequal power distribution in the agency relationship. These result in an interpretation closer to the position favoured by the stronger power. A more even power distribution, as in case (3), is likely to lead to a potentially greater force for a negotiated interpretation – one that is, perhaps, representative of a mid-ground. Here, as Lyotard (1979:8–9) acknowledged, knowledge and power are two sides of the same question: who

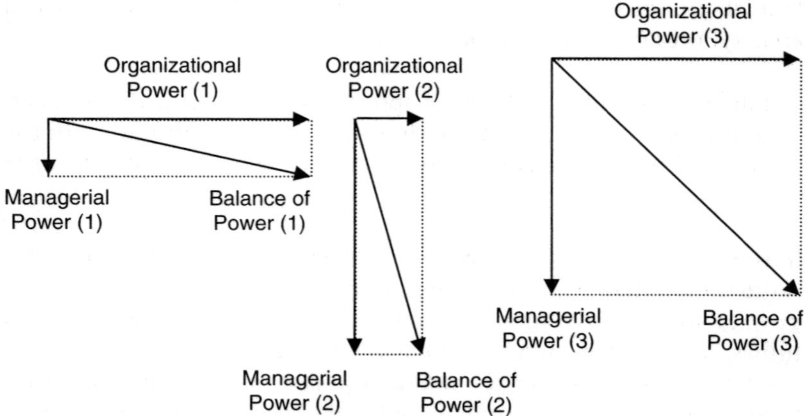

Figure 8.1 Three Views of the Balance of Power

decides what knowledge is, and who knows what needs to be decided? Lyotard also infers a critical distinction between power in the hands of: a) the artist, b) the state and c) the market. Power in the hands of the artists permits them the freedom to express their suspicions. Lyotard (1979:75–76) suggests that:

> [artists] are destined to have little credibility in the eyes of those concerned with "reality" and "identity"; they have no guarantee of an audience. ...Duchamp's "ready made" does nothing but actively and parodistically signify [a] constant process of dispossession of the craft of... [art].

With power in the hands of the state, realism and neo-classicism prevail over experimentalism. This is, according to Lyotard, provided the '..."correct" images, the "correct" narratives, the "correct" forms which the [state] requests, selects and propagates...' can find a public who desire them as an appropriate remedy for the anxiety and depression they might experience. However, power in the marketplace creates a realism of anything goes. Here, as Lyotard continues:

> in the absence of aesthetic criteria, it remains possible and useful to assess the value of works of art according to the profits they yield. Such realism accommodates all tendencies, just as capital accommodates all "needs", providing that the tendencies and needs have purchasing power.

Out of the idealized notion of an art serving the remedy of social anxiety, Lyotard (1979:77) counters that:

> [Modernity,] in whatever age it appears, cannot exist without a shattering of belief [of the social] and without [their] discovery of the "lack of reality" of reality, together with the invention of other realities.

In this postmodern condition, beauty is replaced by the sublime. This is the notion that, whilst our beliefs might be shattered, we might conceive of an "Idea" of our world – our reality – and yet, as Lyotard continues, '...every presentation of an object destined to make "visible" [the] absolute greatness or power [of our Idea] appears to us painfully inadequate.' Such sublime ideas are "unpresentable" and, to Lyotard, it has become the *de facto* project of a "modern art" to present the fact that the unpresentable idea exists – to mediate the sublime. In relation to the concept of *managerial agency* then, the sublime – as an Art-aesthetic of powerful, incomprehensible forces – defines a social creativity through the individual's negotiation of a world that Murphy (1998:574) characterizes with pluralistic cultural complexity, social ambiguity, and daunting political, technological and bureaucratic power.

Between the extremes of *art-for-art's-sake* and *art-for-the-market*, one might envisage a state – perhaps democratic – in which certain *Artists*, exist in a fairly balanced power relationship with the state, cognizant of – but not bounded by – that state's cultural norms and expectations. In this state, art provides a means to both challenge and alleviate social anxiety. In the management world, the balance of power rests on the ability of the *manager-artist* to work towards a resolution of the conflicts of desire and interpretation. This infers a negotiation between parties engaged in an organization where the operation of power is often intentionally obscured. As Murphy (1998:564) notes, this creates a cognitive problematic, rather than presenting a route to understanding. Ultimately, a value in *management art* can only be realized in an organization that is open to the possibilities of the aesthetic, where aesthetic values constitute and legitimate institutional forms and social distinctions. Here, in the period of Degot's (1987) writing, the Bourdieusian rules of cultural engagement privileged an audience with a "social location". As Prior (2005:124) argues, this identifies a social strata through the errors made in the individual's engagement with its *arts*; it therefore identifies a *politics*[109] of *Management Art*.

The audience and the aesthetic of politics

In explicating the potential of a politics of art, Hein (1976:144–146) advances three theories to describe the aesthetic-power relationships within institutions. These are the Contrapuntal, the Propadeutic, and the Propulsive.[110] These theories provide a useful insight into the power-politic relationship inherent in CTA/SNA. Firstly, the Contrapuntal theory – implying the existence of multiple independent voices[111] – sees the balance of power (or, perhaps, the law) in the hands of the state and/or institution. This provides for the "harmonizing" positive ground as well as the negative limitation of individual freedom. As Hein argues, in the Contrapuntal case:

Art serves as a sanctioned counterforce to the mainstream current of society. …The individual is permitted through art (and other forms of controllable aesthetic experience) to purge his feelings of anger, rage, unrequited love, personal inadequacy and impotence – all feelings which, if vented in political action would be disruptive and socially dangerous. ...The political function of [a Contrapuntal] aesthetic experience is... seen to be the conservative maintenance of the status quo – art is used to defuse disgruntled feeling and potentially revolutionary tendencies. ...The anarchy of art is directed against itself – a sacrifice to law and order.

Secondly, in the Propadeutic theory, Hein describes art as a paradigmatic "source of understanding" of the lawfulness and order of the world in which we find ourselves situated. It is here, in the "microcosmic worlds" invented through our art that we are best able to comprehend the larger world that we did not create, and for which we are not wholly responsible. In this sense, the sublimity of the world presents a challenge for comprehension and it is through the suggested ability of the process of art, to produce purposive worlds of our own, that we learn to apprehend and appreciate order in increasingly complex manifestations. As Hein notes:

> The very essence of the propadeutic theory of art lies in the shared conviction that matter, to which the aesthetic experience is ultimately bound, remains on a lesser plane of being than... intellect. ...Art... is thus seen as a model for autonomy, and so as politically justified.

Finally, Hein's Propulsive theory provides that art is a primordial and powerful force for negation. Here the aesthetic is politically destructive – it is a view to be found in the '...*subversive champions of individualistic resistance*'. This is a notion that is singularly well attuned to the nature of capitalism's "interesting times", where art functions as a constant "disturbance". Here, an organization that recognizes the aesthetic politics of a subversive "art-for-art's sake" can either exercise its power and/or authority in the suppression of a *management art* to protect a status quo, or admit it as a force for good. Here, Hein suggests:

> [a *management art* might project] ...new forms [of knowledge], transcending the bounds of the familiar much as scientific "breakthrough" explodes and moves beyond the normal patterns of scientific thought.... Aesthetic experience has the greatest potential for innovative syntheses because the ...scrutiny of forms as well as

the forging of new languages and modes of expression are ...its very essence.

In this *propulsive* case, as my use of Foucault's quote in the opening of this chapter suggests, the *manager-artist* can be seen to be a political force for production, where Hein argues that:

> ...the artist is ...held to be uniquely favoured. Neither an apologist for the status quo nor a house jester who provides relief from pain.... [The artist] is... a critic of the existing system and an architect of the future. The ...artist ...need not be explicitly political; nor need his rebellion be an overtly political one.

Clearly each of Hein's three theories courts its own controversies. However, my interest in them, here, is in broadening the concept of the audience of art in the management context. Intuitively, one might produce a range of examples of management practice that could infer one or other of these aesthetic theories in the context of the politics of an organization. Following Redfield (2003), aesthetics is always, in principle, a political discourse. Here, Redfield (2003:12) argues that:

> Aesthetics... unfolds as a pedagogical, political, and historical model. ...Without question, the sublimation of historical contingency into form constitutes the telos of aesthetic discourse, but much of the political force of aesthetics lies in its historicism, in its projection of a temporal line... [A]n ever-deferred end of history, that aesthetic experience prefigures.

Hein's *aesthetic-politic* theories – as "partial accounts" of *management art's* potential to influence organizational practice – serve to extend the potential interest of *management art* and, therefore, extend its potential audience beyond the organization itself, into the realm of academe.

It is now possible to suggest a positioning of Degot's original *Portrait of the Manager as an Artist* as a contribution to the concept of *management art*. Degot's contribution can be seen as contemporaneous with the Bourdieusian "Field of Cultural Production". Here the schemes and categories used to engage with – in this case management – artworks have a double relationship to the historical context. As Prior (2005:1270) citing Bourdieu (1993) comments, these are the subject of usages that are, themselves, socially marked by the position of the users who are exercising aesthetic choices as a result of some privileged habitus. Degot's own background and personal interest in the arts undoubtedly contributed to the production of his *managerial portrait*. However, from a non-academic point of view, *contrapuntally*, Degot's contribution could be described as an academically sanctioned counterforce to the mainstream current of management writing – in which there was, arguably, no guarantee of an audience.

For the academic audience, *propadeutically*, Degot's contribution can be said to be politically justified along the model of autonomous learning. Here, while an enlightened autonomy might be respected, a concept of *management art* might be said to suffer from its failure to be lifted to the plane of a "privileged intellectualism". Certainly, the weakness of Degot's evolutionary argument does not help his case. However, while a Bourdieusian encounter with Degot's *Portrait* would account, in part, for its relative obscurity, a contemporary rereading is justified.

As Prior (2005:125) observes, the historicity inherent in the concept of an audience presented with any work, plays to the audience's collective cultural and economic capital that activate, *inter alia*, their attitudes, artistic preferences and cognitive competencies. Prior's suggestion of the continually changing nature of the "audience", therefore requires a move from "privileged" conceptual classifications to '...*refined demarcations based on multiple dimensions such as age, gender, ethnicity, sexuality, geography and employment.*' This appeals to a more *propulsive* theory of management art, in which the Schillerian notion of "aesthetic activity as play" is to the fore. Following Hein (1976:148) therefore, the twin audiences of organization and academe are presented with the Marcusean concept of the, spontaneous, aesthetic being who possesses a vision and insight which shapes and designs as it reveals new forms of organizational and managerial order.

The historian and the critic

A *propulsive* aesthetic-politic theory of a management art is also a pendulous notion of an art that might, at one time favour the status quo – finding within it aspects of a reflected realism – whilst at other times favouring an *avant-garde* of the postmodern. While the origin of a management-art work might lie in the vision and insight of the *manager-artist*, artistic power lies in an understanding of the political relationships and imperatives existing in the organizational context, and in knowing how they might be used in the furtherance of organizational goals. As Jameson (1977:196) comments, it is not only political history which those who ignore are condemned to repeat:

Nowhere has this [notion of the] "return of the oppressed" been more dramatic than in the aesthetic conflict between "Realism" and "Modernism", whose navigation and renegotiation is still unavoidable... today, even though we may feel that each position is in some sense right and yet that neither is any longer wholly acceptable. The dispute is itself older than Marxism, and in a longer perspective may be said to be a contemporary political replay of the 17th-century *Querelle des anciens et des modernes*, in which, for the first time, aesthetics came face to face with the dilemmas of historicity.

In the conceptualization of a *management art*, the potential impact of the historicity of its power-politic relations calls for a keen understanding of its history. It is a strength of Degot's thinking that he surfaces the discipline of *management-art historian*. It is, however, blurred in its distinction from its partner discipline of criticism. While Degot (1987:22) initially describes these two separately, his own audience simply resolves to the critic. Following Preziosi (1998:13) I advance the idea that a discipline of a *management-art history* would function to fabricate a historical past that could then be placed under systematic observation for use in the present. Such a discipline would incorporate an amalgam of analytical methods, theoretical perspectives, rhetorical or discursive protocols, and epistemological technologies, of diverse ages and origins. In following Robinson (1981), the *management-art historian* would set about selecting and presenting facts concerning a *management-art work*: who was the *manager-artist*, when and where was the work produced, and under what circumstances. But, could we not, therefore, entertain a history of management without it being a history of *management art*?

As Lamond (2006:6) observes, it has been argued that, with few exceptions, the (non-artistic) history of management is sparse, patchy and unbalanced. Here, as I argued in my Introduction, with the retrenchment of Marxist social theorizing from management and organizational study – with its inherent socio-historic criticism of a bourgeois management's *realpolitik* – there has been a consequential loss of eschatological and teleological purpose to any historical critique. We are left merely with the history of management and organizations as a fertile ground for contemplation, where a Weberian social order might be fascinating in its intricacy, but lacking in its potential to inform the future. As Carson and Carson (1998:38) note, critics of contemporary management history suggest that history lacks utility and is therefore undeserving of attention.

A socio-historic critique, set in the context of a *management-art* history, brings a new utility of its study into being. It reveals the explicit need to elucidate the power-politic relationships that subsisted at the time of the work for the purpose of informing the creation of new narratives of practice. It is "art's" epistemological potential, I argue, that can overcome the problematic of an autonomous Weberian social aesthetic; art's epistemology may be seen to provide new teleological purpose. But this is not teleology in the style of some new grand narrative, but a locally – purposively – derived finality of performativity. One that is intrinsic to the organization in its relationship with its environment.

However, the power-politic question is value laden and not easily interpretable as historical fact. This critique does not discount the proposed utility of management-art history. Recalling Robinson (1981:5), this suggests that there is a need for the role of *the management-art critic* to act in support of *the management-art historian* in the discovery of things that may not seem straightforwardly factual.

It is axiomatic that power-politic distributions, certainly at the *micro-level* of an individual's interaction with the organization, are unique. Power and politics are not given, for example, to the generalizations required for a theory of management performance. As Carson and Carson (1998) argue, history attempts to explain and not predict. History should be used as a guide – as an input to the decision-making process – it should not be mindlessly extrapolated. Potential users of management history must take into account modifications in the contemporary environment – particularly in respect of modified power-politic relationships – that may render the past ineffectual for suggesting, or influencing, future courses of action. Here the potential of a discipline of *management-art criticism* becomes grounded in the need to explain how a history of management ideas and agency relationships can impact the work of management in the future.

The two posited disciplines of *management-art historian* and *management-art critic* are inextricably linked. It would be problematic for the management-art historian to determine a "style" of a management-art work unless it was known that the work indeed had an Art-aesthetic significance. Therefore the management-art historian would rely on the ability of the management-art critic to exercise a value judgement over a particular work's Art-aesthetic. Paradoxically however, following Robinson (1981:10), the management-art critic cannot act without the assistance of the management-art historian in positioning a work within a potential style "setting".

Remapping the management space

By clarifying the nature of the audience of a management art and the inevitability of its politics, the function of Degot's critic can, in a sense, be reversed. Given that a management art refocuses on the individual and their aesthetic sensibilities, the management-art critic may function to inform both the *manager-artist* and the organization how – given certain historical specificities – aesthetically informed management knowledge might be creatively applied. Rather than describe "places and conditions", an Art aesthetic calls to a critical delineation of the management space.

An historio-critical conception of a management-art *style* is inferable from a separation of the process of *management art* from the actual vision that precedes it. This leads to the possibility of observing a variety of specificities. As with the *Fine Arts* previously discussed in Part II, it is possible to intuit, from such specificities, the potential for a range of classifications of various management artforms coexisting within the paradigm of CTA/SNA. This "process" approach to defining management art therefore provides the latitude to develop and accept new, as yet to be discovered, techniques and schools of *management art*. We have, in the same sense previously discussed for *Fine Art*, the facility to delineate the management "space" within which various management artforms might have a credible relationship with the organizational "space" in which they are realized.

I have argued that CTA/SNA provides four dimensions to an artform: innovation, mimesis, craft and temporality. In the context of a management art, the temporal dimension relates specifically to the achievement of progress in organizational understanding through a socially negotiated, mimetic learning experience. This, I have argued, does not occur until there is a closing of the aesthetic gap. This Weberian problematic subsists by virtue of the social's organization of the production and reception of a management art. The gap initiates through the nature of the origin of an aesthetically perceived knowledge as an individualistic phenomenon. It is closed, however, as a function of both the *manager-artist's* ability to portray a certain vision and an afforded facility to negotiate an organizational understanding that is, in turn, subject to a certain *politics of the aesthetic*. In drawing the portrait of the artist in Chapter 6, the lack of an artistic dialogue relevant to this "aesthetically political" process of socialization was not a major concern, since the Artists that I drew on had achieved an *a priori* acceptance in the Artworld. There the problematic of the social aesthetic had been overcome, in whatever manner was necessary of its time. Here, however, the social acceptance of a candidate work of management art, through SNA, is now seen through the functioning of the organizational power-politic relationships of an Art aesthetic.

Having described the field of *management art*, I now draw on my portrait of the artist, and I argue that *management art* may also exist in a fluid state bounded by the four dimensions outlined. Again, this state can usefully be described in a diagrammatic fashion. By assigning a relative value to each of the first three dimensions (*mimesis*, innovation and craft skill) representing the *manager-artist* (or visible within a *management-art work*), the capacity is provided to describe relative spatial positions for various categories of potential manager-artists and their likely organizational settings. An example of such a diagram is Figure 8.2 below. Here, I return to the subjective assignment of a value to the artistic process labels of the artists featured in the framework of Chapter 6. The value is, I acknowledge, wholly subjective and both temporally and contextually sensitive. However, as an explorative device, used to gain insight into *manager-artists* and the *management-art process*, I argue that the arbitrary assignment of such values is appropriate to the conceptual nature of this present text. Although values are inherently discreet, the diagrams produced go some way to retaining a sense of the "fluidity" of a management-art.

Figure 8.2 depicts, for example, a number of arbitrary selections of organizational settings, where the management function is categorized

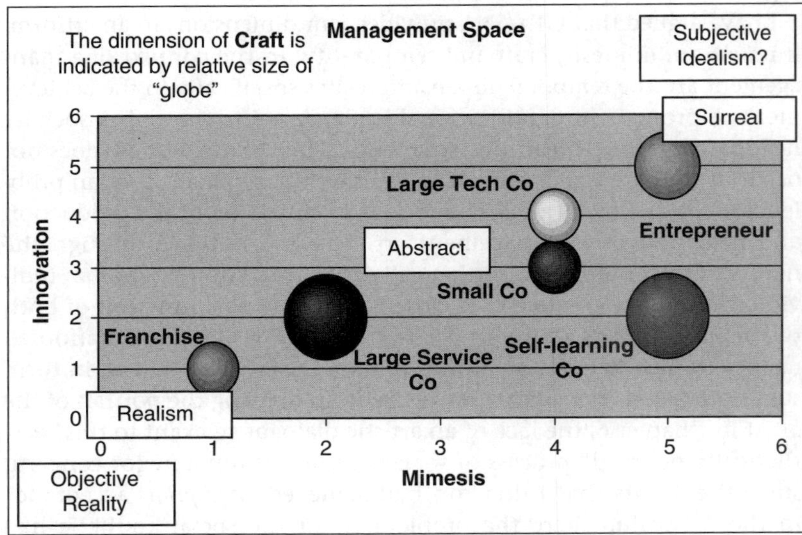

Figure 8.2 Conceptually Mapping the Management Space

in accord with the definition of CTA. My purpose in portraying this hypothetical map of *management art* is not to initiate a critical debate about my particular choice of settings, or to suggest that my allocations of arbitrary values are either accurate or, ultimately, appropriate. I simply depict – following the more empirical nature of the Portrait of the Artist – the type of analysis that is potentially opened up by the conception of a management art. I am, therefore, merely advancing the notion of a generic space within which *manager-artists* (and even non-artists), their work, and their organizational settings – potentially victims of a surfeit of alternative definitions, theories and understandings – can retain a credible relationship with each other.

Figure 8.2 represents a highly subjective and instantaneous view of the *management-art* space. The relative positions of both organizations and their *manager-artists* can (and will) vary, not only in cognizance of Bornstein's (1984) problem of artistic change – as the style of the *manager-artist* responds to changes in technique, craft and other influences such as the political and power relations subsisting in the organizational setting – but also in the temporal dimension. The fluid nature of the *management-art* space can be represented by reference to spatial maps that cover a range of differing temporal and organizational perspectives. The value of this spatial mapping lies, therefore, not in a single view of the relative positions of the various manager-artists or their organizations, but in coming to understand how: organizations; management as an artform; *manager-artists* and their works; and the agential relations of power and politics, move in relation to the total management space over time.

A portrait of the manager as an artist

The manager, in the manner of an *explorer*, is required to employ a full range of faculties and craft skills in mapping *a* path on a journey through his or her own management space and its intersection with the wider social space as the *means* to achieve closure on various given management *ends*. However, the paradox facing the manager is a need to achieve closure in the face of ambiguity and – given the manager's necessary engagement with other individuals in their community – a need to consider potentially competing views of both an *intra-* and *extra*-organizational reality; this appeals for a paradigmatic shift towards image interpretation. Here, I advance the idea that effective managers need to be able to "read" management situations in order to forge appropriate actions. This notion of "reading" an organizational situation aligns with Morgan's (1996) premiss that theories of organization and management are based on implicit "images" that lead us to see, understand, and manage. Epistemically, *Artworks* are, with other image forming devices (for example metaphors), in the wider class of sense-making "objects" that set immediate, concrete, observations within the context of a "subject's" (whether manager or organization) prior cognition.[112] Here, as Adorno (1961:160) has commented:

> In the form of an image the object is absorbed into the subject instead of following the bidding of the alienated world and persisting obdurately in a state of reification. The contradiction between the object reconciled within the subject, i.e. spontaneously absorbed within the subject, and the actual unreconciled object in the outside world, confers on the work of art a vantage-point from which it can criticize actuality. Art is the negative knowledge of the outside world. In analogy... we might speak of the 'aesthetic distance' from existence: only by virtue of this distance, and not [its denial] ... can the work of art become both work of art and valid consciousness.

The *Artwork* is not therefore an object for reification by the subject, either for its own sake as an unreconciled object of the world, or as some concretized "correct" view of an actuality. However, the contradiction presented by both artwork and metaphor – characteristic of Adorno's "aesthetic distance" – is their ability to provide either subjective insight or misplaced reality. In the context of a management *artwork*, the social problematic of the *aesthetic gap* operates as the corollary of the differential *aesthetic distance* between: a state of reconciliation of a plausible management understanding within the management subject, and the potential for an unreconciled, reified objective knowledge. Figure 8.3 depicts the conceptual relationship between aesthetic distance and the aesthetic gap. The differential lies between the *manager-artist* as subject and the *organization* as *audience* subject. As a reified, but unreconciled, objective knowledge (of a misplaced existence) each subject posits *the artwork* on potentially different planes. For the non-aesthetic subject there is an effective denial of an aesthetic distance. The non-aesthete denies the existence of a vantage point from which to critically appraise a plausible management reality beyond what is essentially objectively visible.

In my portrait of the manager as an artist, I do not infer that an *artistic* management action – that is, an action precipitated by a judgement based on an aesthetically informed, plausible knowledge, imparted to the organization by the *manager-artist* – is, itself, to be judged beautiful

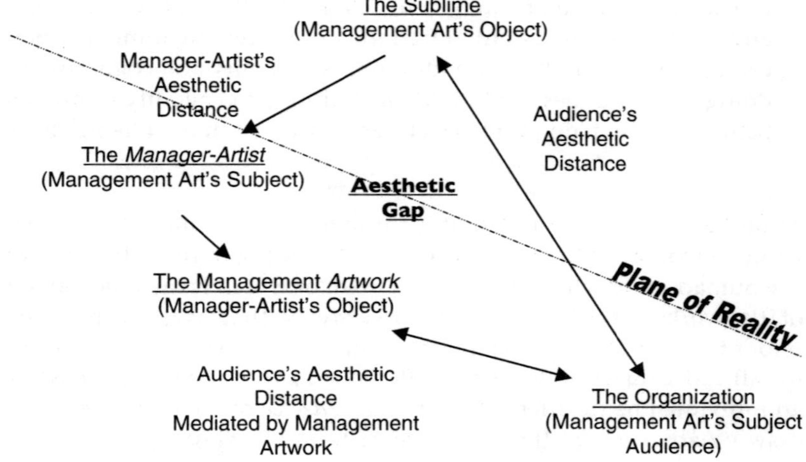

Figure 8.3   The Aesthetic Gap of Management Art

or that it is to be preserved as an object of intrinsic value. This would merely suggest that *management art* is no more than a reified collection of management theories, metaphors, stories, or other artefacts of historic note. Rather, *Art's* importance lies in its potential to facilitate perception formation. Here it is axiomatic that every manager's perceptual system is different. However, whilst managers might prefer Malan and Kriger's (1998) "concrete observations" to abstract concepts – a form of *accuracy* in perception – in the complex, multifaceted, paradoxical organizations they occupy, a manager must frequently exercise choice on the basis of his or her cognition of the moment. What is important, therefore, is a manager's ability to form and impart perceptions that will influence organizational practice. Therefore, although an *accuracy* of perception might be a worthy aim, it is a perceptive ability – set within a context of a communicated aesthetic sensibility – that marks the *manager-artist*.

To make an aesthetic judgement is to make a judgement in advance of "rule or precept". It is, in effect, a judgement that is exercised before any attempt is made to reconcile the (social) aesthetic gap. Here, in Art's tradition, to judge aesthetically is to infer a judgement of taste. As Redfield (2003:11) notes, the notion of "taste" is, however, a subscription to a Burkean metaphoric concept:

Through [the] sleight of hand [of the Burkean conceptual metaphor of taste] that has always threatened to make aesthetics as suspect as it is seductive, aesthetic judgment claims simultaneously to produce and to discover the essential harmony of perceiving mind and perceived world, sensation and idea, phenomenality and cognition. In doing so it inscribes the individual within the generality of human being. For the main point about taste is that all human beings have it.

As Burke (1759:65–73) noted, it is through the metaphor of taste that we are encouraged to reconcile an understanding of those faculties of the human mind which are affected with, or which form a judgement of, the works of the imagination. Burke argued that, as far as the metaphor of taste belongs to the imagination, it is – in principle – the same for all individuals; there is no difference in the manner or cause of an individual being affected, only in the *degree* of affect. However, in drawing attention to the metaphor of taste I suggest that it is not a useful metaphor in the context of a *management art*.[113] Here, what is important to understand from "taste" is Burke's use of the metaphor to highlight the underlying mechanism of the "self" by which individuals come to compare the "excesses or diminutions" of an existent other, when there is no "common measure" available. As Burke argued:

> ...in things whose excess is not judged by greater or smaller, as smoothness and roughness, hardness and softness, darkness and light, the shades of colours, all these are very easily distinguished when the difference is any way considerable, but not when it is minute, for want of some common measures *which perhaps may never come to be discovered.* ...So long as we are conversant with the sensible qualities of things, hardly any more than the imagination seems concerned; little more also than the imagination seems concerned when the passions are represented.... Love, grief, fear, anger, joy, all these passions have in their turns affected every mind; and ...not in an arbitrary or casual manner, but upon certain, natural and uniform principles [of affect] (emphasis added).

I argue that Burke provides a basic understanding of the "sensible" affect in a *management-art*. It is an *affect* arising in the work of the *manager-artist*, through CTA, and of the organizational audience's attention to that work, through SNA. The *manager-artist* is one who can dispel ontological assumptions of a perceived reality and who admits, to their judgement, their aesthetic sensibility; this marks a certain *aesthetic distance*. At the organizational level, the *aesthetic distance* is relative to the audience's sensibility to the work of the *manager-artist*. Here the origin of an aesthetic gap may arise as a function of the differential *aesthetic distance* between manager and organizational audience. The attention to each, of the others sensibility, may necessarily require further critical interpretation. Therefore, in painting my portrait of the manager as an artist, I argue that:

- <u>The Manager-artist</u> is a manager who admits, to their judgement, the plausible knowledge arising from an attention to their own (and potentially an other's) aesthetic sensibility of a given ambiguous or complex situation; who exercises such judgement in the innovative conjunction of an *a priori* knowledge base applied in the mimetic discovery of some aspect (real or imaginary) of their management world; and:
- <u>A Management Artwork</u> is any unique, tangible realization of a thing, concept or idea (for example: metaphor, narrative, story, legend, etc.) resulting from, or depicting, the work of the Manager-artist, and is accepted as such within a given management or organizational context as evidence of the manager's ability to perform as a manager-artist.

Finally, following Burke (1759:72), given either a greater degree of natural sensibility, or a "closer and longer attention to the object", it becomes the role of a management-art *historian* and *critic* to determine the classes and objects of a *management-art* and an understanding for the education of the senses.

9
Stepping Into "Heidegger's Shoes"

> When the creators vanish from the nation, when they are barely tolerated as an irrelevant curiosity, an ornament, as eccentrics having nothing to do with real life; when authentic conflict ceases, converted into mere polemics, into the machinations and intrigues of man within the realm of the given, then the decline has set in.
>
> Martin Heidegger, An Introduction to Metaphysics (1959)

The Model I manager

I have described the perceived gap between management theorizing and management practice within the context of the Mode 1 and Mode 2 knowledge production debate. A perceived failure of Mode 1 academic study to be of direct benefit to practice suggests a certain value to the so-called Mode 2 research. Contra to Mode 1 then, Mode 2 research has been argued as a direct attempt to produce a sophisticated narrative knowledge (NK_S) as an academically rigorous abstraction of practice. However, in advancing a paradigm of *management art,* I suggest that managerial and organizational practice might benefit from an Art-aesthetic theorizing that accepts the paradoxical search for knowledge without such rigour. This is an acknowledgement that, in the unfolding of practice under conditions of ambiguity and complexity, there may well be little time available for the validation of knowledge, before it is called upon as the basis for practical action.

A key question arises: in the socio-cultural environment in which I advance the suspension of a belief in objective truth, by what measure – other than through academic rigour – might we judge the validity of information as a basis of a plausible, actionable knowledge?

How are Lyotard's criterion of efficiency, justice, happiness, and the audio and visual sensibilities to be applied? It is here, I argue, that the value of an Art aesthetic rests in its ability to generate – through the notion of *affective* response – a plausible basis for narrative knowledge production. Here, the mind's processing of aesthetic *affects* provides the "sensible" knower with a natural mechanism for the formation of judgement – remembering that this judgement need only be plausible. The notion of *affect* may be derived by considering the "artistic individual's" *psyche* (see Chapter 6). Here, as Armstrong (2000:109) observes, the rubric of "affect" is inclusive of, *inter alia*, emotions, feelings, passions, moods, anxiety, pleasure, pain, joy and sorrow. To Armstrong, the most important axiom to bear in mind is that *affects* are experienced in consciousness and registered by the body. *Affects* also belong to the mind; they straddle the conscious and the unconscious. In my own reading of what Armstrong calls a "Democratic Aesthetic",[114] *affects* are the consequences of the mind's aesthetic experience of the sublime. Here, attractive beauty is what first draws the mind to become engaged[115] with the sublime; beauty is therefore one trigger to an *affect*.[116]

Drawing from the field of social psychology, Demerath's (1993:136) knowledge-based affect theory (KBAT) suggests that:

> [t]here exists a visceral-level, bipolar, affective response to what the perception of an object does to one's knowledge about that object, to one's certainty and ability to predict things regarding that object. If the perception of an object leads to greater certainty – either by adding to the old knowledge or by replacing lesser knowledge with better knowledge – positive affect will result. If it leads to less certainty and undermines predictive capacity, negative affect will result. …This kind of affect underlies the aesthetic experience… [where the] response may manifest itself as the feeling that an object is good or bad, beautiful or ugly, pleasant or unpleasant.

The manager, then, possesses a certain provisional knowledge concerning his or her organization and their/its position-in-the-world. Through experiences gained while engaged in organizational practice, the manager perceives aspects of their organization – and its relationships with other objects – that serve to trigger an *affective* response. It is this *affective* response that, within the mind of the perceiver, is mediated by a comparison of the newly perceived aspect with a distribution of previously perceived aspects. Affective response is therefore,

I argue, the mind's mechanism for assessing the validity of provisional knowledge within the context of an Art-aesthetic. Therefore, setting Demerath (1993:137) within the context of this text:

> The mean or average of our perceptions of an object [an organization, say] is the most accurate prediction about our future perceptions of that [organization]. The average is an abstraction of [the organization's] meaning, and our certainty of the average indicates the strength of our knowledge (i.e. the reliability of our predictions about the [organization]). Therefore any new perception that strengthens our certainty of the average will increase the power of our predictions and will produce positive affect.

In an Argyrian Model I theory-in-use, the effective manager is able to base his or her judgements for action on the basis of their average perception held – this is an historical conception of NK_n. As Kearney (2002) notes, the organizational narrative develops with a growing allegiance to past perceptions and events. Therefore, as Demerath suggests, provided that the average is perceived frequently in experience, the outcome of any action is relatively easy to predict; predictive power being changed little by yet another observation of the average. In this manner the narrative of organizational practice remains consistent. Where there is an *a priori* equilibrium in the mind of the manager, between what is known by them as knower and what is not, then the average perception may prove historically adequate for the performance of Model I management theories-in-use. Model I organizational practices are therefore adopted as day-to-day routines.

The effective control (that is, the selection and dissemination) of the narrative of the organization "as is" – as organizational learning – will ensure that the organization is perpetuated "as is". Provided, therefore, that the weight of experience is for the continued perception of the average, then the reoccurrence of the average serves to reinforce the currently-held (and historically-based) narrative of organizational existence. The continued perception of the relevance of historical narrative creates and concretizes the boundaries marked by that narrative – but it does not necessarily improve predictive capacity. However, if a manager now perceives a new aspect of the organization, provided this aspect also reinforces the average, there is also a positive effect on predictive ability.

Within KBAT, Demerath argues that a perception must be unique in order to add to existing knowledge and to trigger a knowledge-based affect. I argue, therefore, that organizations that are subject to only little change, and that continue certain practices, on the whole successfully, create strong patterns of economic and social cooperation. Such organizations engender strong cultures. It is the nature of positive affects that reinforce the customs, language, tradition, history, and the networks of moral interdependence and reciprocity observed by Anthony (1994). Whenever a management decision is made which results in a positive affect, the affect can be said to "rationalize" the narrative between decision and outcome. It is, therefore, the nature of positive affect that routinizes (or institutionalizes) even new practices.

The Model II manager

Two issues immediately arise with the Model I scenario of KBAT; both relating to the balance of equilibrium within the mind of the "knower", between the known and the unknown of the organizational object. In the first problematic, a manager may perceive narrative *conflicts* between their own knowledge and that of others. Other organizational members, particularly if recruited from elsewhere, may introduce "stories" about what worked for them previously; new scientific knowledge may suggest that the average is, in fact, now an exception; or "stories of excellence" may hint at the possibility of even greater positive affect: *"90% of the excellent companies we surveyed who did it this way increased their profits; if you do it this way too, you will also increase your profits"*. If managers adopt such "external" perceptions as *a priori* prescriptive knowledge, they risk placing undue weight on them in determining a new average perception. They risk a potential undermining of the predictive power of their extant narrative. History becomes neglected in favour of the promise of the new.

The nature of this first problematic lies, I suggest, in the "causality" of knowledge conversion. The "aesthetic" quality of a certain "external" narrative might, in its own respect, generate a strong affect. The simple "beauty" of a particular narrative as a solution to some problem might trigger strong "feelings" within the mind of a manager. The feeling that the narrative in question is stronger than the extant narrative, might act to skew the manager's predictive ability, causing a revision of his or her narrative with an unvalidated knowledge. The manager, rather than rely on his or her own predictive ability, takes undue account of an external narrative "read" as predictive in its own right. A further, potentially negative, aspect of this first problematic is the question of the manager's agency and the power-politic relationships that exist between the manager and organization. Such relationships can unduly influence the premature prescription of an external narrative. Although such prescription can act as a force for good, clearly it can also be a negative force. It is, I argue, within the notion that any external narrative can be used to influence an extant narrative, that a "belief" in the potential to change organizational cultures arises. If a manager adopts an external narrative as prescriptive, without its mediation with the extant narrative, then there can be no confidence in the manager's predictive power, or indeed in the predictive power of the organizational narrative as a whole.

The second problematic arises where the imbalance between known and unknown is created by levels of increasing ambiguity, owing to the increasing complexities of the organization, its relationships, and the world within which it functions. This growing ambiguity gives rise to the notion of the sublime organization; it can result in unique perceptions (even, potentially, visions) of organizational practice that do not reflect the extant narrative. As Demerath (1993:138) relates:

> Uniqueness is unrelated to the confirmation or contradiction of knowledge. A unique observation can confirm knowledge of previous observations, such as the average of a bimodal distribution, and thus can decrease ambiguity. Alternatively, a unique observation can contradict previous knowledge by being further from the average than previous observations, thus increasing ambiguity. Therefore uniqueness provides the opportunity for knowledge-based affect, but does not determine its valence.

It is in such a manner that the magnitude of change, or of uncertainty, or simply the sense of a great unknown – certainly within the concept of the sublime – may lead to a critical loss of equilibrium in the mind of the knower.[117] I therefore argue that organizations that are subject to great change and uncertainty (internally and/or externally caused) are capable of generating many unique observations (of the senses) that have the potential to contradict the extant narrative and induce high levels of ambiguity through a net negative affect. Faced with such ambiguity, the continuation of certain historically established organizational practices no longer (on the whole) offer the simple prediction of success, and what were previously strong patterns of economic and social cooperation (that is, strong cultures) are undermined. It is, I argue, the nature of negative affects that undermine customs, language, tradition, history, and the networks of moral interdependence and reciprocity.

It is within the concept of the Argyrian Model II manager that the imperative to restore some level of equilibrium within the mind of the manager suggests a necessary and proactive engagement in the production of additional "valid" information. Here Demerath's KBAT also fits the aesthetic agenda. If the application of KBAT as a Model I theory-in-use represents the manager's passive engagement with their organizational environment in a single-loop learning process, then the proactivity of a Model II theory-in-use is congruent with KBAT and double-loop learning. Here the affective consequences of knowledge can motivate the individual to "manipulate" the environment "actively". As Demerath observes, the individual will often manipulate experiences in order to resolve significant ambiguities and to produce positive affect. This "manipulation" is not, however, to be seen in the context of a power-agency relationship – with its possible negative associativity – but in the sense of creative play.[118]

Armstrong's (2000) "Democratic Aesthetic" is grounded in the ceaseless inventiveness of play. Play precludes privileged creation[119] and makes an experimental space for living. Play provides a fruitful possibility for exploration at the boundaries of knowledge. Playful manipulation therefore acts to project knowledge into reality with the implication that individuals build narratives in the course of play, through the experience of positive affect. The narrative knowledge produced by play is, I argue, no different to Kearney's (2002) second branch of narrative. Play is, importantly, fictional – where narrative is developed through a redescription of events in terms of some idealized standard of beauty, goodness or nobility. In its contemporary form, fiction is well referenced by Kearney to the modern *novel*:

> ...[the novel's] extraordinary 'synthetic' power ...draws liberally from such diverse conventions as *lyric* (personal voice), *drama* (presentation of action), *epic* (depiction of heroes or anti-heroes), and *chronicle* (description of empirical detail). But above all, the novel is unique in its audacity in experimenting and evolving, metamorphosing and mutating into an amazingly rich range of narrative possibilities[.]

In a paradigm of management pointillism, the manager who can engage in the production of a fictional narrative concerning their organization – calling on a synthesis of their personal voice, action, (other) characters and empiric detail in experimenting and evolving narrative possibilities – is the Model II manager who can challenge the ontological assumptions that constrain the dissolution of boundaries in the search for positive affect. A Model II requirement for managers to go beyond their effective sub-universe's boundaries, in order to attain new information, provides a *real-time* faculty for the enquiry and testing of information. This now becomes a process by which managers can engage in knowledge production – thereby modifying their "narrative-in-use" and achieving the double-loop learning advanced by Argyris. In the limit that "research time" tends to zero, all that appears required of a "valid" knowledge is a plausible fiction. However, this is problematic: there is a sociological failure to understand and accept a reality that certain organizational representations might merely be fictions – albeit powerful ones – that, as Wolff (1999:500) describes, we do not experience as fictions but as truths. Here, a manager's ability to apply the full range of his or her senses becomes a key limiting factor. The Model II manager, in the *character* of MacIntyre's (1981:107) manager, is, para-doxically, not the hard-headed, pragmatic realist practicing the system-atic perpetuation of misunderstanding. The effective Model II *character* of MacIntyre's manager has a belief in the value of fiction.

Never mind the gap, feel the affect

Let me consider the Management Gap as a fiction,[120] as a *bringing into existence* of an imaginary concept of "the Management Gap" – merely a plausible and provisional perception of an organizational phenomenon. Therefore, managers are merely *perceived* to require further "academic" assistance to help improve the predictivity of their organizational prac-tice, and that current research appears not to meet this requirement. A non-fictional, academic "meaningful" response to this phenomenon is the Mode 1/Mode 2 debate. But, as Demerath (1993) suggests, mean-ingfulness changes when we uniquely perceive objects we already know about. A unique perception revealing an ambiguity of a highly significant meaning will decrease the predictability of much experience and will cause an intense negative affect. Whereas, Demerath contin-ues, when an ambiguity of a highly significant meaning is resolved, much more experience can be explained, and intense positive affect is felt. Meaningfulness, itself, is defined as the individual's conceptual power of understanding over an experience; that is to say, it is the ability of an individual to conceive of an experience using a cog-nitively held set of meanings. Therefore, given my own cognitively held set of meanings concerning the Management Gap, I am able to understand my own experience. As a fiction, the management gap becomes a plausible academic narrative for the failure of certain scientific knowledge in explaining certain experiences of management and organizational practice that I have had as a practicing manager.

Initially, as a practicing manager, I perceive an interest within the academic world concerning the origin of the Management Gap. The suggestion that a different mode of research will assist understanding – and therefore, potentially, lead to better management practice – initially provides a positive affect within my own mind. This affect: A) reinforces my understanding that there are problems with management theory and that it is not a failure of my own understanding, and B) reassures me that progress is being made and that I should continue to maintain an interest in academic research. However, given my own unique perspective as both practicing manager and an academic, I now perceive an ambiguity in the Mode 1/Mode 2 discourse on the Management Gap. Here Watson (2001a) dismisses the Mode 2 concept of a managerially "biased" knowledge that can be used to the advantage of managers as "a nonsense".

As fiction, the Mode 1 and Mode 2 labels merely "sign" fictional boundaries drawn around a specific problem space. The nature of the knowledge that is represented by these signifiers is clearly plausible – as the convention of academic rigour suggests. However, other plausible stories exist. For example, the balance of research funding has, over time, been such that – as government funding reduces and other funding is sourced from commerce – commercial interests are increasingly driving more focused (and shorter) research projects. This prioritization can be seen within the relationship of scientific to narrative knowledge. This perception, a controversion fuelled by the paradox that Mode 2 research is published in Mode 1 language – despite the fact that a Mode 2 project may have successfully solved a "real" problem – now creates an ambiguity in my earlier understanding. The fiction of the Management Gap has now generated a negative affect within my mind that: A) undermines *my* previous understanding through a realization that there are alternative plausible narratives, and that one might be a failure of my own understanding; and B) causes a doubt within my mind that progress in being made; this doubt acts to undermine my interest academic research.

Here I draw a departure from Demerath's (2002) insightful work. Demerath advances KBAT as purely passive; she advocates the necessity for a further *micro*-theory of epistemological culture (ECT) in which knowledge-based affect is framed in manipulation. Demerath argues that we *make* culture in order to see our world as meaningful. Such a theory seeks closure through a conception of knowledge manipulation that, paradoxically, acts to deny the fiction of creative play. My own argument is that we do not *make* culture, but that culture emerges from our collective ability to play creatively. My own premiss is that creative play arises through an individual's desire for positive affect. In my own case, it arises through a desire to counter the negative affect of my (recently undermined) understanding of the Management Gap. While I might seek meaning through playing with ideas about the Management Gap, I certainly do not aspire to *make* culture.

For Demerath's ECT to be of value in reasoning general management and organizational practice, there would need to be a significant, and autonomous, exercise of power in its application. In such a case, the exercise of excessive power would imply that the basis of any consensual meaning would be weak and easily undermined by subversive experience. Whilst it is possible to create a culture under the influence of power, intuitively, the foundations of that culture are unstable and would quickly erode as the power is removed. I argue, therefore, that it is not plausible to lay claim to a (democratic) societal norm in which the creation and maintenance of culture is a prime motivation. I depart from Demerath's ECT in favour of retaining KBAT merely as a meta-extension of SNA's process of social negotiation.

Knowledge through art

I am left with two conceptions of narrative knowledge that are, I believe, essential for understanding management and organizational practice. Firstly, there is the concept of historical narrative knowledge (both NK_n and NK_s), as the basis for what Argyris has termed Model I theories-of-action. The positive affect of the observance of an expected Model I outcome is a strengthened confidence in Model I practice. In this respect, Mode 1 research into management and organizational practice – with a priority on the rigour of its production – has a distinct and valuable service to play in searching for patterns in the universe of management and organization. Such patterns might well represent the potential for new common (sophisticated) narratives based on perceived truths. A Model I manager's expertise is gained through the careful selection, dissemination and control of organizational narratives – their conventions and protocols – within a culturally identifiable boundary. This does not relegate the Model I manager to mere administration, since it is axiomatic that there remain decisions to be made to achieve positive affect and corrective action to be taken under negative affect. It does not denigrate, for example, the existence of formal training such as the MBA. A Model I knowledge-based *affect* also suggests that an autonomous aesthetic agenda might also legitimately influence Model I management and organizational practice. This therefore raises both the importance and the relevance of Mode 1 research into the study of management and organizational aesthetics (for example, Carr and Hancock, 2003 and Linstead and Höpfl, 2000).

Secondly, I argue that the concept of fictional narrative is essential to the growth of NK under conditions of increasing ambiguity and uncertainty. Here complexity, ambiguity and the magnitude of (and scope for) change, creates a sublime environment for management and organization. The search for new narratives of managerial and organizational existence therefore become critical to the reformation of equilibrium between what is currently known (or perceived) and what is required to be known. In this respect, I draw a correlation with Argyris' Model II management. In striving for the positive affect required to restore equilibrium it is, I argue, the prospect of fiction that will enable the manager or organizational practitioner to engage in the production of new narratives through a complex synthesis of their personal voice, action, knowledge of appropriate characters and the observance of empiric detail. I argue that, through fiction, managers and organizational practitioners are enabled to challenge the ontological assumptions that constrain the dissolution of boundaries in the search for positive affect. Here, the negotiated ontological perspective of SNA provides a key concept within a new meta-theory of affect induced narrative.

The expertise of the Model II manager is framed by a requirement to both exhibit and practice Model I expertise – essentially the practice of the craft of a manager – and, in addition, to possess the faculty to produce additional *valid* information; in essence to engage in a mimetic experience. This is for the manager to exercise informed choice and to monitor (in real-time) the effectiveness – that is to say recognize the valence of any affect – of managerial actions, taking corrective action as necessary to reduce negative affect. Here, in using KBAT to describe the mind's capacity to process aesthetic affect, I have argued that *valid* information is that which produces positive affect in relation to its mediation with an extant narrative. I have also argued that the expertise to produce new affects lies in the capacity to engage in play; that is, the creation of fiction. Therefore, my own conception of an Argyrian Model II management theory-in-use is underpinned by a non-autonomous Art aesthetic. Although Model I management invokes a conception of culture that defines and describes its operation – tending (*ceteris paribus*) to a form of cultural stasis – Model II management invokes a conception of culture that will sanction creative play; that is, a conception of a culture that invokes the dissolution of its own boundary in the acquisition of new *affect*.

While Demerath's (1993) KBAT has been instrumental in building my argument so far, it does not however provide an effective mechanism for the synthetic process implied in fictional narrative. Although she expands on KBAT with further discussion of play, games, conversation and other aspects of social psychology, I argue that the true scope of play can better be described by the innovative process that is embedded in art, and particularly through CTA. Here, I argue that a prerequisite to the study of Art's epistemic value lies in Armstrong's (2000) description that *art is saturated in affect.* Through Art – in a transitive, interactive form of disinterested mediation – new possibilities of knowledge emerge. This view requires making explicit the distinction between the production of Art by the artist (*Art-as-Interpretation*) and the interpretation of Art by its audience (*the-interpretation-of-art*). Both, I argue, are valid and necessary within the context of a paradigm of management art (as a communication of meaning); the one describing the potential of a Model II *management art* practice, the other the potential for a Mode 1 research of *management art practice.*[121] The resolution of these two acts of interpretation lies in the process of SNA; this is the communication of meaning – across the organization – as a new organizational narrative of existence.

Management as an artistic process

The conjunctive theory of art addresses the three aspects of mimesis, craft and innovation; *Art-as-interpretation* singles out the "mimetic" component. Here I turn to a closer reading of Kearney (2002), in which I find that the Aristotelian nature of CTA's *mimesis* is also reflected in Kearney's work '*On Stories*'. Mimesis contributes to CTA in the form of a learning process; it provides insight into aspects of a (social) reality and, implicitly, insight into the (sub)universe of management and organization. As Kearney (2002:12–13) would concur, *mimesis*[122] invites both the artist and the audience to engage with a newly imagined way of being-in-the-world. This engagement holds the opportunity of a cathartic experience where, I argue, *catharsis* can be alternatively described as the act of reattainment of an equilibrium-of-mind, between what is known and what is not, through the experience of affect. As Kearney relates:

> [I]t is precisely by... [the mimetic invitation] to see the world *otherwise* that we in turn experience *catharsis*: purgation of the emotions of pity and fear. For while narrative imagination enables us to empathise with those characters in [a] story who act and suffer, it also provides us with a certain aesthetic distance from which to view the events unfolding, thereby discerning "the hidden cause of things". It is this curious conflation of empathy and detachment which produces in us – viewers of Greek tragedy or readers of contemporary fiction – the double vision necessary for a journey beyond the closed ego towards other possibilities of being.

A "socially recognized" process of *Art-as-Interpretation* sanctions (certainly in contemporary western democracies) the artist's capacity to engage with a mimetic experience of the world *otherwise* than what it appears. The artist attempts a representation of that experience within the particular mode of his or her craft skill; be it painting, music, drama, or written narrative and so on. In doing so, in creating new *affective* perceptions of "a" reality, the artist is necessarily playing innovatively with the limits of his or her own extant narrative; mediating between their "space of experience" and a "horizon of expectation". The artist is therefore socially and culturally sanctioned in the production of a fictional narrative concerning their cultural universe. This calls on a synthesis of their personal voice, action, (other) characters and empiric detail in experimenting and evolving innovative, narrative possibilities. The artist is socially and culturally sanctioned to challenge ontological assumptions that constrain the dissolution of cultural boundaries in the search for positive affect and its potentially cathartic effect. The innovation of new (unique) perceptions provides for the possibility of creating new *affects*. This has the potential for causing a cathartic change to the equilibrium within the mind of the artist – between what is known and what is not known by first introducing what *might* be known.

The artist creates the potential to move or modify existing (social) boundaries though the achievement of a similar catharsis within an audience. Through the *manager-artist*, the organization is invited to engage with the world of *otherwise*. However, although *management art* might (potentially) represent a socially and culturally sanctioned "organizational behaviour", the "receiving" mind of an organizational audience (or *organizational individual*) is not necessarily in the same state of mind (that is, equilibrium) concerning their organization world-view, as that of the *manager-artist*. The received affect of the *manager-artist's* representations are neither fixed in valence nor intensity. Here the concept of aesthetic distance becomes important, in which the aesthetic distance of the organization is presented as a mediated resolution of the individual aesthetic distances of its organizational members.[123]

By reference to the boundary that represents the limits of the *individual's* narrative-of-existence, a large aesthetic distance is indicative of a certain immunity from affect. The *individual* who is less aesthetically sensible is, I argue, more immune to the affects caused by changes of narrative beyond their own boundary. Here the *individual* holds a strong belief that their extant narrative will suffice to explain their place-in-the-world. Therefore, when the *organizational individual* is invited to interpret the "new" narrative of the *manager-artist*, the level and valence of affect(s) experienced may not result in the mediation of the extant *organizational narrative* to the extent anticipated. This is particularly so if either or both *individual* and *organization* are given of a large aesthetic distance. The *manager-artist* practices management art as a process of the interpretation of his or her own perception of an organizational reality, while the organization and its individual members (as audience) are engaged in the interpretation of management art as a representation of an other's (the manager's) reality. The resolution of the two aspects of *management-art-as-interpretation*, and the *interpretation-of-management-art*, is therefore a key sociological process in the restoration of equilibrium and the social mediation of new organizational narratives.

An individual's strength of belief in their own narratives acts to position their "plane-of-reality" beyond the conceptual limit of their aesthetic distance. Thus, aesthetically, an individual does not "feel" the affect of what experiences or perceptions might lie outwith their extant "reality". My conception of the manager who is constrained by a Model I practice, is one who possesses a large aesthetic distance and therefore a strong belief in the ability of extant narratives as sufficient to explain the "reality" of their organization and its practice. There is an equilibrium within the Model I mind, between what is known and what is not; the plane-of-reality of the Model I's mind lies outside its aesthetic sensibility. To the Model I manager, all the positive affect required to be "felt", as any necessary counter to negative experience, can be found within the boundaries of their extant narrative. What is not known – what remains the "absent other" – remains beyond a Model I perception and is thus not "affective".[124]

Managers (or *organizational individuals*) who question their narrative beliefs, experience a repositioning of their "plane-of-reality" (the boundary of their narrative) to within their aesthetic distance. This exposes the limits of their aesthetic sensibility to the possibilities of the "absent other" and its "affect". But, the *individual* who questions their own narratives (or has circumstance question them) without a capacity to assimilate new "affects" might be said to experience a "crisis of confidence" in their ability to position their place-in-the-world. A manager who experiences some organizational phenomenon that causes them to question their narrative's predictivity can experience an erosion of confidence in their "managerial ability". Such an experience is, in effect, an introduction of the unknown within their plane of reality causing a loss of equilibrium in the mind. Here, I have already argued that, in order that the unknown becomes quickly assimilated, there is a need to acquire and validate additional information concerning it – mediating that information with extant knowledge to produce a new narrative. This may require the acquisition, validation and mediation of information from many sources. I therefore argue that a manager with a strong aesthetic sensibility (characterized by a small aesthetic distance) is better able to conceptually approach the unknown with a greater awareness of the possibilities it might represent.

A manager with a strong aesthetic sensibility – that is, a small aesthetic distance – is one who engages in an organizational practice that utilizes his or her extant craft skills (for example, Model I theories-in-use), but who also engages in the mimetic activity of learning about the "unknown" that is now a perceived "present other". This now "present other" becomes a new aspect of an existing reality, and the manager becomes engaged in an innovative process of *affect* generation. Such a manager's objective is (either consciously or subconsciously) towards reestablishing an equilibrium of mind, and in producing a new/revised (even if provisional) narrative. I argue, therefore, that with the essential elements of established craft skills, mimetic experience, and innovation, such a manager is engaged in my conception of an Argyrian Model II practice of management as an artistic process – the *manager-artist* practicing a Model II CTA-in-use.[125]

The sociology of management art

The process of the acceptance of knowledge into an organizational narrative, as opposed to its mediation within an individual's own narrative, is a reflection of the "social acceptance" that is a necessary feature of CTA/SNA. While the individual *manager-artist* may or may not exercise a controlling influence over the organizational audience, their work should, nevertheless, be a catalyst to that audience's adoption of a new/revised narrative; one that represents a new shared "reality". Here there is a paradoxical relationship existing between, on the one hand the "ability" and "potential" of the *manager-artist* to be creative, and on the other hand, the exercise of (playful) creativity in the inherently (but not specifically intentionally) conformist-structures presented by organizations. Here, creative play behaviour requires a level of cultural sanctioning for an effective contribution in a social context.[126] As I have argued, the aesthetic gap – in essence the differential between the aesthetic distance of the *manager-artist* and aesthetic distance the organization itself – is a measure of the organization's ability to interpret the work of the *manager-artist* as a relevant contribution to the organization's unfolding narrative. A *manager-artist* who demonstrates an ability to produce net-positive consequential affects within the organization, through a Model II CTA-in-use, is more likely to be effective in overcoming a significant aesthetic gap. The effective *manager-artist* exhibits a capability to shift organizational perceptions. At the extremes, the *almost-Machiavellian* (sanctioned Model II creative play behaviour is likely to be acceptable where positive affects are the outcome of organizational practice. Conversely, non-sanctioned negative affects are likely to receive extreme levels of organizational non-acceptance. Between these two extremes exists a rich variety of managerial performance possibilities.

Becker (1974) referred to art's social character by positing the concept that art is a form of collective action. This is congruent with CTA, where a sociological analysis of any artform implies a division of labour: artist, audience, and so on. Becker argues, however, that in no case does any artform impose a natural division of labour. Within art, any division of labour is held to be a result of a consensual definition of the situation. Some activities, that is to say the generation of new affects, are the province of the artist. However, where the affects that can be produced become commonplace, capable of being produced on demand by other non-artists, the status of the artist may be lost and the techniques of (affect) production become reclassified as additional craft skills.

The conception of *Art-as-Collective-Action* is, I argue, a useful one in the socio-cultural study of management and organization. I might therefore conceive of artistic activities that include: the conception of the "idea" for a management artwork; the making of necessary physical artefacts – in Heideggerian terms, adding form to the matter of the "idea"; the creation of (new) conventions for the communication of affect; the selection and training of "artistically inclined" personnel and audiences to use/appreciate the conventions of communication; and the understanding of the cause/affect relationship in the creation and experience of management artworks.[127] Here a norm of artistic production might well be for the organization, as patron, to sanction the *manager-artist* in the (commissioned) production of a *management artwork* as an interpretation of some (new) aspect of the organization, or its *place-in-the-world*. In this way a new equilibrium is sought in the face of some perceived ambiguity or complexity arising from the unknown. What is then taken, by this organization, to be the quintessential *artistic act*, marking the individual as *manager-artist,* becomes a matter of consensual definition.

If I now consider the range of differing arts, it is axiomatic that – as Becker (1974:771) argues – '*...the possibility of artistic experience arises from the existence of a body of conventions that artists and audiences can refer to in making sense of the work.*' In *Modern Painters*, Ruskin wrote of many conventions for the representation of nature in art – therefore explaining many of the necessary aspects of the communication of affect being employed, at that time, by Turner. As Becker continues:

> Though standardized, conventions are seldom rigid and unchanging. They do not specify an inviolate set of rules everyone must refer to in settling questions of what to do. Even where the directions seem quite specific, they leave much unsettled which gets resolved by reference to customary modes of interpretation on the one hand and by [social] negotiation on the other.

Therefore, in the manner of Ruskin, I argue that the – at least provisional – conventions of a *management art* are those conventions of the "craft" of management. In this respect, the conventions that are to govern a *management art* are synonymous with the craft skills in which lie all those techniques and skills that might be associated with the *five classical functions* of managerial work (after Fayol), including the multitude of their derivations; in short, the accepted limits of Model I management theories-in-use.

I can now illuminate Model II CTA-in-use as a *management art* in diagrammatic form. Figure 9.1 provides that the shaded circle is representative of the "unknown" or "absent other" of the management/ organizational universe. The unshaded portion of the diagram therefore represents what is currently known or knowable. Thus the Craft object "C" is represented by a "convention" of management practice; a

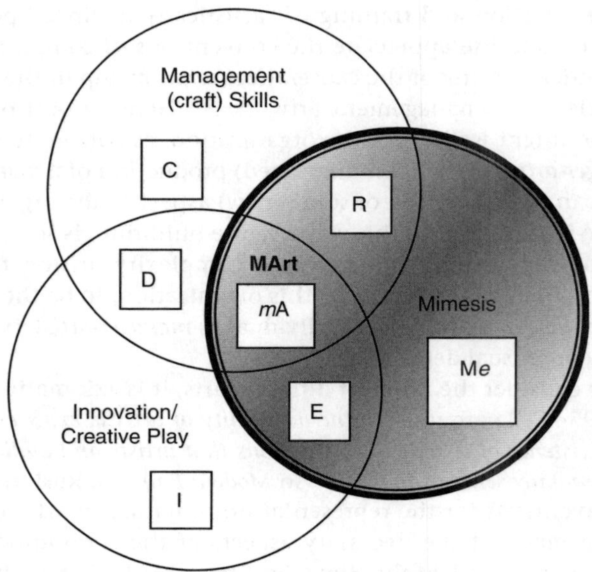

Figure 9.1   Conjunctive Theory of Management Art

design "D" is an adaptation or variation or new instantiation of a management convention that might or might not be then employed in the context of a mimetic experience. The idea "I" is that which is purely new, arising solely from the activity of creative play and the experiment "E" is the application of an idea to the process of mimesis, revealing an aspect of the unknown.

There is a sense in which the mimetic disclosure of an aspect of the unknown, through the application of mere ideas (experimentation), is accidental. The mimetic experience "M*e*" is that which exists in the "unknown" with the potential for affect, and the representation "R" is what is capable of being perceived of the "unknown" by virtue of existing management conventions. While the "object" of the management art process – that is, a *management artwork* – is a conjunction of the three aspects introduced, it may also be seen as the potential outcomes of an innovative representation, a mimetic design or a crafted experiment.

"Heidegger's Shoes"

The efficacy of Heidegger's existential interpretation of the origin of art has been the subject of much commentary. A firm critique is posited by Schapiro (1968) who's factual consideration of Van Gogh's painting *Old shoes* sought to establish, *inter alia*, that Van Gogh's painting was no more than a painting of his own (Van Gogh's) shoes – thus seemingly undermining the basis of Heidegger's narrative. As Stern argues, Heidegger's "off-the-wall" interpretation is merely a projection of what Heidegger saw: a projection of his own views that cannot be seen by others; merely a perceptual property of Van Gogh's painting. An "off-the-wall" interpretation is not within Schapiro's range of "acceptable" interpretations. But, argues Schwabsky (1997), what Schapiro disdains is Heidegger's apparent disrespect for the *Artwork* itself. Certainly, once engaged with a work of art, a "disinterested" interpretation is one that might well, as Heidegger's appears to, present that which is not material to the work; rather such an interpretation arises because of the work.

As Heidegger (1935) argued, '*What art is should be inferable from the work.*' But, Schapiro's assertion that Van Gogh's painting is not of a peasant woman's shoes is a plausible narrative in its own right and, as Schwabsky argues, if we accept this plausibility, Heidegger's narrative is a "fantasia" – apparently owing little to Van Gogh's picture. Yet Heidegger's narrative does not exist in isolation of the picture. The *Artwork* is the essence of the fiction; the fiction itself the essence of a plausible (provisional) truth. Here the conventions of art extend to the conventions of its critique also and, as Becker (1974:772) rightly observes:

> Conventions place strong constraints on the artist. They are particularly constraining because they do not exist in isolation, but come in complexly interdependent systems, so that making one small change often requires making changes in a variety of other activities. A system of conventions gets embodied in equipment, materials, training, available facilities and sites, systems of notation and the like[.]

In the face of strong organizational cultures – that is, where strong patterns of economic and social cooperation have arisen through increased experience of positive affect – the customs, language, tradition, history, and the networks of moral interdependence and reciprocity, instill (Model I) "craft" conventions of management and organizational practice. These conventions appear stable and difficult to change. As with the skills and conventions of painting – for example, the theory of colour and the techniques of shading – all these management conventions can be taught and/or developed as craft skills. But to train in the skills and conventions of painting may only serve to make a person competent in an ability to articulate faithful representations of an extant reality. Craft skills alone do not confer on an individual an ability to represent what is not known. The analogy would be for such a painter to be considered merely a Model I painter.

An ability to interpret a "work" of an artist is undermined where the artist, here the Model II painter, introduces innovative techniques to achieve their interpretation of reality or, equally, where the Model I painter's interpretation of the work induces some other affect. In both senses of management art: *Art-as-Interpretation* and *interpretation-of-art*, the essential element becomes one of interpretation within a socially constrained convention of accepted management skills, where the *manager-artist*, although free to innovate with skills and techniques, can only do so at the risk that his or her work might be misinterpreted through the presence of (or a widening of) the aesthetic gap. Here, the *manager-artist* exercises a (sanctioned) freedom of choice in the process of *management art*. She or he decides the value judgements of what to produce, what to name the productions, and what the relationship(s) between herself/himself, the named artwork and the organizational audience will be. The *manager-artist* therefore has the same responsibility as the *Fine Art* artist to maintain (or provide or have provided) a credible bond between their work and their lived-world. A sanctioned management-art freedom is freedom with a responsibility (albeit limited and even ill-defined). The *manager-artist* therefore exercises freedom in using, adapting, developing or even breaking the conventions of their craft – as by definition they must do through innovation – in the realization of an *a posteriori* representation of their perception(s) of reality. However, this freedom is seemingly bound by the *a priori* conditions established as the currently accepted conventions of management's craft.

If a *manager-artist's* responsibility is disregarded, then any subsequent interpretation will lead to a greater risk of misinterpretation and of unexpected affect. However, neither can the *manager-artist* impose on the organizational audience a correct interpretation. Any socially acceptable interpretation arises through a process of negotiated alternatives – risking, as it must, the possibility that there will always exist other plausible interpretations. Therefore, an object of the process of art that (*in extremis*) breaks totally from the traditions and conventions of its craft roots, is born solely out of an idea – it is an experiment. Arguably, in such an extreme, pure fiction is indeed fantasy and the issue becomes one of identifying whether or not the "idea" might have a basis for consideration through some new convention of management practice. Here, a critical examination of the basis of the idea, in relation to the fiction it offers as a truth, can only be based, *a posteriori,* on the fiction's net organizational affect.

If I am left with interpretation at the root of all that art is (and what it can be) then plausible fiction – the creation of that which is not yet real – becomes the origin of a provisional knowledge to be offered in candidacy for a socio-culturally accepted narrative. This is by virtue of a process of SNA (within an artworld or an organization). I recall, here, the discussion of the first paperweight given in Chapter 7. I argue, therefore, that the essence of fiction lies within its value as a plausible candidate for a negotiated narrative knowledge. As a fiction, any interpretation should be devoid of preconception. As Heidegger (1935) argued:

> What matters is a first opening of our vision to the fact that what is workly in the work [of art], equipmental in equipment, and thingly in the thing comes closer to us only when we think the Being of beings. To this end it is necessary beforehand that the barriers of our preconceptions fall away and that pseudo concepts be set aside.

In reference to Van Gogh's shoes, Heidegger argues that the *Artwork* Van Gogh's *Old Shoes With Laces* lets us know what shoes are in truth (our preconceived notion of the truth of shoes); that is to say it lets us know what is equipmental in equipment. As Heidegger continues:

> The equipment quality of equipment was discovered. But how? Not by a description and explanation of a pair of shoes actually present; not by a report about the process of making shoes; and also not by the observation of the actual use of shoes occurring here and there; but only by bringing ourselves before Van Gogh's painting. This painting spoke. In the vicinity of the work we were suddenly somewhere else than we usually tend to be.

Following accepted conventions of painting, Heidegger recognizes the shoes for what they are: merely equipment. However, his narrative interpretation speaks to a truth that is not visible through convention. By first engaging with the positive affect that is the "attractive beauty" of the painting – that is to say its particularly well executed (by convention) representation of the truth of what shoes are – Heidegger is caused to engage (disinterestedly) with the painting. The (provisional) "truth" of the equipmentality of the shoes falls away to place Heidegger in an *other-place*. The interpretation of the shoes becomes Heidegger's: *"Heidegger's Shoes"*. The collective action of both Van Gogh and Heidegger present the start of a process of social negotiation (SNA) that mediates a plausible narrative of an aspect of our world. In this world we learn something – a provisional truth – about a peasant woman. This interpretation requires neither the "truth" that the Van Gogh's shoes were, in fact, an accurate depiction of real shoes, nor that the shoes were, in fact, those of an actual peasant woman. It merely requires a *social acceptance* that the mediated narrative is plausible in respect of present conventions and that it contributes to an affective positioning of *being-in-the-world*. Therefore, grounding my argument for an art of management in a universal relevance of Heidegger's philosophy of art depends upon a wider understanding of *the world*. As Singh (1990) describes, this world cannot be defined easily, and in the same way that entities are usually defined. The world's nature can only be spoken about as a result of an ontological inquiry.

This inquiry requires a removal of the distortion of current metaphysical thinking. Paraphrasing Singh's reflection on Heidegger's *Being and Time,* the world of management and organization is neither a collection of entities nor an abstraction pertaining to the totality of all "given" entities. If I am to follow convention then I might suggest that the world of management and organization is an "ever-present, non-objective, reality" to which the manager is always subjected. Within this reality, *art*, as a paradigm amongst paradigms merely provides one "means" of synthetic thinking about it, and in which *art* "works" to form its perceptive "ends".

Coming full circle, an artistically grounded inquiry requires methods of investigation that precede ontology itself – here an Art-aesthetic paradigm provides one valid and, I argue, efficacious method. It posits an overall concept of *management art* as a paradigm allowing the extensive redescription of some extant reality of management and organization. That the concept itself is a *fiction* – there being no *a priori* justification for it – does not invalidate the provisional truths concerning management and organization that it is able to disclose. The study of CTA/SNA, and its Art aesthetic of the sublime and attractive beauty, as an epistemic process of fiction production takes form as a valid concept in reconceptualizing management and organization.

10
Into the Far Field

For this is the preoccupation of the artist, to resolve all known abstraction to a particular distance which will, in turn, serve to reinforce the generalization.

Mark Rothko 1940/1941

Beyond simply thinking an art of management

In asking you, the reader, to metaphorically Step into "Heidegger's Shoes" I am suggesting that the provisional "truth" of the equipmentality of this text be allowed to fall away to reveal an *other-place*. The interpretation of the text becomes yours. The collective action of both I, as author, and you, as reader, merely presents the start of a process of social negotiation. This negotiation acts to mediate a plausible narrative within our *shared* world – that of the potentiality, within this world, of considering the *manager-artist*. The task of this book is therefore to facilitate your potential *presence* within a world in which both the study and practice of organizational management can be informed by the basic social process that is *art*. In this respect, this text constitutes a philosophically informed exploration into the question of what, if anything, this world of management and organization can learn from the world of art. In initiating a negotiation with you, this book merely advances a central Art-aesthetic, paradigmatic thesis in which I argue that – given the general and growing uncertainties and constraints inherent in running a business in a "real" world – management might, under certain circumstances, be both legitimately and beneficially practiced as an artform.

In order that insights from this paradigmatic thesis may become of value beyond simply thinking about an Art of Management, there should be some real promise of this paradigm's potential to contribute to an academic research agenda. However, there are many paradigms for innovative research, what is there to be gained from this one? Yet, the mere existence of the so-called Management Gap suggests that extant research paradigms – certainly at the boundaries of current knowledge – fail to view the potentiality of "practice" (management or otherwise) as an epistemic activity in its own right. I argue that both researchers and practitioners alike, within the fields of both management and organization, will benefit from engaging with a theorizing of practice that can lead to a more informed instruction of future practitioners. Such a theorizing should not only addresses the essential core "craft" skills – such as those regularly imparted to students who are subject to the dominant "western-capitalist" MBA curricula of business schools – but should also encourage, within management practitioners, the identification and cultivation of an aptitude to constructively apply all the sensory faculties in meeting their socially conferred responsibility as managers. My argument, here, is that if researchers are not prepared to adopt some existential theorizing, then it is likely that their research output will continue merely to fuel Model I management practice and, given management's malaise – where a Model II practice is seemingly required – managers will continue to reach for popular texts in search of the naïve narratives of the apparently successful "others".

In the opening of my introduction I expressed the idea that, if for no other reason than some managers appear to be able to manage well, without being exposed to formal management training, there must be a non-formal, but nevertheless "instrumental" knowledge that contributes to managerial success. I might say that such knowledge is borne out of the seemingly irrational. Certainly, while "instrumental" in terms of a contribution to success, this is not to say – in the sense given by the "instrumentality" of an autonomous theoretical knowledge – that such non-formal knowledge bends to that of rational, enlightened thought. The *Enlightenment* of a management science indeed appears to be the root of an "evil" that suggests autonomous thought can rationalize the socio-cultural phenomenon that is often a perception of an irrational management and organizational practice. I have argued that this is particularly so in the seemingly irrational context of a complex, ambiguous situation.

Management, I have argued, is not solely a science; neither is management solely a craft nor is it solely an artform. Management, properly considered in the whole, and under the paradigm I have described, involves a full range of activities. Some of these activities may indeed be scientific – taught and practiced as an exercise of an acknowledged craft skill(s) – and yet other management activities can appear worthy of considering as "artistic". Ultimately, the responsibility of the manager, to the socio-cultural grouping that gave accord to that role, is to facilitate – as that socio-cultural group's agent – a "means" to achieve a given "end". This responsibility is exasperated by a reality of practice that is increasingly irrational; the more irrational the real appears, the more the socio-cultural grouping expects of its managers. As social agents, managers remain responsible for achieving the desired "ends". Yet paradoxically, managers are increasingly prepared solely with a means that is derived empirically from a study of a bounded rationality and are thus ill-prepared for what appears, in reality, to be characteristically irrational.

I have argued, and recalled above, that Management itself cannot be an autonomous activity – the idea of management is wholly reliant on a socially and culturally sensitive acceptance of a particular worldly context that calls for the character of a manager. It is, however, abundantly clear that those who have come to be known and accepted as managers, in general, do a great many things. This gives rise to many aspects of management that can, indeed, be traced through the writings of a great many scholars from Ancient Chinese history to Fordist America, and beyond, to contemporary postmodernistic views. Yet, there is one vital ingredient missing. If we were to start with conceptualizing the first manager, a fictional concept – for, at the time of its conception, no one person knew what it was to be a manager – where might we have started? Who cast the first paperweight? How do we think beyond where we might, at any point, be?

The hope of an invisible college

Art, I argue, provides one efficacious means for thinking beyond our present position; Art facilitates our presence within a reality beyond. However, if we are to study and act beyond merely thinking an Art of Management, where shall we best position ourselves? In what research agenda is an Art of Management best aligned? It is within this context that I have set this present text within the field of *Critical Management Studies (CMS)*. Here I propose the Art-aesthetic paradigm of CTA/SNA as a potential candidate for framing what some might consider is a requirement for a new CMS agenda. As Grey (2005:17) has argued, the contemporary CMS agenda is, essentially, a political phenomenon: it is a left-wing movement nestled within the right-wing institution of "the business school". This right-wing institution is characterized, *inter alia*, by a goal of enhancing a firm's profit-making performativity. This is a goal that Zald (2002:379) has observed as been morally suspect in many intellectual discourses. We therefore see that, as Clegg, *et al* (2006:8) also argue, the performative realism of the non-CMS right, opposed by the social ideology of the CMS left, represents a fertile ground for the theoretical and cultural dichotomizing of a "for" and "against" management. As Clegg, *et al,* continue, this ideological root acts to separate CMS from other forms of critique, on the basis of the taken-for-granted assumptions that:

> …managerial domination is abundant, that employees suffer from this domination, and that CMS researchers are needed to reveal this domination and devise strategies to undo it, since the employees are unable to do so by themselves.

The dominant[128] CMS narrative positions itself as the critical "other" to those that practice a non-CMS, performative, management theorizing. However, in summarizing an extant position on CMS, Grey (2005:3) also notes that:

> …CMS [invokes] two related but slightly different propositions. One is a critique of management. The other is a critique of the study of management. …[T]hese are linked, for if the critique of the study of management is successful then a new form of studying management emerges – one which engages in the critique of management.

This present work is, *de facto*, an engagement with the later sense of CMS, in which I argue that a paradigm of *management art* is potentially a valuable contribution to the critique of management and organizational study – specifically for the benefit of its practice. Here, as Pfeffer (1993:602–603) has argued, a key leverage to such study is offered through the concept of *paradigm development*.[129] In a field where there is significant consensus across its researchers, concerning the technological certainty of knowledge production, the field is held to be highly paradigmatically developed. However, Pfeffer argues that the study of organizations is not well developed, and, as a consequence, it is characterized by both a deficit and dispersion of research talent and resource. The suggestion is that, in order to redress this apparent deficit to the advantage of an increased organizational knowledge (at least as it was seen in the 90's), it is necessary to reach what Pfeffer has argued is a "vital" paradigmatic consensus. But, citing Marsden (1993), Pfeffer (1993:617) also suggested that:

> Paradigmatic [development]... depends on the outcome of political conflicts between the custodians and opponents of a paradigm. Resistance to change is the norm; breakthroughs typically occur when the hegemony of the "invisible college" is broken.

Marsden's own suggestion was, however, that resistance to consensus is a necessary part of knowledge development; but Pfeffer rationalizes this conflict with his own thinking through advancing the premiss that the "invisible college" of (management and) organization is not representative of a paradigmatic consensus. Pfeffer's "invisible college" is representative of those who foster theoretical dissent. If this is the case, from where might this "invisible college" of dissent have originated, and of what importance to a paradigm of *management art* is it?

Management and organizational studies is an eclectic activity – as eclectic as its practice. Here, I have outlined that the "cultural turn" in studies saw an increased importation of a leftist agenda. Certainly from the 1980's, the formation and growth of business schools within the UK was driven, in part, by recruitment from the junior faculty of the social sciences. As Grey (2005:7) notes, this growth brought with it '...*a collection of people, trained to be hostile to positivism, trained in critical traditions in social science, and often radicalized by the class, feminist and ecological politics of the 1980s.*'.[130] The very nature of the importation of this agenda acted to create a multi-paradigmatic field of study that, rather than being detrimental to the advancement of knowledge, has considerably enhanced its scope. Following the form of Marsden's argument, I argue that it was the social agenda of this cultural turn in management thought that created a breakthrough in organizational understanding through the gradual but unrelenting dismantling of the hegemony of an instrumental rationalism. But this has not been without cost.

The down-side of a multi-paradigmatic field is analogous to Lyotard's postmodern condition. Here, social theorists seeking social "truths" within the narratives of organizational and management practice – through whatever paradigm might be argued as relevant to their needs – have created a vast body of contextually related SK. But, a surfeit of SK serves to undermine management and organizational practice through its systematic deconstruction of prescriptivity. The extent of our knowledge, today in the first decade of the 21st century, really does suggest to us – as Adler (2006) so aptly observes – that we can do anything. Yet our postmodern crisis is that we know not what to do. While Adler's "hope of humanity" wrestles with "mere prediction", her Artist's conflation with business practices may appear a noble, but too simplistic a notion in the echo of *Cézanne's Doubt*. What, then, of such hope – at least in the academic sense? While some renewed consensus might appear to be beneficial, any desire for a purge of low-consensus paradigmatic fields – in seeking enhanced resource allocation, power and prestige for a few high-consensus fields – amounts to what Van Maanen (1995) has referred to as a "Stalinist" agenda. Additionally, a politics of the social left becomes centred on challenging the dominant authorities and the distribution of power, status and material claims surrounding the organization and its management. However, set against any socially informed desire for consensus, with its tendency to be critical of the achievement of the profit making goal, is the mainstream rationale for business schools. Here, particularly in the UK, funding for business school research agendas is necessarily, and increasingly, being sought from the very sources it seeks to support with its teachings of SK. Therefore, although providing new and valuable insights beyond the scope of rationalistic managerialism and organizational practice, an overtly critical CMS agenda can act to marginalize its own prospects.

In considering the Management Gap that informs this work, I have highlighted the lament of some academics over their perceptions of the failure of much SK to influence practice. This lament might be interpreted as a less overt call for consensus in enhancing management and organization research talent and resource. Here, as Zald (2002:375) notes, in a social theorizing of management and organizations, the tendency is to measure the firm. Such theorizing is therefore more likely to deal with the internal structure of the firm and its policies, than it is to focus upon the problematics of organizational performance in the political economy at large. Paradoxically then, rather than the *Realpolitik* of a business school's capitalism being faced with combating "Stalinist desires" for anti-management research power and prestige, if an "appropriate" call for paradigmatic consensus merely implicitly tends, in any event, towards the social, there is the potential danger of a further marginalization of research activities – away from management's concern – and the risk of a future reduction in resources in the business school environment. Is academe's lament over the Management Gap simply the frustrated voice of an "invisible college" of socialism? As Zald (2002:380) observes:

Those who explicitly challenge the central institutions of capitalism or the perquisites of management will have a tougher time [with their scholarship and teachings] than those whose work does not directly challenge [the] central practices [of management].

One might observe that a focus on the "rights of the individual" lies at the root of contemporary leftist thinking (as opposed to an origin in, say, Marxism). A left-critical focus on managerialism and organizational study, in the context of the power/politic structures and the abuse of the individual worker's relationship with the firm – witnessed in contemporary views on gender and racial segregation, and of equality in the work-force – challenges the profit motive of capitalism. Yet, as Zald (2002:380) confirms, capitalism's contribution as a system has largely triumphed, and its contribution to both economic welfare and freedom is justified.

In the maturity of the cultural turn, rationalistic management thinking appears to have hijacked at least some of the left's social agenda. The remaining left, perhaps in a protest movement, now appears to have rallied its troops: a call to arms to protect its ideology. The growth of CMS can be rationalized out of the "retained other" of the original social agenda. As Clegg *et al* (2006) have noted, the dominant voices within CMS devote their interests to a continued dismantling of the power that management exercises over their employees and stakeholders. The potential "hope" for a revised CMS agenda becomes the potential to direct understanding towards the issues faced by management in its relationship to its wider society. As Zald (2002: 380) contributes:

[w]hen the issues facing management have to do with the responsibility of management and the corporation to society and the community [and not the individual – a return to a Marxist ideology perhaps], CMS may be seen as a more useful part of the dialogue [of scholarship].

My argument here is that the potential value of the CMS project moves beyond any mere rationalization of an Argyrian Model I/Model II (or Gibbons *et al*'s Mode 1/Mode 2) debate as instrumental in determining the relevance of knowledge to practice. My argument, however, calls for a new paradigm of NK construction in order to be able to rationalize a surfeit of SK, as required by increasing conditions of complexity and ambiguity. This calls to the enlightened rejoining of the Enlightenment's autonomous spheres of thought – it posits a value to the Art-aesthetic paradigm of CTA/SNA. But, it is not enough to "hope"; hope is not a strategy, it is merely an emotional belief in a positive outcome.

The question of (management) art's value

The nature of a gap in understanding between management and organizational study and its practice, arises in the perceived inability of the two worlds of academe and practice to share a common understanding of the "use value" of a base of SK. That is to say the gap arises where there is little common understanding of the value of SK as part of a sophisticated narrative of practice (NK_S). Here it can be rationalized that much of a social research agenda, critical of certain management practices, can create, within academe, frustration at its lack of adoption by practitioners.

I have argued that, under rationalism, the limits of an *a priori* (therefore finite) knowledge base are reached under excessively complex and ambiguous situations – where an immediate correlation between, on the one hand an "abstraction" of reality and on the other, an "unknown" or "incomprehensible" reality, is not easily reached. Here, I have suggested, management and organizational practice is no longer an operationalization of narrative (either naïve or sophisticated) but it becomes an epistemic activity in its own right, in which new knowledge must be formed as part of the practice itself. Knowledge under such conditions becomes emergent, *a posteriori*, where much of the complexity and ambiguity of management and organizational practice lies in Zald's (2002) problematic of organizational performance in the political economy at large. However, despite the rational notion of pragmatism, where working knowledge is also developed *a posteriori* through experience, I have argued that a desired Model I theory-in-use is hindered by pragmatism's failure to necessarily admit existing SK. As I have described, in the manner of Mode 2 research, with little apparent practical call for the rigour of scientific knowledge, academic study is merely seen to resort to the direct, or consultative, production of NK_S. Here the only academic potential becomes a secondary language translation from NK_S to SK, in order to preserve academic capital. A study of management and organization, informed merely by a rational pragmatism, tends to a catalogue of history with, arguably, little to satisfy any requirement for prescriptivity or for academic rigour.

In the absence of any generally accepted conception of a managerial artform, my departure from the rationalistic views of organizations and their management was a perception of their collective inadequacy in dealing with conditions of complexity and ambiguity. In this respect I have argued that, hitherto, the concept of "art" has been related – as an avoidance strategy – merely to the "idea" that management is more like an art than a science, in justifying that there are effective managers and effective organizations operating in complex and ambiguous situations, for which no generalized, prescriptive, insight can be found. However, within this text, following the form of art defined by CTA and its non-foundational philosophy of SNA, an *art of management* provides for a practice that, indeed, tends towards an epistemic function of (plausible) knowledge development. In this respect, the arguments I have presented have allowed me to confirm the value of the concept of an *Art of Management* through a discussion of the emergent thematic insights from Degot's (1987) *Portrait of the Manager as an Artist*. The emergent themes of historicity, creativity, management (art) works, management-art's philosophy, and management-art's audience, provide the value proposition to CTA/SNA, through their potential to make more explicit the aesthetic, power and politic relationships with which management and organizational practice are inextricably bound – both to each other and to the *social-environment-at-large*.

In terms of an underlying philosophy of CTA/SNA, I argue that the concern of any theorizing or practice of management as an artform is likely to lead to a greater potential for a manager being better able to resolve ambiguity and complexity within management situations, and to manage to successful outcomes. The manager, in the manner of an *explorer*, is required – under such circumstances – to employ a full range of faculties and craft skills in mapping *a* path on a journey through management life as the means to achieve closure on various ends. Although only a theoretical position at this stage, CTA/SNA at least gives the potential to address the managerial paradox of achieving closure in the face of ambiguity and complexity through an imperative to consider potentially competing views of both an *intra-* and *extra-*organizational reality. This suggests a paradigmatic shift from rationalism towards an artistic paradigm of image interpretation. A paradigm of management art facilitates an understanding of the study of fiction production as the basis for new narrative knowledge. Here, the appropriateness of the concept of an art of management, as defined by CTA/SNA, lies in its paradigmatic "value", in which the study of (perhaps fictional) managerial and organizational perceptions of reality can be further explored.

In following Singh (1990), I suggested that the world of management and organization is an "ever-present, non-objective, reality" to which the manager is always subjected, and that within this "reality", a paradigm of managerial art provides just one "means" of synthetic thinking. Art, in this respect, allows the question of aesthetics to surface within the formation of perception. New narratives of practice emerge though a negotiated synthesis of action and the playful conflict of fiction in overcoming the ambiguity in a perceived reality. But these narratives of practice, based in the negotiated action and play of individuals who are inherently diverse, are only ever "local". They align with Costea's (2000:24) argument that practice itself is irreducibly local. This is a conclusion also supported by Strati (2005:920) who suggests that:

> ...aesthetics highlights the ongoing negotiation that take place among the multiple and diverse *personal knowledges* that pervade organizational life and "give form" to an organization's distinctive skills. Similar to logical and intellectual understanding, aesthetic forms of knowing, constructing – and even destroying – organizational life, undergo social and collective negotiation.

In reflecting on Heidegger's comments on Van Gogh's painting *Old Shoes with Laces* I have observed that an artistically grounded inquiry requires methods of investigation that precede ontology; in which a conception of *management art* as a paradigm allows the extensive (and creative) redescription of some extant reality of management and organization. Therefore, in suggesting a new paradigm of management art, I also offer a heuristic analogy from the field of Fine Art. In *Impressionistic* terms, I have envisaged a paradigm of *management and organizational pointillism*. This is one that offers the ability to construct and infer new meanings from fragmented, objective and aesthetic knowledge; it offers an ability to infer new narratives through visualizing connectedness in complex structures. The *management-artist's* exercise of aesthetic judgement, in realizing a pointillistic *mimetic* representation of managerial reality, appeals to Polany's observation of where the focus of analysis shifts from a dynamic of explanation to a dynamic of tacit knowledge.

In addressing this book problematic, my conclusion of the value gained from learning about cognition from the role of the Artist and Spectator, and the artistic process, provides a significant contribution to the question of whether or not the concept of an art of management has a role to play in reconceptualizing both the study and practice of management and organization. This "value" in the concept of an art of management is, in no small part, built on the foundation of Degot's early work. In arguing a "value proposition" for the concept of managerial art, there is, then, a promise that the invocation of the word "art" need no longer be an avoidance strategy: one used to signify that which cannot properly be understood. A paradigm of management art – within which the perception forming faculties of certain effective managers and effective organizations might be studied – provides a new means for studying that which previous prescriptive theorizing held little potential to offer substantive insight about. It provides a paradigm within which lies the potential to create, and to call upon the disciplines of (management) art history, and (management) art criticism.

In general terms, as an interpretivist paradigm of narrative construction, CTA/SNA advances the notion of fiction production as essential part of the managerial process. Such a constructivist paradigm appears as an antithesis of the postmodern condition. However, crucial to positioning this paradigm as a contribution to the CMS research agenda, is the fact that CTA/SNA also advances, and makes explicit, other concepts (such as power and politics) that are fundamental to the CMS project. Therefore, while CTA/SNA admits to the potential for power and politics to be either subversive or corruptive, as a constructivist paradigm of interpretation it also explicates how (through the notion of the managerial audience) power and politics can act to influence the creative space required for the growth of knowledge. It further adds a purposiveness to management's historicity and critique. I suggest, therefore, that CTA/SNA offers a distinct, paradigmatic value proposition that addresses the problematic of conceptualizing a management artform. Art, properly envisaged, is a strategy for "hope". But it is an art to be practiced by managers, rather than for managers. While managers may learn from art (*Art and Management*), an Artist is no substitute for an *artistic* manager (*the Art of Management*).

From theory to policy and practice

I have positioned this present text as an engagement with the CMS project in a critique of the theorizing of management and organizational practice. It is not a critique of practice itself. Here, as Grey (2005:4) notes:

Understood as a critique of management *studies*, CMS... has a much shorter history and denotes a much more limited terrain [than its critique of management]. Relatively speaking, it also makes CMS a much more original set of ideas, to the extent that most of management studies in this meaning has [hitherto] been "uncritical".

However, Grey (2005:16) does not suggest that CMS should not continue to develop new insights from a whole variety of perspectives, but that the purpose of those insights should be part of an attempt to shift understandings (perceptions) within the orthodox and managerialist majority of business schools, and more extensively than hitherto. This outlines the importance of developing a theorizing of management and organizational practice that is of benefit to the practice itself. Here, as (Zald, 2002:369) describes, those engaged in management practice are engaged in a process of routinization and differentiation, where:

> High status and reputation *within* the profession [are] reserved for those handling what are perceived to be the most difficult cognitive challenges, those close to the "core" of the discipline or those representing important but unsolved problems. Those tasks whose uncertainties have been removed... are handled by lower-status professionals or... delegated to technicians and assistants with lesser credentials.

Intuitively, at the point of departure from the rationalistic paradigm – where extant narratives fail to act as prescriptive guides to management and organizational practice – we might reasonably expect the increased uncertainty of managerial action to be the responsibility of higher-status professionals. Intuitively, those higher-status professionals who appear "successful" under complex and uncertain conditions appear to possess an epistemic ability to engage in (creative) knowledge production. This is Watson's "creation and adoption of pragmatic truths as the basis for action". But, the guiding hypotheses of rationalistic managerial practice fall short in their ability to legitimize such pragmatism. As I have argued, even *pragmatism* itself suggests that managers are simply the product of evolutionary practice.

Contra to any rational theorizing about pragmatic management, if there is now to be an artistic paradigm, it is apposite to consider how theorizing from within such a paradigm will impact upon management and organizational policy and practice. Here, given CTA/SNA's implicit requirement for a creative epistemic ability, policy and practice can be addressed at two levels: specifically the actual practice of management and the support that the academic world provides –

through its business schools – to managers. Thus, alongside building an understanding of how a paradigm of management art might influence practice, if we now need to build an appreciation of an "Art" of managing into the focus of our Business School's, what policies and practices do we now need to consider? Here, a paradigmatic view of management as an *artform* simply considers a preference for the artistic process of CTA/SNA at the boundaries of knowledge, where new narratives of prescription are required to inform practice. Therefore, in only certain circumstances, do I suggest that the study and practice management as an artform becomes a legitimate concern. For example, Zald's comment that high status and reputation amongst managers is to be reserved for those handling the most difficult cognitive challenges, when seen through a paradigm of management art, suggests the operation of a "natural" and/or "organizational" selective process within which the performance and rise of senior managers is to be cultured and/or managed. Here, the implication is that any policy and practice of an art of management is necessarily, and paradoxically, to be considered limited in scope.

Paradigmatically, the performance and rise of senior managers practicing their craft as an artform indicates that, aside from the possession of management craft skills they must also possess an ability to do so innovatively and with mimetic learning. A process of natural selection, in which certain managers appear to rise to the challenges of complexity and ambiguity suggests that those managers possess an innate (aesthetic) sensibility and, knowingly or otherwise, possess an innovative/mimetic capacity to participate in the CTA/SNA process. Under a paradigm of management art, faced with a process of natural selection, the key implication for managerial policy and practice becomes an internal focus on the identification of managers that might possess such "artistic" ability (an Art-aesthetic attitude of disinterested contemplation about their reality) and in identifying the organizational conditions, including the power/politic relationships that subsist under such enhanced performance. There is, therefore, an imperative for the study of organizational history and of identifying its heroes, heroines and legends. Here "cases" of managerial work under such conditions becomes the historicity of successful managerial performance. However, the study of such historicity, as Watson (2001a:387) might concur, is not for the development of guides for future action *per se*, but the development of knowledge and insights which can be used in deciding "how" effective managers act within specific contexts.

While natural selection represents one aspect of managerial practice, the notion of improving an organization's collective performance under conditions of ambiguity and complexity suggests a need to be selective in the recruitment, retention, training and promotion of managers to situations that invoke the most difficult (and uncertain) cognitive challenges. Here, the artistic process of CTA/SNA suggests a need for organizational policies that respect a practice of "talent management" that is cognizant of the artistic process. This is a process that requires, for example: an Art-aesthetic sensibility; an ability to engage in negotiated knowledge practices; and an appreciation of the power and politics that subsists within the twin concepts of aesthetic distance and the aesthetic gap. Furthermore, organizational policies and practices themselves need to address their own limiting effect in terms of the creation and maintenance of suitable "managerial" space within which the appropriate conditions can foster rather than restrict an artistic process. Strategies, policies, procedures, protocols and other rule-based initiatives to foster creativity and innovation within organization, under the Art-aesthetic paradigm, merely act to close down the space for creative play. It is from such creative play that "desirable ends" or other such outcomes become emergent between organizational players negotiating a current reality, rather than the missed objective of some formulaic *faux*-art craft process – dare I mention "brain storming".

Clearly, within academe's support for the paradigmatic challenges of a management practice influenced by, say, management pointillism, there is a significant implication in the perceived importance of the CMS agenda itself. Reframing CMS's traditional (negative) critique of ideological challenge within a new creative, constructivist paradigm, the business-school potential for CMS becomes demarginalized; it becomes representative of the "absent other" of the management and organizational reality that managers are taught within business schools to practice within. Here, CTA/SNA offers the promise of a contribution to performativity that is irrefutably distinct from normative rationality – providing a valid new voice for a "social aesthetic" agenda. The inclusion of a refined CMS ideology in mainstream management and organizational teaching – rather than merely contributing to a surfeit of validated, postmodernist contextual knowledge – offers the promise of a closing of the gap between management theorizing and practice. This is I argue, achievable by contributing to a greater, shared understanding of the management process at the limits of knowledge; it promises to foster – within appropriately sensible individuals – abilities to recognize and exercise management as an epistemic as well as operational activity.

As I have previously noted, the convergence of many functions in the gamut of public and private, profit and non-profit organizations ensures that the implications of Art-aesthetic paradigm of CTA/SNA extend well beyond the commercial context. Here, as a new paradigm, I simply note the extent of these implications. An artistic paradigm suggests that business school policies and practice must become inclusive of a constructive (CMS) agenda, grounded in understanding how pragmatic knowledge might be developed through the "artistic" process. Fundamentally, such an artistic agenda cannot be subject to typical examination (pass/fail) criteria, neither (I suggest) is it one for detailed undergraduate study.

Before any policies and practices are set, however, the limitations of this philosophical study need to be addressed. I have merely set out to explore the central question: what might be learnt from the subject of Art, in addressing the problem of how useful the concept of an Art of Management might be in reconceptualizing the broad-field of management and organization studies. As an exploratory study therefore, I have made no specific limiting assumptions within this text. The emergent conclusion of the study is, in essence, the explication of the concept of a *management artform*, set in the "value" context of a paradigmatic view. It remains one paradigm amongst many paradigms. Therefore, as well as the limitations that arise from a philosophical/ exploratory research approach, a paradigm of *management art* also inherits limitations that belong to the model "class" of *paradigm*.

Chief amongst the limitations of this present study is the derivation of Art's CTA definition itself. My approach to defining CTA, through an assessment of past and distinguished artworld writings, is not an attempt to surpass the theorizing of philosophers from Plato to, for example, Croce and Carroll. There is a clear limitation in the idea of coming up with a comprehensive, historically and philosophically generic, definition of art, capable of withstanding the full range of counter-examples and artistic diversity. However, in accepting the philosophical limitations to the derivation of CTA, this work is most definitely not done for mainstream art-philosophical purposes; CTA and its philosophy of SNA is simply offered in support of a critical rationale. I argue that accepting this emergent limitation allows me some latitude in leaving aside the major worries that a mainstream philosopher of art might have concerning the efficacy of CTA.[131]

Secondly, I note the limitations of explicating management art as a Paradigm. Here, I accept that I have necessarily developed and argued concepts at a high level of abstraction. Therefore, rather than further develop some of these concepts – for example Organizational Sublimity, Aesthetic Distance, Aesthetic Gap and so on – I have chosen a strategy that has attempted to provide, within this book, a description of the paradigm as a whole. Furthermore, in developing the high-level concepts required of this paradigm I have necessarily engaged in a degree of disciplinary eclecticism that will rightly attract critique. I have attempted to balance this necessary eclecticism through a broad basis of informed reference. Yet, as a paradigm, I also set this book's content firmly against the critique of the "Paradigm Wars" – as, for example, delineated by Pfeffer's (1993) argument for a paradigmatic consensus and Van Maanen's (1995) extreme, self-confessed, anti-theoretical position. Considering my own paradigmatic view in the context of either extreme, attracts the critique of either further paradigm proliferation (and its unwelcome limitations of uncertainty) or a critique of theoretical "style", in which Van Maanen's (1995:139) limitations of a "consensual", "stylistic" approach to describing theories, ultimately restricts the range of inquiry and speculation that I advocate in so essential in concepts such as "play".

Art – a new critical agenda?

As Hatchuel (2005: 36) comments, the academic status of management research may be critiqued at three levels: its (lack of) scientific unity ("the paradigm wars"); its lack of prescriptivity ("the relevance gap"); and a critique of business school curricula and effectiveness. These critiques amount to a consequence of the "epistemological trap" of the import, to management and organizational study, of a traditional ontological-epistemological framework. This, as I argued in my Introduction, is also consequential legacy of the Enlightenment project; it is representative of a classical foundational epistemology. However, as I have also argued, the derivation of CTA/SNA, as a paradigm of *management art*, leads me to a non-foundational epistemology. Such an epistemology at least offers the promise of a degree of deconflicting Hatchuel's three critiques. It advances a plausible knowledge of management and organization's *absent other*. However, as the above, brief, discussion of the paradigm's limitations indicates, there is an emergent requirement for further research – in particular, in respect of CTA/SNA as a "candidate" agenda for a revised CMS project.

The paradox of paradigm development, certainly rooted – as this present text is – in a tradition of philosophy, is that such development raises more questions than it immediately offers answers. That is to say that such a development – at least initially – opens more avenues for further research than it closes. Here I would like to pick up on just two themes that might be taken up by future study. Firstly, I suggest that there is a need for further research to overcome the philosophical limitations of CTA/SNA. For example, an empirical study – as suggested by the "artistic" mapping of managerial space – suggests one avenue for fruitful research in which a further validation of the concept of CTA's definition of management art might be advanced. With the nature of typical empirical research being bounded by the "here and now", the potential of mapping the "artistic" managerial/organizational space provides one possible approach to correlating changing managerial perspectives. Here notions of market value might also be empirically examined in a management and organizational context. That is to say, for example, that we might start to study the idea of the spread of a "success story" as an *artwork*, and how such works become the subject of *"faux"* representation across competing firms and industries. Here there is an analogy within the curious phenomenon of the "Shark Factory" where scaled down copies of Damian Hirst's *Shark Set in Formaldehyde* sell at multiples of the original's value.[132] Do we see, here, aspects of management consultancy offering high value solutions that are mere imitations of success offered under dubious circumstances? In Tolstoy's words we might even conceive the fiction:

> [*The consultant*] had a talent for understanding [management artworks] and for imitating [them] with accuracy and good taste, and he imagined that he possessed the real power [a manager] needs. After wavering for some time between various kinds of [management art – six-sigma, business process reengineering, entrepreneurialism, or corporate innovation – he began to advise his client]. He understood all the different kinds and was able to draw inspiration from all, but he could not imagine that it is possible to be quite ignorant of the different kinds of [management art] and to be inspired directly by what is in one's own soul, regardless of whether what one [does] belongs to any particular school. As he did not know this, and was not inspired directly by life but indirectly by life already embodied in [management art], he found inspiration very readily and easily, and equally readily and easily produced [management artworks] very similar to the school of [management art] he wished to imitate. He liked the... effective [Knowledge Management School] best, and in that style began [advising his client in the model of a previous client] and he, as well as every one else who saw [his work], considered [it] to be a great success.

A second avenue for further study lies in the critical management context. Almost regardless of how or why a CMS field has arisen, there is, I believe, a need to clarify a new agenda. Here, as Grey (2005:4) notes, business schools are, perhaps, one of the last battle grounds for political ideology. They present a significant nodal point within contemporary society. As Grey suggests, a mature politics of CMS is required; one that is inclusive, outward facing and that utilizes the strategic possibilities of its business school location. It is not that the "political" movement that is CMS is saying anything different to those in other areas of the academic world who also hold to ideologies of happiness, satisfaction, social responsibility, justice, and environmental stewardship; it is that, as Grey continues, the cadre of CMS has the potential to say it in places, and to individuals within shouting distance of where power, if it lies anywhere, lies. It is this issue, that CMS has a distinct political and institutional context, that needs to be understood in advancing any new CMS agenda. It is in respect of the perceived need for such a new agenda, that further research becomes not only interesting but necessary. For CMS then, there is a need to move away from an antagonistic approach to management studies in order for CMS scholars to carry influence. As Clegg *et al* (2006) would concur, CMS needs to be reflexive of its own theoretical certainties, including those that hold management as being both totalizing and "bad".

The promise of a paradigm of management art is the promise of shifting not only managerial and organizational perspectives, but also the perspectives of those that study management and organizational theory. Perhaps CMS, and an agenda based on CTA/SNA, might provide a useful "neo-modernistic" core for what Volkmann and De Cock (2005:20) hinted at in their comment on a "Bauhaus" idea within an extant MBA curriculum. From a paradigm of artistic management practice, an aesthetic "Bauhaus" adjunct to the MBA curriculum might be developed; one that does not debase – as Volkmann and De Cock might fear – the epistemic value of aesthetics, but encourages its facility in allowing the experience of things other than they are. Might this (with some modification) have been a revised agenda for Lancaster's now disbanded M.Phil in Critical Management: a management and organizational "Bauhaus" set in the land beloved of John Ruskin?

The purpose of this chapter is, then, a misnomer; I offer not a conclusion in a traditional sense, but the opening up of a possibility – a system of concepts in which we can consider the theory and practice of management and organization from a new perspective that is at once creative, in the broadest of senses, yet remains cognizant of some of the major concerns of the social problematic that gives both management and organization its *raison d'être*.

Therefore this book ends with a beginning – with the Bauhaus idea. To paraphrase an excerpt from the official Bauhaus website[133] we have a utopian definition: "The building of the future". Could it be envisaged, within a paradigm of management art, that an Institute might be formed to combine all of a management art's potential in an ideal unity? This suggests a new type of manager-artist beyond academic specialization, for whom such an "Institute" would offer a new form of management education. In order to reach this goal, as for the Bauhaus (and its founder, Walter Gropius) such an Institute would need to acknowledge a necessity to develop new teaching methods. Building on the Bauhaus idea however, the Institute could conceive that the base for any "art of…" is a conjunction of craft skills, innovation and mimetic learning. The Institute would seek to provide an environment within which all three elements could be brought to bear on the education of future managers and leaders. Indeed, artists, craft experts, innovators and visionaries would all act together to direct and produce classes for students of this utopian ideal. Key to such an Institute's agenda would be the notion, developed from both the thinking of Ruskin and Merleau-Ponty, of the manager-artist's twin responsibilities: a responsibility to the artist's integrity and a responsibility to his or her audience. The philosophy of such an Institute would be to provide the executive student with a peer-level forum within which the conceptual thinking required to manage this otherwise negative conflict can be fostered in the furtherance of future Management Art.

Notes

1   For example see: van Aken, 2005; Ford *et al*, 2005; Aram and Salipante, 2003; MacLean and MacIntosh, 2002; Wilkerson, 1999; and Grayson, 1973.

2   As Garber (1998:2) observed: '... *[a] syndrome is a category of naming, not a category of analysis.... To name is to control, or to assert control, even over that which we cannot fully explain or understand.*'

3   Here I adopt a sociological definition of universe that, broadly stated, delineates the totality of a given social population that is the object to be measured. The measures generated are intended to reflect the behaviour of that population. Within this book both the terms universe and world are generally synonymous.

4   For examples of writing on the "cultural turn" see Wolff, 1999 and Chaney, 1994.

5   I use the term rational in the sense that Curley (1992:411) describes as an epistemological rationalism in which '...*the rationalist gives undue weight to reason at the expense of something else.*'

6   I refer to positivism in the epistemological sense of logical positivism (or logical empiricism), where Stroud (1992:264) notes that theorizing should exhibit the structure, content and basis of human knowledge in accordance with empiricist principles.

7   I define ontology, in sociological terms, as a philosophical sub-field focusing on the question of what actually exists and what does not (for example Johnson, 1995:195).

8   Sun Tzu – The Art of War, Translated by Samuel B. Griffith, Oxford University Press, 1963.

9   Mintzberg's three poles of management are Art, Craft and Science.

10   In the early 1800s, Schopenhauer worked on a metaphysical system in which art was granted a uniquely important position; in which aesthetic experience granted an access to '*ideas behind the appearances of nature*', where the artist has a '...*privileged position by virtue of his [sic] capacity to beyond the limitations of striving and reasoning humanity.*' (Harrison *et al*, 1998:13).

11   The notion of *mimesis* is at least as old as Plato's comparison of the painter with a person who captures the appearances of things by holding up a mirror to the world (Blinder, 1986).

12   Unlike *mimesis*, *poiesis* is only interpretable in an ontological sense. This precludes a poietic sense of "bringing forth" an aesthetic knowledge, since aesthetic perception is held to precede ontology.

13   Van Gogh made a number of still lives with old shoes in the period to 1889. One of these is generally referred to under varying titles, for example "A Pair of Shoes", "Old Shoes" or "Old Shoes with Laces", by Heidegger and Schapiro in appropriation for their respective discourses.

14   See, for example, works by the French artist Georges Seurat (1859–1891); notably "Une Baignade, Asnieres" (1883–84) and "Sunday Afternoon on the Island of La Grande Jatte" (1884–86). Seurat's method – first named *Divisionist,* later as *Pointillism* – became known as part of the *Neo-Impressionist* group. His technique was achieved with regular tiny particles of pure colour; like small dots in a mosaic. These dots blend as an image in the eye and, perhaps, predict the structural discipline of later abstract and modern art to come. Seurat's technique provided a reflection of social and economic change. Today, with the advent of computer technology, we can perhaps grasp his technique easier when we relate it to the pixels of colour that make up a digital image.

15   Aside from Björkegren's (1993), 'What Can Organization and Management Theory Learn from Art', one other attempt at explicating the concept of art – as it might be applied outside the traditions of Art – is Martin's (1993) empirically informed study of Appraisers as Artists. Martin reported that a definition of art remained elusive. He merely concluded with the view that art is the antithesis of science in which '...we attribute to the artistic domain that which is not science.'

16   I use the term critical, here, in the sense of a perceived need to manage overly complex and/or ambiguous commercial scenarios.

17   Introduction to Arthur Young's 'The Manager's Handbook: The Practical Guide to Successful Management'

18   A universe, in this context, implicitly defines its own boundary. But this boundary – even if conceptually recognizable – delineates a universe that can intuitively be described as beyond a complete (empirical) measure – even if only in terms of its mathematical greatness (bounding the totality of the elements of the population) and/or its dynamic complexity (bounding the totality of the interrelationships of the elements of the population). The concept of a *bounded universe* implies a secondary level of "fictitious" boundary definition, the purpose of which is to create a more measurable (identifiable, potentially understandable, & logistically manageable) sub-universe that is assumed to be representative of the totality. Scholarly social research that attempts a feat of universalization by making an assumption that <u>a</u> (fictitiously constructed) sub-universe is truly representative of <u>the</u> universe might thus be construed as naïve.

19   It is not my intention to introduce the detail of Argyris' (2004) Model I/ Model II concept; there are many aspects of this concept that go beyond any requirement to illuminate my own argument.

20   The characteristics of Argyris' (2004) Model I theory-in-use comprise the organization's governing variables or values such as: exercising control, maximizing gain and minimizing loss, suppressing negativity and rational action.

21   The dominant Model I Management strategies include: advocating one's position; evaluating the action of the self and others; and the making of attributions concerning the intentions of the self and others. (Argyris, 2004:9)

22   Much of Argyris' discussion of Model I theories-in-use appears in the context of its limiting potential. My own view is that, as with any process oriented model, the consequences are determined by the nature of

the conditions antecedent to its use. Model I theories – in Argyris' defensive application – might well be construed as limiting organizational learning. However, Model I may also have a positive effect, through the careful selection, control and dissemination of narratives, in extending internal learning of an "as-is" effective NK.

23   As Ford, *et al* (2005) cite, in the US alone, managers' consumption of non-academic "knowledge" has created a $15 billion consulting industry and a $1 billion/year business-book industry.

24   Berkeley argued that some abstract ideas are intrinsically impossible objects, the descriptions of which are contradictory, and so they cannot exist. Also, he argued that abstract general ideas are not needed to adequately explain the function of general terms. Berkeley argued that Locke was right to think that such "linguistic" matters needed explanation, but wrong to think that the only explanation was to be given through abstraction. (Papas, 2002:55). However, Berkeley's own account of *general ideas* encompassed the essentials of abstraction and his critique can be seen merely as a critique of one version of abstraction only. (Taylor, 1978:98).

25   Penley *et al's* (1991) findings did not generally support a hypothesis that a social cognitive perspective was linked to managerial performance. However, they accepted that their findings were at variance with other studies, where that variance merely indicated that additional investigative work was required in this area. However, their finding of self-monitoring (as a further form of social cognition), does indicate the complexity of the field of social cognition and that, in abstraction, social cognition is not invalidated as a managerial trait.

26   I shall maintain this link with emotivism as a valid perspective for an aesthetic understanding of management. MacIntyre's Emotivism can be subsumed within an overall social aesthetic (for example the "Democratic Aesthetic" of Armstrong, 2000) and the general concept of "affect" (see Chapter 9).

27   Watson is preempted by Gergen (1973) who argued that, because the social world is so bounded by cultural, spatial and temporal specificities, and that since our knowledge cannot easily transcend these boundaries, any global truth claims are subsumed in local knowledge. Here, local knowledge is analogous to naïve narrative, reaffirming an inability to see narrative as, in any sense, universally prescriptive.

28   Even naïve narrative has a value. Peters and Waterman's sub-universe of excellent companies can be said to have represented a "provisional truth", subject to progressive revision until the story of excellence became yet another story of culture. As Bush (1908:184) noted, '[t]he bounded universe is a sufficiently evident fact in the eyes of primitive folk, ...it was appropriate to the theology of St. Thomas and the poetry of Dante, but our own experience and science hardly reveal anything of the sort.'

29   There is a paradox within the phenomenon, often used in encouraging creativity in employed workforces, of "thinking outside the box". The abstract construct of the "box" is typically framed in the context of an organizational boundary that is itself a construct signified by an extant narrative. The box becomes a culturally "sanctioned" problem space

within the organization and is (necessarily) controlled by the limits of the organizational narrative "as is". To sanction "thinking outside the box", through legitimizing and encouraging "freedom of thought" outside the box, does not necessarily sanction a dissolution of the organizational boundary itself. This does not, therefore, necessarily lead to a revision of the extant narrative. The concept of the "box" can act to strengthen rather than dissolve limits to organizational creativity.

30 Here I admit a notion of chance that subsumes aspects of what Grint (1997:57) describes as Luck (events are random), and Chaos Theory (in the short term anything can happen but in the long term certain patterns – strange attractors – are discernable).

31 I use the term *naïve* in order to place "research" in the context of "practice", where perhaps the term "pure" would both apply equally and court less controversy. In this sense, "pure" research is naïve of the requirements of management and organizational practice.

32 For example see Gibbons *et al* (1994) and Starkey and Madan (2001).

33 For example see van Aken (2005), Ford *et al* (2005), Aram and Salipante (2003), MacLean and MacIntosh (2002), Wilkerson (1999) and Grayson (1973).

34 As an example of what I term sophisticated narrative, Denyer and Tranfield (2006) look at the qualitative synthesis of management research in an attempt to produce better accessibility to its content for practicing managers.

35 MacIntyre (1981:88) describes the vindication of management expertise through a '*justified conception of social science as providing a stock of law-like generalizations with strong predictive power.*' However, MacIntyre goes on to suggest that the salient fact about social science is the absence of the discovery of any law-like generalizations; thus any claim to a management expertise lacks authority.

36 Given the state of a contemporary education system that, at least in the United Kingdom, exposes even high-school students to aspects of formal management training.

37 For example see Aram and Salipante (2003), MacLean and MacIntosh (2002), Starkey and Madan (2001), Wilkerson (1999), and Grayson (1973).

38 Cited in Chia and Morgan (1996).

39 I will refer to Degot's (1987) text with the simplified page referencing of (D:*nn*).

40 For example see Parker & Ritson (2005).

41 In the sense given by the aesthetics of art, the history of art and art criticism.

42 Here, there is a conceptual link to the requirement, developed in Chapter 2, for an effective manager to possess the capability to (re-)map culturally constructed boundaries in creating new narratives; indicating a form of managerial vision.

43 For example see Ford (1996, 1999) and Higgs & Hender (2004).

44 This is despite the fact that much research in the field of creativity stems, in practice, from an educational environment focused on traditional "creative activities" such as painting and music. (Higgs and Hender, 2004:1).

45   The respondents within Higgs and Hender's (2004) study were, in fact, drawn from the categories of senior management and DBA students.

46   The form of a management artwork is discussed subsequently, but here we can envisage that: commercial myths and legends, company histories, executive biographies, press releases, success stories, the company itself, or many other forms of realization or abstraction of a project, large or small, may be representational of the conclusion of an "artwork". Much like performance art, it may be a "record" or some other "representation" that lives on for posterity.

47   Recalling Booth's Gergenian observation that the social world is so bounded by cultural, spatial and temporal specificities that our knowledge cannot transcend these boundaries, a Weberian social aesthetic, while problematic to Weberian philosophy, might indicate a new value in art and an art historical perspective, in providing new possibilities of transcending socially contrived specificities.

48   For example, the fine (or plastic) arts of painting, sculpture, and so on; the performance arts of theatre, music and the like; and the literary arts of the poet and author.

49   For example see Tsang and Kwan (1999) and Fleetwood (2005).

50   For example, Anthony's (1994) organizational cultures.

51   In an address to the Royal Academy of Arts, quoted in Time, 11 May 1953.

52   I note that the aesthetic experience is, itself, more than just an experience of art. This, often neglected, aspect of aesthetic understanding is typical of the bias towards art shown within the study of aesthetics over the last century (see for example Brady, 2003:7). However, while accepting that the contemporary study of aesthetics is broader than I infer here, I will assume that it is axiomatic that any theory about the nature of art is inextricably linked to the field of aesthetics.

53   While Weitz acknowledged that this "primary concern" is widely held, he nevertheless developed the argument that "art" is not amenable to any real or true definition.

54   Taken from 'Art Critic London' Turner Prize 1999 (Tate Gallery, 20 October 1999 – 6 February 2000), http://www.theartnewspaper.com

55   The data for Table 4.1 is derived from collected observations of the Art54 class (2003) of Santa Rosa Junior College, www.santarosa.edu/art, an online Art class exploring the Internet for research and display of image and text.

56   Collingwood (1938:20) notes that an essential characteristic of craft lies in the fact that there is a visible distinction between its "means" and its "end". Collingwood writes that '[t]he craftsman's [sic] skill is his knowledge of the means necessary to realize a given end, and his [sic] mastery of these means.' To Collingwood, an *object* of an activity that does not exhibit qualities of the activity's craft cannot therefore be associated with that craft.

57   I acknowledge that, in Aesthetics, *mimesis* retains very strong connotations of Platonic imitation. However, as Cascardi (1986:39) has observed, there has been a shift, over time, in the concept of *mimesis* from imitation to representation. *Mimesis* may have therefore gained several

literal meanings over the years. As Sartwell (1992:364) notes, '...*Gadamer, among many others, has pointed out the translation of "mimesis" as "imitation" is problematic, and at the least too narrow. "Mimesis" has the sense of "making the absent present"*...'. In clarifying my own reading of *mimesis*, it is this notion that *mimesis* is a process that involves making the absent present – realizing the previously unseen – that I advance. The process (or means) *mimesis*, in this context, implies a specific "function" (or end): *to make the absent present* – it is a process of learning and discovery.

58   A similar relegation of the *object* artwork (and its creator – the artist) lies at the root of Schapiro's (1968) vehement criticism of Heidegger's (1935) interpretation of Van Gogh's *Old Shoes*. I shall return to this in Chapter 9.

59   There is an important link here, through my introductory argument, to the (moral) responsibility of the artist. I shall develop this further in Chapter 6.

60   Here, I would argue that production might legitimately include skills of arrangement – as in the representation of "found" objects, or (for example) the objects comprising Emin's *My Bed*.

61   The notion of a complex definition is also to be identified in Parker's Voluntarism (Parker, 1953) – see Table 4.2.

62   This is pure discovery: the object exists – even if unseen – within the social world, it is not a product of a craft.

63   Innovation as defined, for example, in Webster's (Dictionary) as the act of finding out or inventing; contrivance or construction of that which has not before existed.

64   The conjunctive definition is not prescriptive of a specific craft therefore, as Dewey (1934:5) observed, '[t]*he intelligent mechanic engaged in his job, interested in doing well and finding satisfaction in his [work], caring... with genuine affection, is artistically engaged. ... [The] product may not appeal to the esthetic [sic] sense of those [consumers] who use the product ... [but this is more] with the conditions of the market... [at that time].*'

65   Gaut (1993:602) argues that an *intentionalist* theory of art falls victim to the critique of global theories of interpretation; in which the meaning of a work of art is assumed to be embedded within some internal property of the work.

66   The creation of a wholly new craft is, I argue, a separate matter of a "social" acceptance (as art object) of an instantiation of an *experimental* consequence. New crafts can only be introduced *a posteriori* to an *Art object*.

67   Compare this with Björkegren's (1993:107) description of the process by which a painter strives to become acknowledged as a "serious painter" in Sweden, through the Academy of Arts in Stockholm. '*When the aspiring painter has gained acceptance as a legitimate artist, the artistry becomes a 9–5 business.*'

68   My argument for CTA should, in no sense, be construed as exclusive; that is, I do not suggest art as the only method for explicating a social knowledge, nor that art cannot be used to explicate a knowledge of the natural world.

69   Kant's Critique of Judgement. Hereafter I reference the translation of Pluhar (1987) as, for example, (CJ:98).

70   I do not suggest the sublime as some "absolute" concept against which art is the only means available to reveal an undisclosed other; nor that art is exclusively related to the mediation of the sublime. In the spirit of a paradigm, art merely provides one conceptual framework for understanding our social phenomena. Art also provides other "functions", for example decorative and investment potential.

71   Concentrating on just two aesthetic categories might be argued as oversimplifying an aesthetic discourse. Strati (1992:568) notes that, with beauty at the core, there are several aesthetic categories, ranging from 6 to 64 in the aesthetic literature: the ugly, the sublime, the graceful, the sacred, the comic, the picturesque and so on.

72   Despite Kant's distinction between the *mathematically* and *dynamically* sublime, my own use of the term relates to both categories as – in relation to an unknown "other" – it is not possible to categorize, *a priori,* a sublime experience.

73   As included in the Anthology: Romanticism, Duncan Wu (1994).

74   For Kant, the sublime surpasses senses and overwhelms – thus, the notion of "super" sensibility is an attempt to square my own account of the sublime with that of Kant's. This super-sensibility will form the basis for what I shall later explicate as function of an individual's aesthetic distance.

75   There is a sense in which primary qualities might be regarded as (objective) phenomena, whereas secondary qualities would by typified by experiential phenomena. I have already noted Kant's view of the sublime as, in a sense, beyond phenomena, positions the sublime experience – that is, in the realm of the *super*-sensible – beyond the senses. As I have previously noted, I respond to this super-sensibility by positing the notion of an aesthetic distance, in which certain individuals are able, sensually, to experience that which appears beyond the senses of others.

76   The conception of a "dark side" of beauty lies in the dichotomous relationship between individual notions of a "power of beauty" and a "beauty of power". I make this observation less the reader question the open-endedness of my reading of Brand's comments.

77   Tolstoy's conception of beauty is perhaps best reflected in the Russian word *krasotá* (beauty), by which is meant only that which pleases the sight; it may relate to a man, horse, house or movement. (Knox, 1931:486).

78   This is the (almost) traditional sense of aesthetic judgment, posited by Burke, and regarded by Kant as empirical.

79   From the original manuscript *The Artist's Reality: Philosophies of Art* (Rothko, 1940/41:Plate 2).

80   This further introduces the notion of power as relevant to the discussion of art (certainly in a Foucauldian/Derridian sense; see for example Richardson, 1991:173–174).

81   This does not preclude a craft product becoming, at some subsequent moment in time, an accepted artwork. In such a circumstance, a secondary conjunction is deemed to be operative – see Chapter 4.

82   Noting that an artwork itself need not be representational (certainly in a classical sense) of the object referenced by the artist.

83   Anonymous Book Review, "Münsterberg, H. (1915), 'Business Psychology', Chicago: LaSalle Business Texts", in *Journal of Political Economy,* Vol. 24 No. 2: 205–206 (1916).

84   Although I would accept that, given the concept of an "aptitude" for certain skills, some individuals might benefit over others from certain "learning" experiences.

85   Rothko observes that (at the time of the writing of his philosophy) the word *art* had already achieved a legitimacy applied to other skills: '...the Art of Love, the Art of War, as well as the Art of Cooking.' Rothko is critical of this diversity in the ambiguous nature of art. However, it is through a transcendence of the actual craft skill that CTA can deliver an argument that even the advertising executive can practice his craft as an artform – certainly advertising purports to communicate aspects of a product's qualities that may or may not be visible. This is more so the case as I consider replacing the craft of painting with the craft of management and organizational practice.

86   I would accept here, a Popperian position, that it cannot be excluded that some case might be found that refutes such a theory as CTA. However, CTA merely aims to provide a paradigmatic tool with which a pragmatic (and an acknowledged subjective) insight can be gained into the world of management and organization. As a theory, CTA simply presents a framework for viewing social phenomenology, rather than any purport to offer one for a systemic and/or objective analysis.

87   Archived interviews providing material for this section were accessed through the UK's public broadcasting organization, the BBC, from their website: www.bbc.co.uk/bbcfour/audiointerviews/professions/painters. shtml, during November 2004 (Atkinson, 2006). The set of Artists is, in a sense, arbitrary – their selection being based merely on the criterion of availability. However, the Artists do represent a cross section of established 20th-century Artists whose works have reached axiomatic recognition as *Artworks.*

88   The open source encyclopedia: http://en.wikipedia.org notes Dialogic as a term used by the Russian philosopher Mikhail Bakhtin in his literary theory, *The Dialogic Imagination.* Bakhtin contrasts the "dialogic" and the "monologic" work of literature. The dialogic work is in continual dialogue with other works; it is not merely a work that answers, corrects, silences, or extends a previous work, but one that is being informed and informing the previous work. The term "dialogic", however, does not just apply to literature. For Bakhtin, all language – indeed, all thought – is dialogic. As a result, all language (and the ideas which language contains and communicates) is dynamic, relational and engaged in a process of endless redescriptions of the world. Dialogism has been seen by many as doing away with the idea of knowledge as emanating from single, authoritative, closed (or "monologic") sources; instead it embraces the idea of knowledge as collective, relational and dynamic.

89   The term *fiction* is not used here in the sense of its popular association with the written narrative, but in a more general sense of a *bringing into existence* of (imaginary) characters, events or places (or entities/concepts) in words, pictures or actions. (Proudfoot, 1992:152). In this sense fiction

subsumes such pessimistic interpretations as lies and untruths. Such negative fictions are perhaps more characteristic of MacIntyre's pessimistic outlook of managerial authority. However, in this present work I merely exaggerate the positive aspect of fiction.

90   By transitory I use Cruickshank's (2004:579) sense of the transitive being open to revision and replacement.

91   Kelly's CA was radical at inception and is still a popular concept (see, for example, Anderson, 2001 and Adams & Krockover, 1999).

92   I make this intuitive observation on the basis that not all individuals would reasonably be given to the preconditions required of the scientific rationality implied by the *individual-as-scientist*. Although it might be argued that Kelly's idea used the term "scientist" in the rather loose sense of "finding out about things", when I turn to the possibility of CA informing the notion of an *individual-as-artist*, the idea that the CA individual's *scientific-action-in-the-world* could be determined by a conscious application of an ontology of bi-polar constructs – a key methodological characteristic of CA's philosophy – raises more questions that it answers.

93   A predisposition to a *"malleability of ontology"* can be reasoned as analogous to a cultural, societal, religious or other defined belief system, in which sense-making sets immediate observations, both the concrete and the aesthetic, within the context of an individual's prior (internalized) knowledge. Compare this with the discussion, for example, on 'Prejudices as Conditions of Understanding' within Gadamer's (1989:240) essay on the Hermeneutic Circle. Here, also, the notion of any *power* (or authority) promoting or upholding a certain (strong) belief system will significantly impact the extent to which an individual may exercise *Alternativism*.

94   At this point I make no distinction between the words abstraction and representation; finding them to be synonymous within this discussion. However, my preference is for abstraction, on the basis of a consistency of use within developing the *portrait of a manager*.

95   I do not suggest that research of non-real fictional entities is impossible, merely that the question of research itself should concern a positive focus on possibility rather a negative focus on refutation.

96   We see here, the notion of the concretization of an "organizational boundary" in which emergent patterns of naïve narrative might act to either confirm or allay concerns over the usefulness of management and organizational research to its practice. Such narratives depend on information at hand about "the gap". But, any claim to a generalization of this knowledge as a "science" of the management gap is undermined by the existence of further information about the gap that remains outside the boundary.

97   As an exemplar, this text cannot purport to offer an objective truth and neither, I argue, do I present it as such. This text merely offers, to *an other* – the reader – an interpretation (mine) of *a* reality, in the language of academe. It merely offers a plausible *possibility of a truth* as a basis for engagement – through the process of SNA – within the infinitely malleable (academic) world. Prior to a process of editing, review, publication, reading and critique – a process of SNA – this text exists as a self-dependent

entity (DE_{sf}). It is a narrative, philosophical argument, comprising (*inter alia*) verifiable DEs – excerpts from previously negotiated entities – that is, references to other texts. As a candidate DE, the construction and presentation of this text is required to be in a form of language given by the conventions of academic writing that are commonly held to represent the norms of representation accepted by the academic audience I wish to engage.

98   New York: Random House, (1978) cited in Warner (1991).

99   This argument recalls Gergen (1973) and Booth (2003) from Chapter 3.

100   This is not, however, to suggest that the organization or management environment is a sublime object.

101   This is a narrow, subjectively non-artistic application of the concept of creativity. Although Degot's "Creative" Manager has an aesthetic undertone, "aesthetic creativeness" is not highlighted. Rather, Degot uses the term merely in the sense of an ability to "creatively" overcome the difficulties of expressing, and gaining an acceptance for, some new idea or project – "creatively" overcoming the aesthetic gap.

102   Any attempt to categorize such a subjective concept as creativity into a certain number of explicit characteristics acts to undermine the very nature of the concept being labelled "creative". Certainly, from the *art-aesthetic* view, there is evidence to suggest that the only thing that can be agreed on amongst artistic individuals is that a creative person should have *many* ideas. (Glück *et al*, 2002).

103   For Degot, a *management artwork's* thematic root lies in the act of decision-making, suggesting the link between a decision and its outcome is the most obvious evidence of a management work. However, what is there to separate the management artwork from the ordinary management work? For Degot, it is the basic creative design that can be attributed to one individual – the manager as artist. My reservation concerning Degot's work in this respect is that, in his concentration on the "successful" outcome, the full potential of the concept of a *management art* is lost.

104   Carl Rogers (1961), *Theory of Creativity*.

105   All things being equal, would firm "M" achieve a better performance than firm "N" if its managers were of type P1, P2, P3, or P4? Could it be that "M's" profit performance would increase by 25% if its management team included 10% more managers of type P4? Empirically testing these arguments is problematic in a direct sense; how are we able to create an experiment in which the antecedent can be varied under a *ceteris paribus* assumption in order to study its effect on the consequent? In Atkinson (2006) I offer a tentative argument, in *reductio ad absurdum*, based on propositional logic in support of H4.

106   Giddens (1990) describes "Risk" as related to the avoidance of danger; where the world is seen as a "fraught and dangerous place". A distribution of risk might be adequately defined as a distribution of presumptions of danger resulting from the (potential) consequences of actions and operations of the organization and its individuals, within the environment in which they exist. A possession of, or lack of, knowledge prior to some action does not, however, imply a knowledge of danger or thus a

presumption of risk. An appreciation of, or sensibility for, the sublime where the sense of pleasure is mixed with the sense of pain (Lyotard, 1979:77) would, however, infer a respect for the possibilities of danger, even if not a certain knowledge of its existence.

107   I use the term here broadly, in that the organization itself, as principal, might be represented as a body corporate, a management board or an individual in a superior/subordinate relationship with the *manager-artist*.

108   The notion of Trust, as Giddens relates (1990:34–35), is intertwined with risk, with trust serving to reduce or minimize the dangers to which, in this case, the activities of the organization are subject. Here trust is defined as the confidence (of the organization) in the reliability (of the *manager-artist*) regarding a given set of outcomes where that confidence expresses a faith in the correctness of an abstract knowledge.

109   Here "politics" refers to the patterns of hierarchical relationships that a society/institution fosters (Hein, 1976:144).

110   Hein makes a point that the labels: Contrapuntal, Propadeutic and Propulsive, are her own appropriation of these terms, and their use in this context does do not infer any scholarly import.

111   See, for example, the concept of polyphony in Clegg *et al* (2006).

112   Although Morgan famously explicates a theory of "metaphor" as images that facilitate "*a way of thinking*" and "*a way of seeing*", I argue that he is also outlining (certainly in part) a theory of aesthetic perception. A metaphor is also an abstracted concept around which a complex scenario can be imagined. Thus, in contrast to my conception of artworks, management metaphors are, I posit, similar in their affect to artworks, even if they are conceptually separate; both facilitate comprehension by stimulating perception.

113   As inferable from Redfield, the choice of metaphor – certainly in extending aesthetics outside of *Fine Art* into a study of management – acts to undermine the concept of a *management art*. That a manager, or his organizational "audience", might be referred to as having "a taste" for some work or other does not foster a suitable basis for either the origin of an episteme, or of a critical management study. Extending the concept of art into management does not call for a blind acceptance of all that field's terminology. Any metaphor may be safely replaced by either its underlying *raison d'être*, or by an alternate metaphor, without violating any associated theory.

114   In Armstrong's "Democratic Aesthetic", the components of aesthetic life are practices of consciousness: playing and dreaming, thinking and feeling and so on. These are common to everyone. (Armstrong, 2000).

115   I chose the word *engaged* to differentiate between the individual who exhibits a desire to understand and perhaps resolve a sublime environment or situation, and the individual who merely exhibits a reaction to the sublime.

116   My own concentration on the aesthetic categories of the sublime and beauty appears to abandon the other distinctions in aesthetic discourse; for example the ugly, the graceful, the sacred, the comic, the picturesque. This abandonment is intentional; it gives rise, as noted by Armstrong, to

the dissolution of boundaries between affects and knowledge. (Armstrong, 2000).

117   It might be argued, in this respect, that a (future) vision of the organization represents the potential for the greatest organizational affect and the potential for the greatest threat of change.

118   As Costea *et al* observe, '[p]lay is a universal phenomenon but with no universal definition.' It may concern games, humour, irony, sarcasm, gambling, chance, the arts, role playing, carnival, dance and many more aspects of imagination and expression. However, play makes most sense in a "local" context and within its own horizon of interpretation. (Costea, *et al*: 2005:1). I therefore refer to play, here, as the playing (in the mind) with concepts, in the sense of a concept being a mediation between a certain "space of experience" and a "horizon of expectation".

119   The inference of such preclusion acts to level "scientific" knowledge to the provisionality of "narrative" in order that it may be considered in a mediative process. It is a reminder of the fictionality to be observed in (certain) social representations, often regarded as a sociological truth. (c.f. Wolff, 1999).

120   The act of stepping beyond the "constructed" boundary of the individual's knowledge changes perspective and creates an opportunity to draw in new information and cause narrative revision. The act of achieving a new equilibrium is reaffirmed as a dissolution of the constructed boundary and a removal of the obstruction to exploring new affects that are received as positive or negative and used through knowledge-based affect theory in the progressive revision of narrative. If creative play is fundamental to the generation of narrative, then the management gap may be no more than an academically derived and concretized fiction; a "sociological" truth.

121   I do not address Mode 2 research here – in either a Model I or Model II context. I argue that Mode 2 research is a special case, best considered as "consultative" research; one that may (or may not) lead to a Mode 1 output (M1K). Mode 2 has its roots in specific problems – while academic rigour is certainly achievable, I question whether such rigour is a *de facto* requirement for the solution of an immediate problem. In taking this stance, I avoid the danger of the dichotomous form of the Mode 1/Mode 2 argument observed by Pettigrew (2001).

122   Kearney relates to mimesis in a narrative realization as *mimesis-mythos.*

123   The concept of an organizational aesthetic distance is, I argue, an aspect of the "cultural" definition of any given organization or, indeed, any other socio-cultural grouping of individuals. (C.f. The concept of Aesthetic Muteness advanced by Taylor, 2002).

124   For the Model I manager, the concept of the sublime is irrelevant, since the possibility of the negative affect of a fear of a perceived unknown does not occur. Providing that such a manager exercises effective selection, dissemination and control over their organizational narrative, and continues to experience reaffirming consequences of action (that is, no significantly unexplainable events occur), then such a manager certainly has a capacity to perform effectively.

125   The outcome a Model II CTA-in-use, that is to say any new/revised (provisional) narrative, is a contender for signification as a *management artwork*. At its point of origin it is a fiction. A *management artwork* is thus constituted by an identifiable original contribution to an organizational narrative – it is the fiction behind a narrative knowledge. Thus, the value of the artwork lies in its contribution to a sociological process of mediated narrative; the essence of which is a negotiated, "concretized" interpretation of a fiction.

126   I again refer to Costea's observation on defining play earlier, noting that play is not always creative, but in the local context of this text, I argue that my use of the term play in this sense is not inappropriate.

127   Although, with no *a priori* concept of a *management artwork*, examples of such artworks are not evidenced here, it is not difficult to imagine that suitable "conventions of communication" will admit the organizational conventions of policy, processes, procedures, guidelines for presentations, meeting structures and any other norm of organizational practice such as might be learnt under the general rubric of the craft skills of management.

128   While this may be a dominant narrative within CMS it is by no means the only narrative. A fair overview of the range of CMS narratives can be gleaned from a review of the conference proceedings from the CMS conference series.

129   The state of paradigmatic development in the 1990s is noted by Pfeffer as related to a consequence of the discipline's social structure, culture and power relations, i.e. how organizational studies is itself organized and the factors that create and perpetuate that organization. (Pfeffer, 1993:615). However, as Hassard (1990:220) has noted, a surfeit of "inconsistently applied paradigms" within the field of organizational theory has acted to undermine the Kuhnian value of the paradigm concept. Thus my own strategy in advancing a paradigmatic thesis is to explicate the correspondence between the Art-aesthetic paradigm model and the philosophical principles upon which it is based.

130   However, it is to be recognized that the growth of sociological thinking within an organizational context extends beyond its importation into the climate of business schools. For a review of organizational sociology see Scott (2004).

131   This limitation was discussed in personal correspondence between myself and Dr Jonathan Vickery following my first airing of the CTA at the 2nd Art of Management and Organization conference in Paris, 2004.

132   The Sunday Times, March 19, 2006: 'Hirst earns £2m at the shark factory'. It was reported that Damian Hirst is to earn £24m [sic] by turning out versions of the works that made his name in the 1990s as the leader of the Young British Artist movement. A version of the "pickled shark", ⅓ size, sold for £2.28m, 45 times more than the artist first received for the original work.

133   Bauhaus 1919–33: http://www.bauhaus.de/english/bauhaus1919/index.htm – accessed January 2007.

Bibliography

Adams, P.E. and Krockover, G.H. (1999) 'Stimulating Constructivist Teaching Styles through Use of an Observation Rubric', *Journal of Research in Science Teaching*, Vol. 36 No. 8: 955–971.

Adler, N.J. (2006) 'The Arts & Leadership: Now That We Can Do Anything, What Will We Do?', *Academy of Management Learning & Education*, Vol. 5 No. 4: 486–499.

Adorno, T. (1961) 'Reconciliation Under Duress', in Taylor, 1980: 151–176.

Alvesson, M. and Willmott, H. (eds) (1992) 'Critical Management Studies', London: Sage.

Anderson, L. (2001) 'Is Management Beauty in the Eye of the Beholder? Implications of Perceptions of Effective Management for Learning Transfer', *Proceedings, Teaching & Learning Research Programme Conference*, Leicester, download www.tlrp.org/pub/conf00.html June 2005.

Anthony, P. (1994) 'Managing Culture', Buckingham: Open University Press.

Aram, J.D. and Salipante, P.F. Jr. (2003) 'Bridging Scholarship in Management: Epistemological Reflections', *British Journal of Management*, Vol. 14: 189–205.

Argyris, C. (1973) 'Some Limits of Rational Man Organizational Theory', *Public Administration Review*, Vol. 33 No. 3: 253–267.

Argyris, C. (2004) 'Reasons and Rationalizations: The Limits to Organizational Knowledge', Oxford: Oxford University Press, 2006.

Aristotle (1996) 'Poetics' (Transl. Heath. M.) London: Penguin.

Armstrong, I. (2000) 'The Radical Aesthetic', Oxford: Blackwell.

Atkinson, D.M. (2006) '"Heidegger's Shoes": On Management, Art and an Art of Management', *PhD Thesis*, Lancaster University.

Austin, R. and Devin, L. (2004) 'Successful Innovation Through Artful Process', *Leader to Leader*, Vol. 32: 48–55.

Barglow, R. (1994) 'The Crisis of the Self in the Age of Information: Computers, Dolphins, and Dreams', London: Routledge.

Bartlett, C.A. and Ghoshal, S. (1997) 'The Myth of the Generic Manager: New Personal Competencies for New Management Roles', *California Management Review*, Vol. 40 No. 1: 92–116.

Baudrillard, J. (1970) 'The Consumer Society: Myths & Structures' (Transl.) London: Sage, 1998.

Baudrillard, J. (1981) 'Simulacra and Simulation' (Transl.) Michigan: University of Michigan Press, 1994.

Baudrillard, J. (1983) 'Fatal Strategies', Paris: Editions Grasset (Transl.) London: Pluto Press 1999.

Beardsley, M.C. (1983) 'An Aesthetic Definition of Art', in Lamarque and Olsen, 2004: 55–62.

Becker, H.S. (1974) 'Art as Collective Action', *American Sociological Review*, Vol. 39 No. 6: 767–776.

Bhaskar, R. (1975) 'A Realist Theory of Science', London: Verso (2nd edn) 1997 cited in Cruickshank, 2004.

Björkegren, D. (1993) 'What Can Organization and Management Theory Learn From Art?', in Hassard and Parker (eds) 1993: 101–113.

Blinder, D. (1986) 'In Defense of Pictorial Mimesis', *The Journal of Aesthetics and Art Criticism*, Vol. 45 No. 1: 19–27.

Booth, C. (2003) 'Does History Matter in Strategy? The Possibilities and Problems of Counterfactual Analysis', *Management Decision*, Vol. 41 No. 1/2: 96–104.

Bornstein, M.H. (1984) 'Developmental Psychology and the Problem of Artistic Change', *The Journal of Aesthetics and Art Criticism*, Vol. 43 No. 2: 131–145.

Bourdieu, P. (1993) 'The Field of Cultural Production', Cambridge: Polity.

Brady, E. (2003) 'Aesthetics of the Natural Environment', Edinburgh: University Press.

Brand, P.Z. (1999) 'Beauty Matters', *The Journal of Aesthetics and Art Criticism*, Vol. 57 No. 1: 1–10.

Brewer, K.B. (1997) 'Management as a Practice: A Response to Alasdair MacIntyre', *Journal of Business Ethics*, Vol. 16 No. 8: 825–833.

Burke, E. (1759) 'A Philosophical Enquiry into the Sublime and Beautiful', 2nd Edition (Womersley, D. ed.) London: Penguin 1998.

Bush, W.T. (1908) 'Provisional and Eternal Truth', *The Journal of Philosophy, Psychology and Scientific Methods*, Vol. 5 No. 7: 181–184.

Carr, A. and Hancock, P. (eds) (2003) 'Art and Aesthetics at Work', Basingstoke: Palgrave Macmillan.

Carroll, N. (1999) 'Philosophy of Art', London: Routledge.

Carroll, S.J. and Gillen, D.J. (1984) 'The Classical Management Functions: Are They Really Outdated?', *Academy of Management Proceedings*: 132–136.

Carson, P.P. and Carson, K.D. (1998) 'Theoretically Grounding Management History as a Relevant and Valuable Form of Knowledge', *Journal of Management History*, Vol. 4 No. 1: 29–42.

Carter, R.W. (2000) 'Cultural Change and Tourism: Towards a Prognostic Model', The University of Queensland: PhD Thesis.

Cascardi, A.J. (1986) 'Genre Definition and Multiplicity in Don Quixote', *Cervantes: Bulletin of the Cervantes Society of America*, Vol. 6 No. 1: 39–49.

Chaney, D. (1994) 'The Cultural Turn: Scene-Setting Essays on Contemporary Cultural History', London: Routledge.

Chaney, D. (2002) 'Cultural Change and Everyday Life', New York: Palgrave.

Chia, R. (2003) 'From Knowledge-creation to the Perfecting of Action: Tao, Basho and Pure Experience as the Ultimate Ground of Knowing', *Human Relations*, Vol. 56 No. 8: 953–981.

Chia, R. and Morgan, S. (1996) 'Educating the Philosopher-Manager: De-signing the Times', *Management Learning*, Vol. 27 No. 1: 37–64.

Clegg, S.R., Kornberger, M., Carter, C. and Rhodes, C. (2006) 'For Management?', *Management Learning*, Vol. 37 No. 1: 7–27.

Collingwood, R.G. (1938) 'The Principles of Art', Oxford: University Press, 1958.

Cooper, D. (ed.) (1992) 'A Companion to Aesthetics', Oxford: Blackwell.

Costea, B. (2000) 'Representations of Human Diversity in Mainstream Management Education: Critique and Development', *PhD Thesis*, Lancaster University.

Costea, B. and Introna, L. (2004) 'On Cognition and Action in Organization Life: Management and the Situated Body in-the-World', *Lancaster University*

Management School: Working Paper, 2004/019 download from http://www.lums.co.uk/publications.

Costea, B., Crump, N. and Holm, J. (2005) 'Play at Work: Questions of Historical Interpretation', *Proceedings: 4th Critical Management Studies Conference, Cambridge, July 2005*, pagination as downloaded www.mngt.waikato.ac.nz/ejrot/cmsconference/ 2005 Jul 2006.

Cowan, R. and Foray, D. (2002) 'Evolutionary Economics and the Counterfactual Threat: On the Nature and Role of Counterfactual History as an Empirical Tool in Economics', *Journal of Evolutionary Economics*, Vol. 12: 539–562.

Cruickshank, J. (2004) 'A Tale of Two Ontologies: An Immanent Critique of Critical Realism', *The Sociological Review*, Vol. 52 No. 4: 567–585.

Cuff, R. (1996) 'Edwin F. Gay, Arch W. Shaw, and the Uses of History in Early Graduate Business Education', *Journal of Management History*, Vol. 2 No. 3: 9–25.

Cunliffe, A.L. (2002) 'Social Poetics as Management Inquiry: A Dialogical Approach', *Journal of Management Inquiry*, Vol. 11 No. 2: 128–146.

Curley, E. (1992) 'Rationalism', in Dancy and Sosa (1992): 411–415.

Cussins, A. (1992) 'Content, Embodiment and Objectivity: The Theory of Cognitive Trails', Mind, Vol. 101 No. 404: 651–688.

Cuthbert, N. (1970) 'Fayol and the Principles of Organization', in Tillett, A., Kempner, T. and Wills, G. (eds) (1970): 108–139.

Dancy, J. and Sosa, E. (eds) (1992) 'A Companion to Epistemology', Oxford: Blackwell, 1993.

Danto, A. (1964) 'The Artworld', *The Journal of Philosophy*, Vol. 61 No. 19: 571–584.

Das, T.K. (2003) 'Managerial Perceptions and the Essence of the Managerial World: What is an Interloper Business Executive to Make of the Academic-Researcher Perceptions of Managers?', *British Journal of Management*, Vol. 14: 23–32.

Davidson, M.J. and Burke, R.J. (eds) (1994), 'Women in Management: Current Research Issues', London: Paul Chapman Publishing.

Davies, S. (1991) 'Weitz's Anti-Essentialism' (ed. from Davies 1991, Ch. 1 'Definitions of Art', Ithaca, NY: Cornell) in Lamarque and Olsen, 2004: 63–68.

Deetz, S. (2003) 'Reclaiming the Legacy of the Linguistic Turn', *Organization*, Vol. 10 No. 3: 421–429.

Degot, V. (1987) 'Portrait of the Manager as an Artist', *Dragon* (Paris: Ecole Polytechnique), Vol. 2 Pt. 4: 13–50.

Demerath, L. (1993) 'Knowledge-Based Affect: Cognitive Origins of "Good" and "Bad"', *Social Psychology Quarterly*, Vol. 56 No. 2: 136–147.

Demerath, L. (2002) 'Epistemological Culture Theory: A Micro Theory of the Origin and Maintenance of Culture', *Sociological Theory*, Vol. 20 No. 2: 208–226.

Denyer, D. and Tranfield, D. (2006) 'Using Qualitative Research Synthesis to Build an Actionable Knowledge Base', *Management Decision*, Vol. 44 No. 2: 213–227.

Dewey, J. (1934) 'Art as Experience', New York: Perigee, 1980.

Dickie, G. (1983) 'The New Institutional Theory of Art', Proceedings of the 8th Wittgenstein Symposium, reprinted in Lamarque and Olsen, 2004: 47–54.

Dickie, G. (1992) 'Definition of Art' in Cooper, 1992: 109–113.

Dickie, G. (1997) 'Art: Function or Procedure: Nature or Culture', *The Journal of Aesthetics and Art Criticism*, Vol. 55 No. 1: 19–28.

Dixon, J. and Dogan, R. (2003) 'A Philosophical Analysis of Management: Improving Praxis', *The Journal of Management Development*, Vol. 22 No. 6: 458–482.

Dobson, J. (1999) 'The Art of Management and the Aesthetic Manager: The Coming Way of Business', Westport, CT: Quorum.

Ducasse, C.J. (1928) 'What has Beauty to do with Art?', *The Journal of Philosophy*, Vol. 25 No. 7: 181–186.

Easterby-Smith, M., Thorpe, R. and Lowe, A. (1991) 'Management Research: An Introduction', London: Sage.

Eaton, M.E. (1999) 'Kantian and Contextual Beauty', *The Journal of Aesthetics and Art Criticism*, Vol. 57 No. 1: 11–15.

Eco, U. (1997) 'Kant and the Platypus' (Transl.) London: Vintage, 2000.

Eisenhardt, M. K. (1989) 'Agency Theory: An Assessment and Review', *Academy of Management Review*, Vol. 14 No. 1: 57–74.

Eisner, M. (1999) 'Work in Progress', New York: Hyperion.

Eyerman, R. (2004) 'Jeffrey Alexander and the Cultural Turn in Social Theory', *Thesis Eleven*, No. 79: 25–30.

Fayol, H. (1916a) 'Administration Industrielle et Générale', Dunod.

Fayol, H. (1916b) 'General and Industrial Management', (Storrs tans.), Pitman, 1949.

Ferrario, M. (1994) in Davidson, M.J. and Burke, R.J. (eds), (1994).

Fleetwood, S. (2004) 'An Ontology for Organization and Management Studies', in Fleetwood, S. and Ackroyd, S. (eds) 'Critical Realist Applications in Organization and Management Studies', London: Routledge, 2004: 27–53.

Fleetwood, S. (2005) 'Ontology in Organization and Management Studies: a Critical Realist Perspective', *Lancaster University Management School: Working Paper 2005/003*, downloaded http://www.lums.co.uk/publications.

Fleetwood, S. (2005) 'Ontology in Organization and Management Studies: A Critical Realist Perspective', *Organization*, Vol. 12 No. 2: 197–222.

Ford, C.M. (1996) 'A Theory of Individual Creative Action in Multiple Social Domains', *Academy of Management Review*, Vol. 26 No. 2: 1112–1142.

Ford, C.M. (1999) 'Interpretive Style, Motivation, Ability and Context as Predicators of Executives' Creative Performance', *Creativity and Innovation Management*, Vol. 8 No. 3: 188–196.

Ford, E.W., Duncan, W.J., Bedeian, A.G., Ginter, P.M., Rousculp, M.D. and Adams, A.M. (2005) 'Mitigating Risks, Visible Hands, Inevitable Disasters, and Soft Variables: Management Research that Matters to Managers', *Academy of Management Executive*, Vol. 19 No. 4: 24–38, reprinted from Vol. 17 No. 1, 2003.

Friedman, G. (1986) 'Eschatology vs. Aesthetics: The Marxist Critique of Weberian Rationality', *Sociological Theory*, Vol. 14 No. 2: 186–193.

Fuchs, C. (2002) 'Some Implications of Anthony Giddens' Works for a Theory of Social Self-Organization', *Emergence*, Vol. 4 No. 3: 7–35.

Gadamer, H.G. (1989) 'The Hermeneutic Circle', in Alcoff, L.M. (ed.) 'Epistemology: The Big Questions', London: Blackwell, 1998: 232–247.

Garber, M. (1998) 'Symptoms of Culture', London: Penguin (UK Edn.), 1999.

Gaut, B. (1993) 'Interpreting the Arts: The Patchwork Theory', *The Journal of Aesthetics and Art Criticism*, Vol. 51 No. 4: 597–609.

Geiger, D. (1961) 'Tolstoy as Defender of a "Pure Art" That Unwraps Something", *The Journal of Aesthetics and Art Criticism*, Vol. 20 No. 1: 81–89.

Gergen, K.J. (1973) 'Social Psychology as History', *Journal of Personality and Social Psychology*, Vol. 26: 309–320.

Gerwen, R.C.H.M. van. (1996) 'Art and Experience', *PhD Thesis*; University of Utrecht.

Ghoshal, S. (2005) 'Bad Management Theories Are Destroying Good Management Practices', *Academy of Management Learning & Education*, Vol. 4 No. 1: 75–91.

Gibbons, M., Limoges, L., Nowotny, H., Schwartman, S., Scott, P. and Trow, M. (1994) 'The New Production of Knowledge: The Dynamics of Science and Research in Contemporary Societies', London: Sage.

Gibson, J.W., Hodgetts, R.M. and Blackwell, C.W. (1999) 'The Role of Management History in the Management Curriculum: 1997', *Journal of Management History*, Vol. 5 No. 5: 277–285.

Giddens, A. (1984) 'The Constitution of Society: Outline of the Theory of Structuration', Cambridge: Polity.

Giddens, A. (1990) 'The Consequences of Modernity', Cambridge: Polity Press.

Glaser, B.G. (2002) 'Conceptualization: On Theory and Theorizing Using Grounded Theory', *International Journal of Qualitative Methods*, Vol. 1 No. 2, Article 3. Pagination as retrieved 20.04.05 from http://www.ualberta.ca/~ijqm/.

Glaser, B.G. and Strauss, A.L. (1967) 'Discovery of Grounded Theory: Strategies for Qualitative Research', Hawthorne, NY: Aldine de Gruyter.

Glück, J., Ernst, R. and Unger, F. (2002) 'How Creatives Define Creativity: Definitions Reflect Different Types of Creativity', *Creativity Research Journal*, Vol. 14 No. 1: 55–67.

Golden, L. (1969) 'Mimesis and Katharsis', *Classical Philosophy*, Vol. 64 No. 3: 145–153.

Gombrich, E.H. (1950) 'The Story of Art' (16th ed), London: Phaidon Press, 1995.

Goodman, N. (1976) 'Languages of Art' (2nd Ed), Indianapolis: Hackett.

Goodman, R.S. and Kruger, E.J. (1988) 'Data Dredging or Legitimate Research Method? Historiography and Its Potential for Management Research', *The Academy of Management review*, Vol. 13 No. 2: 315–325.

Grayson, C.J. Jr. (1973) 'Management Science and Business Practice', *Harvard Business Review*, Jul–Aug: 41–48.

Grey, C. (2005) 'Critical Management Studies: Towards a More Mature Politics', *Proceedings: 4th Critical Management Studies Conference, Cambridge, July 2005*, pagination as downloaded www.mngt.waikato.ac.nz/ejrot/cmsconference/ 2005 Jul 2006.

Grint, K. (1997) 'Fuzzy Management: Contemporary Ideas and Practices at Work', Oxford: Oxford University Press.

Guillet de Monthoux, P. (2000) 'The Art Management of Aesthetic Organizing', in Linstead and Höpfl (eds), 2000: 35–60.

Gutting, G. (2001) 'French Philosophy in the Twentieth Century', Cambridge: Cambridge University Press.

Hales, C. (1993) 'Managing Through Organization: The Management Process, Forms of Organization and the Work of Managers', London: Routledge.

Hands, D.W. (1998) 'Conjectures and Reputations: The Sociology of Scientific Knowledge and the History of Economic Thought', *History of Political Economy*, Vol. 29 No. 4: 695–739.

Harrison, C., Wood, P. and Gaiger, J. (eds) (1998) 'Art in Theory: 1815–1900', Oxford: Blackwell.

Hart, C. (1998) 'Doing a Literature Review', London: Sage.

Harvey-Jones, J. (1991) 'Getting it Together: Memoirs of a Troubleshooter', London: Mandarin, 1992.

Hassard, J. (1990) 'An Alternative to Paradigm Incommensurability in Organization Theory', in Hassard and Pym (eds), 1990: 219–230.

Hassard, J. and Parker, M. (eds) (1993) 'Postmodernism and Organizations', London: Sage.

Hassard, J. and Pym, D. (eds) (1990) 'The Theory and Philosophy of Organizations: Critical Issues and New Perspectives', London: Routledge.

Hatchuel, A. (2005) 'Towards an Epistemology of Collective Action: Management Research as a Responsive and Actionable Discipline', *European Management Review*, Vol. 2: 36–47.

Heidegger, M. (1935) 'The Origin of the Work of Art', in Preziosi (1998): 413–426.

Heidegger, M. (1959) 'An Introduction to Metaphysics' (Transl. Manheim, R.), New Haven: Yale University Press.

Hein, H. (1976) 'Aesthetic Consciousness: the Ground of Political Experience', *The Journal of Aesthetics and Art Criticism*, Vol. 35 No. 2: 143–152.

Higgs, M. and Hender, J. (2004) 'The Characteristics of the Creative Manager', *Journal of General Management*, Vol. 29 No. 4: 1–20.

Hofstede, G. (1994) 'Cultures and Organizations', London: HarperCollins Business.

Hughes, W. (1996) 'Critical Thinking: An Introduction to the Basic Skills' (2nd edn), Ontario: Broadview Press.

Jahn, G.R. (1975) 'The Aesthetic Theory of Leo Tolstoy's What is Art?', *The Journal of Aesthetics and Art Criticism*, Vol. 34 No. 1: 59–65.

Jameson, F. (1977) 'Reflections in Conclusion', in Taylor, 1980: 196–213.

Johnson, A.G. (1995) 'The Blackwell Dictionary of Sociology', London: Blackwell.

Johnson, G.A. (ed.), (1993) 'The Merleau-Ponty Aesthetics Reader', Evanston, Ill: Northwestern University Press.

Kant, I. (1790) 'Critique of Judgement', in Pluhar, W.S. (Transl.), Indianapolis: Hackett, 1987.

Kearney, R. (2002) 'On Stories', London: Routledge.

Kelly, G.A. (1955) 'The Psychology of Personal Constructs', New York: Norton.

Kelly, M. (ed.) (1998), 'Epistemology and Aesthetics', in 'Encyclopedia of Aesthetics', Vol. 2, Oxford: University Press: 120–122.

Kemple, T.M. (2005) 'Instrumentum Vocale: A Note on Max Weber's Value-free Polemics and Sociological Aesthetics', *Theory, Culture & Society*, Vol. 22 No. 4: 1–22.

Knapp, P. (1986) 'Hegel's Universal in Mark, Durkeim and Weber: The Role of Hegelian Ideas in the Origin of Sociology', *Sociological Forum*, Vol. 1 No. 4: 586–609.

Knights, D. (1997) 'Organization Theory in the Age of Deconstruction', *Organization Studies*, 18/1: 1–19.

Knox, I. (1931) 'Beauty and Art', *The Journal of Philosophy*, Vol. 28 No 18: 484–489.

Kotler, P., Armstrong, G., Saunders, J. and Wong, V. (1999) 'Principles of Marketing', 2nd European Edition, Harlow: Prentice Hall Europe.

Lamarque, P. and Olsen, S.H. (eds) (2004) 'Aesthetics and the Philosophy of Art: The Analytic Tradition – An Anthology', London: Blackwell.

Lamond, D. (2004) 'A Matter of Style: Reconciling Henri and Henry', *Management Decision*, Vol. 42 No. 2: 330–356.

Lamond, D. (2006) 'Management and its History: the Worthy Endeavour of the Scribe', *Journal of Management History*, Vol. 12 No. 1: 5–11.

Lamoreaux, N.R. (2001) 'Reframing the Past: Thoughts About Business Leadership and Decision Making Under Uncertainty', Enterprise and Society, Vol. 2 No. 4: 632–659.

Liddane, J. and Chandler, B. (consulting eds) (1986) 'The Arthur Young Managers Handbook', London: Marshall Editions Ltd.

Lind, R. (1992) 'The Aesthetic Essence of Art', *The Journal of Aesthetics and Art Criticism*, Vol. 50 No. 2: 117–129.

Linstead, S. and Höpfl, H. (eds) (2000) 'The Aesthetics of Organization', London: Sage.

Linstead, S., Fulop, L. and Lilley, S. (2004) 'Management and Organization: A Critical Text', Basingstoke: Palgrave Macmillan.

Loesberg, J. (2005) 'A Return to Aesthetics', Stanford: University Press.

Lopez, F.M. (1970) 'The Making of a Manager: Guidelines to His Selection and Promotion', American Management Association.

Lui, A.Y.L. (1996) 'Trends in International Business Thought and Literature: Parallels Between the East and the West: The Teachings of Ancient Chinese Philosophers and the Echoes from Western Management Theorists', *The International Executive*, Vol. 38 No. 3: 389–401.

Lyotard, J-F. (1979) 'The Postmodern Condition: A Report on Knowledge', (Bennington & Massumi, Transl.), Manchester: Manchester University Press, 1984.

Lyotard, J-F. (1982) 'Answering the Question: What is Postmodernism?', (Durand, Transl.) in Lyotard (1979) 1984.

MacIntyre, A. (1981) 'After Virtue' (2nd edn, Corrected) London: Duckworth, 1985.

MacLean, D. and MacIntosh, R. (2002) 'One Process, Two Audiences; On the Challenges of Management Research', *European Management Journal*, Vol. 20 No. 4: 383–392.

Magee, B. (1973) 'Popper' (3rd edn), London: Fontana Press, 1985.

Magretta, J. and Stone, N. (2002) 'What Management Is: How it Works and Why it's Everyone's Business', London: Profile 2003.

Malan, L.C. and Kriger, M.P. (1998) 'Making Sense of Managerial Wisdom', *Journal of Management Inquiry*, Vol. 7 No. 3: 242–251.

March, C. (1896) 'Evolution and Psychology in Art', *Mind*, Vol. 5 No. 20: 441–463.

Margolis, J. (1961) 'Describing and Interpreting Works of Art', *Philosophy and Phenomenological Research*, Vol. 21 No. 4: 537–542.

Marsden, R. (1993) 'The Politics of Organizational Analysis', *Organization Studies*, Vol. 14: 93–124.

Martin, M.M. (1993) 'The Appraiser as an Artist', *The Appraisal Journal*, Vol. 61 No. 3: 316–322.

Mason, J. (2002) 'Qualitative Researching' (2nd edn), London: Sage.

Mathews, R.J. (1979) 'Traditional Aesthetics Defended', *The Journal of Aesthetics and Art Criticism*, Vol. 38 No. 1: 39–50.

McNeilly, M. (1996) 'Sun Tzu and the Art of Business: Six Strategic Principles for Managers', New York: Oxford University Press.

Merleau-Ponty, M. (1945) 'Cézanne's Doubt', in Johnson, 1993: 59–75.

Merleau-Ponty, M. (1952) 'Indirect Language and the Voices of Silence', in Johnson, 1993: 76–120.

Mezias, J.M. and Starbuck, W.H. (2003) 'Studying the Accuracy of Managers' Perceptions: A Research Odyssey', *British Journal of Management*, Vol. 14: 3–17.

Mintzberg, H. (1971) 'Managerial Work: Analysis from Observation', *Management Science*, Vol. 18 No. 2: 97–110.

Mintzberg, H. (2004) 'Managers Not MBAs', Harlow: Pearson Education.

Mir, R. and Mir, A. (2002) 'The Organizational Imagination: From Paradigm Wars to Praxis', *Organizational Research Methods*, Vol. 5: 105–125.

Mohun, S. (2003) 'Ideology, Markets and Money', *Cambridge Journal of Economics*, Vol. 27: 401–418.

Morgan, G. (1996) 'Images of Organization' (2nd edn) London: Sage, 1997.

Moscovici, S. (1988) 'Notes Towards a Description of Social Representations', *European Journal of Social Psychology*, Vol. 18: 211–250.

Mothersill, M. (1992) 'Sublime', in Cooper (ed.), 1992: 407–412.

Mueller, G.E. (1958) 'The Hegel Legend of "Thesis-Antithesis-Synthesis"', *Journal of the History of Ideas*, Vol. 19 No. 3: 411–414.

Mulhall, S. (1992) 'Expression', in Cooper (ed.), 1992: 144–149.

Mure, G.R.G. (1932) 'Aristotle', London: Ernest Benn.

Murphy, W.P. (1998) 'The Sublime Dance of Mende Politics: an African Aesthetic of Charismatic Power', *American Ethnologist*, Vol. 25 No. 4: 563–582.

Nash, K. (2001) 'The "Cultural Turn" in Social Theory: Towards a Theory of Cultural Politics', *Sociology*, Vol. 35 No. 1: 77–92.

Novitz, D. (1998) 'Epistemology and Aesthetics', in Kelly, 1998.

Papas, G.S. (2002) 'Abstract Ideas and the *New Theory of Vision*, British Journal for the History of Philosophy*, Vol. 10 No. 1: 55–70.

Parker, D. (1953) 'The Nature of Art', reprinted in Vivas, E. and Kreiger, M., 'The Problems of Aesthetics', N.Y., 1953.

Parker, L.D. and Ritson, P.A. (2005) 'Revisiting Fayol: Anticipating Contemporary Management', *British Journal of Management*, Vol. 16: 175–194.

Pelzer, P. (2002) 'Art for Management's Sake? A Doubt', *Proceedings, The 1st Art of Management and Organization Conference*, pagination as downloaded www.essex.ac.uk/AFM/emc/conferences.htm.

Penley, L.E., Alexander, E.R., Jernigan, I.E. and Henwood, C.I. (1991) 'Communication Abilities of Manager: The Relationship to Performance', *Journal of Management*, Vol. 17 No. 1: 57–76.

Pepper, S.C. (1962) 'Evaluative Definitions in Art and Their Sanctions', *The Journal of Aesthetics and Art Criticism*, Vol. 21 No. 2: 201–208.

Peters, T. (1987) 'Thriving on Chaos', London: Macmillan, 1989.

Peters, T. and Waterman, R.H. (1982) 'In Search of Excellence', New York: Harper and Row.

Pettigrew, A.M. (2001) 'Management Research After Postmodernism', *British Journal of Management*, Vol. 12 Special Issue: S61–S70.

Pfeffer, J. (1993) 'Barriers to the Advance of Organizational Science: Paradigm Development as a Dependent Variable', *The Academy of Management Review*, Vol. 18 No. 4: 599–620.

Pluhar, W.S. (Transl.) (1987) 'Immanuel Kant – Critique of Judgment', Indianapolis: Hackett.

Polanyi, M. (1958) 'Personal Knowledge', London: Routledge and Kegan Paul, 1962.

Polanyi, M. (1966) 'The Tacit Dimension', Garden City, NY: Doubleday.

Popper, K.R. (1963) 'Conjectures & Refutations: The Growth of Scientific Knowledge', London: Routledge & Kegan Paul (5th edn) 1989.

Postone, M. (1990) 'History and Critical Social Theory', *Contemporary Sociology*, Vol. 19 No. 2: 170–176.

Preziosi, D. (ed.) (1998) 'The Art of Art History: A Critical Anthology', Oxford: Oxford University Press.

Prior, N. (2005) 'A Question of Perception: Bourdieu, Art and the Postmodern', *The British Journal of Sociology*, Vol. 56 No. 1: 123–139.

Proudfoot, D. (1992) 'Fictional Entities', in Cooper, D. (ed.), 1992: 152–155.

Rancière, J. (2000) 'The Politics of Aesthetics' (Transl: Rockhill, G.), London: Continuum, 2004.

Redfield, M. (2003) 'The Politics of Aesthetics: Nationalism, Gender, Romanticism', Stanford: Stanford University Press.

Reed, M. and Anthony, P. (1992) 'Professionalising Management and Managing Professionalisation: British Management in the 1980s', *Journal of Management Studies*, Vol. 29 No. 5: 591–613.

Rhodes, C. and Brown, A.D. (2005) 'Narrative, Organizations and Research', *International Journal of Management Reviews*, Vol. 7 No. 3: 167–188.

Richardson, L. (1991) 'Postmodern Social Theory: Representational Practices', *Sociological Theory*, Vol. 9 No. 2: 173–179.

Robinson, J.M. (1981) 'Style and Significance in Art History and Art Criticism', *The Journal of Aesthetics and Art Criticism*, Vol. 40 No. 1: 5–14.

Rogers, C.R. (1961) 'On Becoming a Person: A Therapist's View of Psychotherapy', Boston: Houghton Mifflin.

Rogers, N. (2004) 'Giving Life to Carl Rogers Theory of Creativity', Unpublished work downloaded from www.nrogers.com, February 2006.

Rothko, M. (1940/41) 'The Artist's Reality: Philosophies of Art' (Rothko, C., ed.), New Haven: Yale University Press, 2004.

Rowe, M.W. (1991) 'The Definition of Art', *The Philosophical Quarterly*, Vol. 41 No. 164: 271–286.

Ruskin, J. (1873), [MPI], 'Modern Painters: Volume I, Part I–II' (3rd edn), New York: John W. Lovell.

Ruskin, J. (1856) 'The Harbours of England' (with drawings by Turner, J.M.W.), London: Gambart.

Sartre, J-P. (1943) 'Being and Nothingness: An Essay on Phenomenological Ontology' (Transl. Barnes, H.E.), London: Routledge Classics, 2003.

Sartwell, C. (1992) 'On Representation', in Cooper, 1992: 364–369.

Schapiro, M. (1968) 'The Still Life as a Personal Object – A Note on Heidegger and Van Gogh', in Preziosi (1998): 427–431.

Schmidt, J. (1998) 'Civility, Enlightenment, and Society: Conceptual Confusions and Kantian Remedies', *The American Political Science Review*, Vol. 92 No. 2: 419–427.

Schopenhauer, A. (1844) 'Originality and Genius: Extract from the World as Will and Representation', in Harrison *et al*, 1988: 15–22.

Schwabsky, B. (1997) 'Resistances: Meyer Schapiro's Theory and Philosophy of Art', *The Journal of Aesthetics and Art Criticism*, Vol. 55 No. 1: 1–5.

Scott, W.R. (2004) 'Reflections on a Half-Century of Organizational Sociology', *Annual Review of Sociology*, Vol. 30: 1–21.

Searle, J.R. (1995) 'The Construction of Social Reality', London: Penguin.

Simon, H.A. (1959) 'Theories of Decision-Making in Economics and Behavioural Science', *The American Economic Review*, Vol. XLIX No. 3: 253–283.

Singh, R.R. (1990) 'Heidegger and the World in an Artwork', *Journal of Aesthetics and Art Criticism*, Vol. 48 No. 3: 215–222.

Sircello, G. (1975) 'A New Theory of Beauty', Princeton: Princeton University Press.

Sircello, G. (1993) 'How is a Theory of the Sublime Possible?', *The Journal of Aesthetics and Art Criticism*, Vol. 51 No. 4: 541–550.

Stallknecht, N.P. (1936) 'Semblance and Substance in Esthetics', *The Journal of Philosophy*, Vol. 33 No. 26: 707–714.

Starkey, K. and Madan, P. (2001) 'Bridging the Relevance Gap: Aligning Stakeholders in the Future of Management Research', *British Journal of Management*, Vol. 12, S3–S26.

Strati, A. (1992) 'Aesthetic Understanding of Organizational Life', *Academy of Management Review*, Vol. 17 No. 3: 568–581.

Strati, A. (2000) 'The Aesthetic Approach in Organization Studies', in Linstead and Höpfl (eds) (2000).

Strati, A. (2005) 'Designing Organizational Life as "Aesth-hypertext": Insights to Transform Business Practice', *Organization*, Vol. 12 No. 6: 919–923.

Strati, A. (2007) 'Sensible Knowledge and Practice-based Learning', *Management Learning*, Vol. 38 No. 1: 61–77.

Stroud, B. (1992) 'Logical Positivism', in Dancy and Sosa, 1992: 262–265.

Stubbart, C.I. (1989) 'Managerial Cognition: A Missing Link in Strategic Management Research', *Journal of Management Studies*, Vol. 26 No. 4: 325–347.

Sumpf, D. (2002) 'Management & Art – Changing Perception', *Proceedings: The 1st Art of Management and Organization Conference*, pagination as downloaded from www.essex.ac.uk/AFM/emc/conferences.htm, 2005.

Sypher, B.D., Bostrom, R.N. and Seibert, J.H. (1989) 'Listening, Communication Abilities, and Success at Work', *The Journal of Business Communication*, Vol. 26 No. 4: 293–303.

Taylor, C.C.W. (1978) 'Berkeley's Theory of Abstract Ideas', *The Philosophical Quarterly*, Vol. 28 No. 111: 97–115.

Taylor, R. (Transl. Ed.), (1980) 'Aesthetics and Politics', London: Verso.

Taylor, S.S. and Hansen, H. (2005) 'Finding Form: Looking at the Field of Organizational Aesthetics', *Journal of Management Studies*, Vol. 42 No. 6: 1211–1231.

Taylor, S.S. (2002) 'Overcoming Aesthetic Muteness: Researching Organizational Members' Aesthetic Experience', *Human Relations*, Vol. 55 No. 7: 821–840.

Thompson, C.J., Locander, W.B. and Pollio, H.R. (1989) 'Putting Consumer Experience Back into Consumer Research: The Philosophy and Method of Existential-Phenomenology', *Journal of Consumer Research*, Vol. 16: 133–146.

Thurston, C. (1947) 'Major Hazards in Defining Art', *The Journal of Philosophy*, Vol. 44 No. 5: 129–132.

Tierney, P., Farmer, S.M. and Graen, G.B. (1999) 'An Examination of Leadership and Employee Creativity: The Relevance of Traits and Relationships', *Personnel Psychology*, Vol. 52 No. 3: 591.

Tillett, A., Kempner, T. and Wills, G. (eds) (1970) 'Management Thinkers', Harmondsworth: Penguin, 1978.

Tolstoy, L. (1873/1877) 'Anna Karenina', Ware: Wordsworth Editions, 1999.

Tracy, H.L. (1941) 'An Intellectual Factor in Aesthetic Pleasure', *The Philosophical Review*, Vol. 50 No. 5: 498–508.

Tsang, E.W.K. and Kwan, K.M. (1999) 'Replication and Theory Development in Organizational Science: A Critical Realist Perspective', *Academy of Management Review*, Vol. 24 No. 4: 759–780.

Van Aken, J.E. (2005) 'Management Research as a Design Science: Articulating the Research Products of Mode 2 Knowledge Production in Management', *British Journal of Management*, Vol. 16: 19–36.

Van Maanen, J. (1995) 'Style as Theory', *Organization Science*, Vol. 6 No. 1: 133–143.

Vermeulen, F. (2005) 'On Rigor and Relevance: Fostering Dialectical Progress in Management Research', *Academy of Management Journal*, Vol. 48 No. 6: 978–982.

Volkmann, C. and De Cock, C. (2005) 'The Bauhaus and the Business School: Analogies and Antinomies', *Proceedings: 4th Critical Management Studies Conference, Cambridge, July 2005*, pagination as downloaded www.mngt.waikato. ac.nz/ejrot/cmsconference/2005 July 2006.

Walsh, J.P. and Weber, K. (2002) 'The Prospects for Critical Management Studies in the American Academy of Management', *Organization*, Vol. 9 No. 3: 402–410.

Warner, W.B. (1991) 'Social Power and the Eighteenth-Century Novel: Foucault and Transparent Literary History', *Eighteenth-Century Fiction*, Vol. 3 No. 3: 185–203.

Watson, T.J. (2001a) 'Beyond Managerialism: Negotiated Narratives and Critical Management Education in Practice', *British Journal of Management*, Vol. 12: 385–396.

Watson, T.J. (2001b) 'In Search of Management (revised edition)', London: Thompson Learning (originally Routledge, 1994).

Weitz, M. (1956) 'The Role of Theory in Aesthetics', *The Journal of Aesthetics and Art Criticism*, Vol. 15 No. 1: 27–35.

Whewell, D.A. (1992) 'Tolstoy, Leo', in Cooper (ed.), 1992: 429–431.

White, R. (1997) 'The Sublime and the Other', *Blackwell: The Heythrop Journal*, Vol. 38 No. 2: 125–143.

Whitton, B.J. (1988) 'Herder's Critique of The Enlightenment: Cultural Community versus Cosmopolitan Rationalism', *History and Theory*, Vol. 27 No. 2: 146–168.

Wilkerson, J.M. (1999) 'On Research Relevance, Professors' "Real World" Experience, and Management Development: Are we Closing the Gap?', *Journal of Management Development*, Vol. 18 No. 7: 598–612.

Wolff, J. (1999) 'Cultural Studies and the Sociology of Culture', *Contemporary Sociology*, Vol. 28 No. 5: 499–507.

Wren, D.A. (1990) 'Was Henri Fayol a Real Manager?', *Academy of Management Proceedings*: 138–142.

Wu, D. (ed.) (1994) 'Romanticism: an Anthology', 2nd edn, Oxford: Blackwell.

Zald, M.N. (2002) 'Spinning Disciplines: Critical Management Studies in the Context of the Transformation of Management Education', *Organization*, Vol. 9 No. 3: 365–385.

Zangwill, N. (1999) 'Art and Audience', *The Journal of Aesthetics and Art Criticism*, Vol. 57 No. 3: 315–332.

Zangwill, N. (2001) 'The Metaphysics of Beauty', New York: Cornell University Press.

Index